Go Your Own Way
Joerg Kuehn

Go Your Own Way

Joerg Kuehn

Go Your Own Way
How to get unstuck and transform your life –
lessons from an 800 km walk and beyond

ISBN: 979-8-89034-082-5

JK Coach Publishing
Hogarth Road, SW5 0PT, London, UK
www.jkcoach.com

Editor: Sebastian Michael
Newsletter Editor: Tom Wadenfels
Cover Designer: Karen Sawrey
Design and Layout: Andrea Päch
Illustrations: Jörg Metze
Proofreading: David Haviland and Sebastian Michael

For information about special discounts for bulk purchases, please contact the publisher at info@jkcoach.com.

Table of Contents

Introduction

About ten years ago, my life looked very successful and positive from the outside. I had a good job as a senior supply chain director at Procter & Gamble, I was being paid a handsome salary, and lived in a high-end property overlooking the Singapore skyline. But something was missing. I somehow felt unfulfilled, lost, and trapped. After a string of spectacularly failed relationships, with my health not the best and 'handcuffed' to the golden cage of my well-paid job, I was at the crossroads of a classic midlife crisis.

And so, on the 5th of May 2012, I set out to walk 800 kilometres on the Camino de Santiago in Spain. This strenuous adventure transformed me: it broke me apart, it rebuilt me, and it gave me the courage to find and go my own way.

Today, nearly everything in my life is different, and one of the key transformations was to quit my stable corporate career and become a full-time executive coach. Working with my clients, I discovered a variety of common challenges we seem to face in our professional and personal lives. I felt compelled to understand them better and to share their learnings in the form of engaging anecdotes and stories through a monthly newsletter. Over the years I have produced more than 60 such bulletins.

The feedback I have received has been positive, and so during a regular philosophical walk with my friend Sebastian in London in December 2021, I shared with him the crazy idea of gathering these newsletters together into a book. Being a professional writer, Sebastian did not find this idea crazy at all, and he challenged me right there and then to sit down and develop an overarching storyline for a book.

As a German mechanical engineer, I went about this systematically: I created a little 'thumbnail' for each newsletter, each personal milestone during my walking experience, as well as the ten years of transformational change since. And then, on a cold and rainy Sunday in January 2022, I printed and cut out all these thumbnails and laid them out on the floor in our living room in London. This was carefully watched over and guided by my CEO (Chief Enjoyment Officer) cat Rosie (see image on previous page).

When all the paper slips were on the floor, a flow emerged, a common thread. I saw that there was something that linked the mosaic of personal learning experiences to the learning topics of the newsletters: the common thread was my life. It was my own personal journey with its knocks, transformations, and changes, which appeared to magically weave the two strands together, and thus the structure was in place and the book came about.

The first part of the book, *The 800 km Walk,* describes my experiences during the life-changing journey on the Camino de Santiago. In the second part, the book talks about all the changes and transformations the walk triggered in my personal and professional life in the decade that followed. This part, therefore, is called *Walk of Change.* The third part has evolved from its original concept thanks to a 'divine' intervention by philosopher and workhorse Dr Detlef Thiel (aka Pfeffi). This part talks about how I work with clients in my coaching practice, and as it puts all the learnings into action, it is called *Walk the Talk.*

Each part of the book is enriched with a selection of newsletters, which are placed there to further illustrate learnings and to provide you with intuitive tools, reflective ideas, and a personal strategy for your own 'walk of life'. To differentiate the main story from the newsletters, these sections are highlighted with a small grey bar on the left and right-hand side, as shown for this paragraph here.

My overarching insight from this book is that we are all on our own 'Life Camin-os'. At times this is challenging and hard. At other times it is pleasant and fulfilling. Like a walk on the Camino de Santiago, our life is divided into many unique adventures, experiences, and learnings which together fold into our life story. And for me, one of the most important things to realise is that we are not alone. There are people around us who walk with us, who can help us at times of need, and to whom we sometimes can give our own support, no matter how small.

This book is meant to be a good friend, offering to walk with you side by side, helping you to find your very own direction, and supporting you in taking your own life compass firmly into your own hands, so that you achieve whatever it is that you are searching for.

With this, I would like to invite you to come on an inspiring personal development journey with me. Enjoy your walk, and, as the pilgrims say when they greet each other in Spain, I welcome you with *"Buen Camino!"*

Part One
The 800 km Walk

Why?

It was Friday morning, the 5th of August 2011, when I happened to glance over the shoulder of my girlfriend. She had just received a text message, and reading the message, my heart sank, my stomach churned, and I struggled to breathe as if someone had punched me in the gut: "I cannot imagine a life without you any longer!" That message was not from me.

I asked her what this was about, and it turned out she had met someone else. Just like that my life situation was different, underlining the fact how quickly things can change. We had recently bought an apartment together in Singapore for a large sum, but with this message our relationship would come to an abrupt end. In an instant, all kinds of fears rose in me, such as how to manage the mortgage, how to explain this to my friends and family, how to start my life all over again.

Some dark days and weeks followed, during which I was glad to have good friends around me who helped me work through the pain and confusion. When the dust began to settle, I felt it was time to take a step back and evaluate my life, looking carefully at where I was, what I really wanted, and what could be next.

It was during that time that one of my friends introduced me to the Wheel of Life, a very simple but powerful tool to get a quick snapshot of how well-rounded your life looks.[1] Taking stock of the various areas of my life made me realise that it was far from 'rolling smoothly'. On the positive side, I had always been surrounded by a good network of friends and was also very close to my family. I was earning good money in a steady job, and I loved my physical environment as I had just moved into the newly bought apartment, alone.

Looking at my career though, I was not happy. Every week when preparing for Monday at the office I felt the Sunday Blues. I was working in a high-pressure senior supply chain role for Procter & Gamble, a large global corporation that manufactures and distributes – among many other things – skin care products. Olay and Safeguard were my brands, and I was responsible for ensuring the supply of their products for a business worth roughly 500 million USD in revenue. Whilst I loved working with my team, helping them to be successful and to develop themselves further, I constantly wondered whether there wasn't something else I should be doing with my life, rather than helping a billion-dollar money-making machine get a little richer every day.

My health was also not that good. A recent health check had revealed that I was one centimetre shorter and five kilos heavier than at the previous check-up. Obviously, this was not a good trajectory for my BMI to be on, and it coincided with having more or less given up playing football, owing to knee problems.

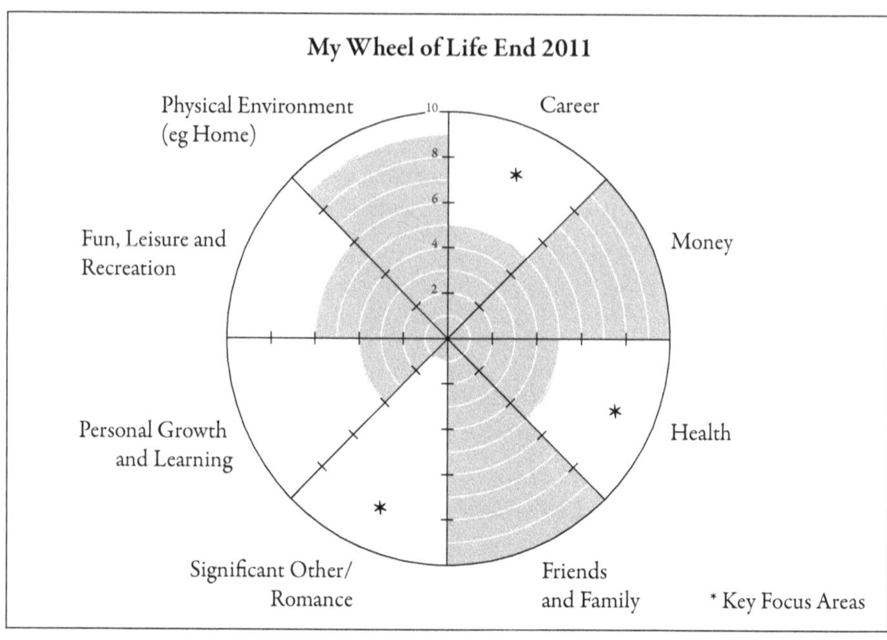

The starting point of my personal development journey

But the area I struggled with most was 'significant other/romance'. I had been in and out of relationships too long, and now here I was, 41 years old and starting all over again. Getting into a stable and fulfilling relationship was the thing in my life I wished for most. Perhaps even having my own family, although I somehow could not really imagine being a father at that point.

Lastly, the areas of 'personal growth' and 'fun/leisure' did not score highly either, as I felt stuck in my job, without a clear plan for how to grow and find meaning, working crazy hours with very little time for myself. From the Wheel of Life it was clear something needed to change, especially with regard to my work, my health, and my romantic relationships.

If I were to ask you: What does your Wheel of Life look like right now? What would you like to change? What are your top three priority areas? Perhaps take a few minutes to quickly sketch your own life evaluation using the Wheel of Life exercise on the next page.

After I had completed my Wheel of Life, I wondered how do I now re-engineer my personal situation whilst working in a busy and demanding full-time job? I struggled with that for several months, and it was not until March 2012 that things started to take a new direction, when I attended a mindfulness workshop.

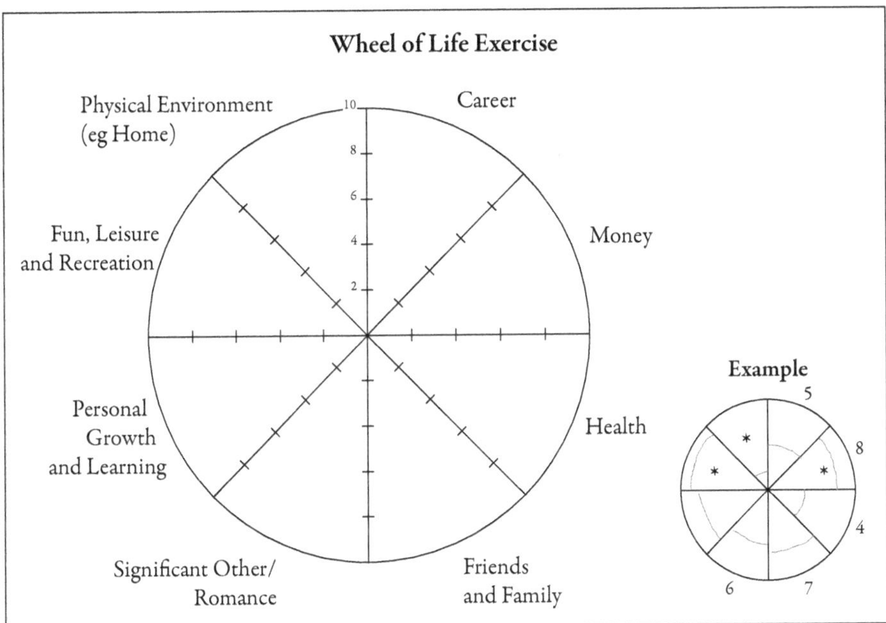

Take a few minutes and draw your own Wheel of Life

If you had asked the German mechanical engineer in me ten years earlier to sit down, calm my mind, listen and – even worse – begin to 'trust the things bubbling up' when the brain is in something known as the 'alpha state', I would have shaken my head in complete disbelief. But here I was, sitting quietly amongst my fellow meditators, desperate for some new insights about what to do with my life.

And suddenly it turned out that my inner voice was indeed there. In fact, during the meditations it was pretty active and speaking to me quite loudly, repeating the following scary message over and over again: "Go for the walk! Go for the walk! Go for the walk!"

The walk my inner voice was referring to was the Camino de Santiago in Spain, about which I had read a book several years ago, by a German comedian named Hape Kerkeling. In this book – a Christmas present in 2006 from my good friend Juergen – Kerkeling very humorously describes the ups and many downs experienced by a couch potato like himself as he was struggling to hike nearly 800 km across Spain while strapped into a heavy backpack.

Reading the book, I felt how deeply this journey must have touched and changed his personal life. He wrote: "This path is hard and wonderful. It is a challenge and an invitation. It destroys and empties you and it completely rebuilds you. It takes away all your power and gives it back, making you three times stronger!" I don't know if my friend Juergen knew the impact this gift would have on my life, but to me it was much more than just words strung together on a page.

Here now, in the workshop, voicing out loud the 'crazy message' from my inner voice and sharing it with my fellow mindfulness students, I was surprised when they smiled, nodded, and asked me when I would start the walk?

People say, "Visions without actions are hallucinations," and for me there was a big hurdle to overcome: how would I get four weeks off work? Asking for that amount of time at senior management level was basically unheard of in my company at the time.

But I was determined to give it a shot, and on the Monday after the workshop – doubtless still in my 'alpha state' – I walked up to my boss and asked him whether I could get four weeks off in July, as I was invited to the wedding of my good friend Jesus in Zaragoza.

I half expected my boss to turn around and suggest I might want to see a psychiatrist, but to my surprise he said that was a great idea. But he cautioned that the company was going through a massive restructuring, and so July was not a good time to go.

Alright, I thought, let's put the dream back into the shoe box and wait for a better time, when there is no restructuring or other pressing activity happening in the company – which realistically might not be until after my retirement ...

But, as Paolo Coelho said, "If you really want something, the universe conspires," and one week later I received an invitation to a meeting in London during the week starting April 30th. And so, on Sunday, 1st April 2012, I sent my boss the following note: "Hi Jeffrey, we will be having a global LT Meeting in Europe in the week of April 30th. I could use this opportunity to take off May and do my walk, being back in Singapore beginning of June ready to work on the organisational restructuring. What do you think about that scenario? Happy to have a quick cup of coffee tomorrow if this is more appropriate."

He replied one hour later, and it was not an April Fool: "Hi, Joerg, Thx for sharing. I think the May walk plan is doable. Let's talk tomorrow. Enjoy the rest of the weekend."

Gulp. Here I was on my balcony, jumping up and down and not believing that in only four weeks' time I would be off to fulfil a big, exciting, adventurous dream, which – as I can now say with hindsight – was to completely change the course of my life. I can't thank Jeffrey Chen enough for letting me go, and I hope he will read these lines one day. Thanks boss!

And now I had one month to get my act together for the walk of my life.

The Preparation

First, I had to find out more on what the Camino de Santiago is about and how best to get myself ready for it. As I began to study it, I learnt that it is a pilgrimage which has existed since the 9th century. At that time, pilgrims started to travel to Santiago de Compostela in north-western Spain, where tradition holds that the remains of one of Jesus' apostles, Saint James the Elder, are buried. While it originated as a Catholic pilgrimage to atone for personal sins, it has since become increasingly popular, today attracting hundreds of thousands of pilgrims of all faiths who go on their personal journeys on 'The Way of St James' every year.

Hundreds of years ago it was not possible to take a train or hop on a plane, and so pilgrims had to literally start walking from their doorsteps and take the gruelling route there and back home on foot. Because of this, there now exists a remarkable web of thousands of kilometres of Camino pathways across Europe, all of which eventually lead, like a network of small rivers, into Santiago de Compostela.

One of the key decisions I had to make was which path to take, and here I happily got some help from a Camino expert, Hans-Valentin Kirschner (HVK), the father of my good old buddy Christian. In a phone call, HVK suggested to me the Camino Frances, which is one of the main routes starting in Saint-Jean-Pied-de-Port and then crossing into Spain over the Pyrenees. He said, "This route is the spiritual route," which I think in hindsight was right for me, and I shall explain why in due course.

HVK also informed me that I would need a Camino Pilgrim Passport (Credencial del Peregrino), which would enable me to stay in pilgrim hostels, known as *albergues,* for a moderate charge of €10–15 a night, which sometimes even included a pilgrim dinner. The nice thing about the Pilgrim Passport (see image below) is that you collect a stamp in each of the hostels and eventually show this in Santiago where you receive the *Compostela,* which is a certificate to show you have walked at least the last 100 km of the Camino. One pilgrim told me that in Spain some people even include this certificate when applying for jobs, as a sign of their determination and tenacity.

The other major preparation to be done now was to purchase the right footwear. I have to say that I completely failed here, and only three days into the walk I started to absolutely hate myself for my own stupidity. How on earth could I have selected these boots?

To get them, I visited two outdoor sports shops in Singapore and then bought a brand that was called 'Hi-Tec', which looked pretty cool and was on sale for a whopping €49. I walked three laps of the shop and then asked the cute shop as-

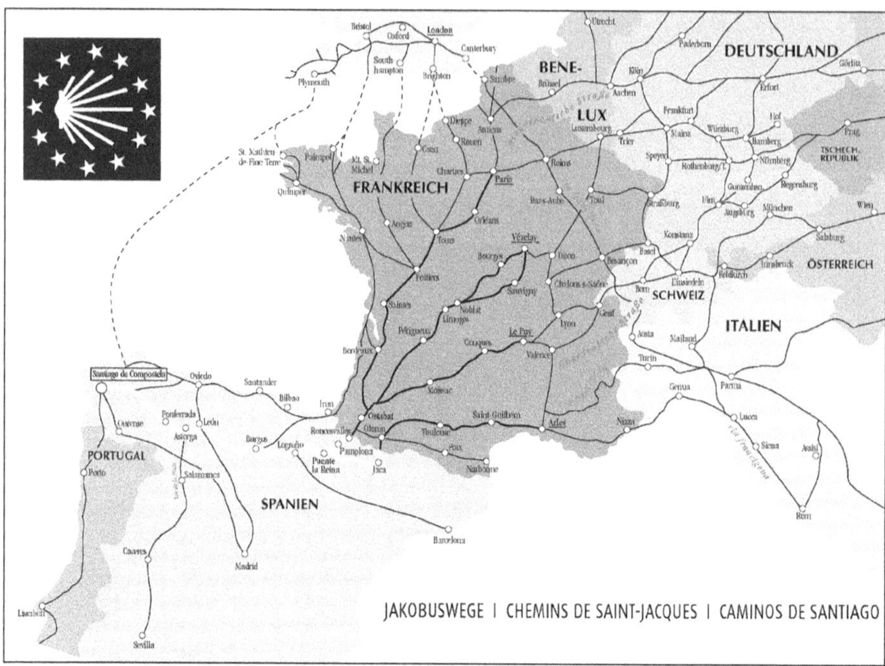

Map of the Camino de Santiago

My Pilgrim Passport

sistant from the Philippines whether I could walk 1000 km with those shoes. In broad Singaporean and with a big smile on her face she said, "Sure, can do lah!" I guess if I had asked her whether I could walk to the moon with these boots, she would also have answered, "Sure, can do lah!" I will tell you more about the struggles this mis-purchase caused me soon.

The next key challenge for my preparations was to get physically fit, even though there was probably not too much to be expected from the four weeks that remained before setting off. Still, in good German tradition, I first of all made a plan! And this genius plan had three sophisticated stages which I executed meticulously.

Meckes' T-shirt

At Stage One, still in Singapore, I walked 10 km in flipflops from Tiong Bahru to Mt Faber, which is a towering elevation of 106 metres above sea level. Having passed this stage with flying colours, I approached Stage Two the following weekend. I put on my fancy new walking boots and walked about 20 km from Tiong Bahru to the MacRitchie reservoir. This was already a bit more challenging, now with 1.5 kg of 'Hi-Tec' on my feet.

But I also passed this hurdle well and so felt ready for my final qualification hike of 25 km from Tiong Bahru to Tampines, this time with 8 kg of stones in my backpack. This, too, passed off without any hitches and so, together with some walking I then did in Germany just before departing for the Camino, I clocked up probably about 90 km of training in total. This doesn't sound too bad, but it still is a completely different ballgame compared to the relentless average of 30 km per day for 26 consecutive days I was about to subject myself to. I had no idea how difficult this would be, but I would soon discover this in a very painful manner.

The last item, which made my preparation complete, was a specially made T-shirt from my close friend and 'philosophical advisor' Captain Meckes. On the front it had the Camino map, so that I wouldn't get lost, and the very philosophical Erich Kaestner quote: *"Es gibt nichts Gutes, ausser man tut es,"* which roughly translates as 'There is no good [in the world] unless you do it'.

The back of the T-shirt said, 'Camino de Santiago 2012 – *Mach Dein Ding*'. *'Mach Dein Ding'* is the title of one of my favorite songs by Udo Lindenberg and literally translates as 'do your thing', or, as we would most likely say in English: 'Go your own way'. Along the walk I was often asked where I had bought this perfect T-shirt, but I only smiled and answered that this was a very, very special edition. Thank you, Meckes! With this, I was now ready to 'rock and roll' and pack my bag, which is where I learnt my first key lesson.

What Do We Really Need?

To make sure I had everything that I thought I would need on an 800 km walk, I first created a list and then gathered all the items together on my bed. I felt that I would definitely need several books to help me fill the evenings and the breaks along the journey. I also thought that a lot of different clothes would be required for varying types of weather and that I should also bring a change of shoes. A proper sleeping bag had to be in the pack, as well as a well-stocked medicine pouch for all kinds of potential medical emergencies.

Once I had assembled all these items, I tried to squeeze them into my new backpack. Somehow they all fitted in, but when I tried to put it on my back I nearly fell over. I looked very similar to the man in the next picture. Stepping carefully onto the scales in my home, I realised the backpack weighed a whopping 27 kg. I was wondering how on earth I would be able to walk 800 km with such a heavy load on my back, but at the same time I thought that perhaps that's just how it is ...

Fortunately, I phoned HVK one more time for advice. He laughed out loud when I told him the story and he quickly sent me a very short list of what I should take "at a max." He said that my backpack should be no more than 8–10 kg as I also needed to consider carrying around 1–2 kg in weight of water.

Now, to cut down my backpack from 26 kg to 10 kg I had a lot of uncomfortable letting go to do. I have to say I really struggled to ditch some of the items I had preselected. But eventually I gave up and just trusted the expert that his list would be sufficient. With this I reduced the weight to 9.5 kg, packing only the items listed further below.

Now, one might question whether in this context the ukulele was really an 'essential item', especially if, like me, you can only play three songs, and even more so in the light of my spectacular failure in a recent Singapore busking audition. They had rung the bell while I was singing my lungs out on my third song, and a few weeks later told me in a very polite letter that 'my singing needed just a little bit

How my backpack would have looked
initially

3 underpants	1 rain poncho	1 mascot
3 T-shirts	1 tube of travel detergent	1 camera
4 pairs of socks	1 tube of foot cream	1 book
2 long-sleeve shirts	several plasters	1 Pilgrim Passport
2 long walking trousers	1 small towel	1 Camino map
1 long-sleeve jumper	1 ultralight sleeping bag	2 mobile phones
1 rain jacket	(250 g)	1 ukulele

Table of all the things I really, really needed

more work'. Still, and irrational as it was, I felt this little indulgence was essential, and so I carried my ukulele with me all the way to Santiago, occasionally playing *Over the Rainbow* or *Mr. Tambourine Man*. To my surprise, doing so some mornings in the hostels helped bring a smile to several worn-out and tired pilgrim faces: it was certainly worth the effort.

All the other items on my list and in my backpack were truly essential, and whilst initially I had struggled to see how I could walk 800 km with only three pairs of underpants, it worked out very well. I washed my clothes every evening, quickly settling into the rhythm of wearing one set whilst one was drying, and one was ready to wear. In hindsight, I cannot thank HVK enough, as even the 10 kg at times felt like carrying a full Marks & Spencer store on my back. I do not know how far I would have made it if I had started with the 26 kg I had spread out on

Picture of all the things I really, really needed

my bed initially. Most likely I would have done what many pilgrims end up doing: give away stuff to reduce the weight. Thus, and before even starting the walk, I had learnt my first lesson: what do we really need?

I lived for four weeks out of this backpack and strangely enough never had the feeling that something essential was missing. So how can it be that we are able to declutter our life down to 10 kg and not sense that we are lacking anything much? Applying this metaphor to our lives, I feel the following thought-provoking story attributed to Paolo Coelho[2] can help us reflect on what we really need, and perhaps even more importantly ask the question:

How Much Is Enough?

Every day the fishermen of an idyllic Brazilian village went out to sea in their boats to catch fish. The sale of the fish provided a decent living, but none of the fishermen were rich. Over time this charming and peaceful village started to attract tourists, among them Jack, an investment banker from New York, who was looking to escape the rat race for a while.

One morning, Jack saw a fisherman rowing a small boat towards the shore with quite a good catch of fish aboard. Jack was very impressed and asked the fisherman how long it took him to catch so many fish? The fisherman replied, "Oh, not that long, just a short while."

"Then why don't you stay longer at sea and catch even more?" asked Jack. Without hesitating, the fisherman replied: "This is enough to feed my family and give me the money I need." Jack was puzzled and questioned further: "So, what do you do for the rest of the day?"

"I go back and play with my kids. In the afternoon, I take a nap with my wife Maria. In the evening I then join my buddies in the village. We have a drink, play guitar, sing and dance."

This baffled Jack. He found it difficult to comprehend and weighed in: "I'm an investment banker from New York. I can help you become a more successful person. From now on, you should spend more time at sea and try to catch as many fish as possible. When you have saved enough money, you can buy a bigger boat and catch even more fish. Soon, you will be able to buy a fleet of boats, set up your own company, your own production plant for canned fish, and have a distribution network. You can then move out of this village to São Paulo and manage the business from there."

The fisherman listened carefully and asked: "And after that?"

"After that, you can go public and float your shares on the Stock Exchange and you will be rich," replied Jack.

"How long will all that take?"

"Well, several years of hard work." Jack responded.

The fisherman repeated his question: "And after that?"

Jack beamed: "Oh, that's the best part. After that, you can retire and move to a small fishing village, catch a few fish in the morning, return home to play with your kids, have a nice afternoon nap with your wife, join your buddies for a drink in the evening, play guitar, sing and dance."

The fisherman went silent and nodded sagely to himself.

This short tale, which I have adapted slightly, speaks powerfully of the critical flaw in how we sometimes approach life. Many of us work to buy what we think will make us happy. But shouldn't being happy come first?

Now, working hard is fine if we enjoy our work. But what if we don't enjoy it or if we work so hard that we have no time to enjoy our lives, or worse become stressed and sick? What price are we paying to have more? And since when does having more money automatically translate into being happier?

Sure, we need a certain amount of money, some material possessions, food, healthcare, and shelter to be comfortable and safe. But what we want and what we really need are two different things. Once we have what we need, is it really worth getting caught up in the rat race just to have more?

Nigel Marsh, author of the book *Fat, Forty & Fired*[3] crystallises the thought this way: "There are thousands and thousands of people out there leading lives of quiet, screaming desperation, where they work long, hard hours at jobs they hate to enable them to buy things they don't need to impress people they don't like."

How would you change your life to be happier if you determined that what you need is a lot less than what you are currently striving for? What, if anything, could you take out of your 'life backpack', letting it go and leaving it behind to walk with a much lighter weight on your shoulders?

Hold Your Own, Know Your Name, and Go Your Own Way!

Once I had completed all my preparations, I flew to Germany for a few days and from there attended the company workshop in London, which finished on Thursday 3rd of May. By Friday I was ready to fly to France directly from London thanks to the great help of my colleague Andy Spencer who had agreed to send my computer and some work clothes over to my parents in Germany so that I would not have to carry around this surplus weight. Sadly, Andy was diagnosed with a brain tumour in 2020 and passed away a year later. I wish I could thank him for his act of kindness which was one of many in his life and which helped me a lot to fulfil my dream of walking the Camino de Santiago.

I took a Ryanair flight from Stansted to Biarritz in France, followed by a short bus ride to Bayonne, where I had a couple of hours before my train to Saint-Jean-Pied-de-Port. I used the time in Bayonne to visit the cathedral. Sitting down in this church I began to feel peace and calm rise inside myself. Afterwards, indulging in a cappuccino in the old market square of Bayonne brought home the unforgettable feeling of having a stretch of four weeks ahead of me, just for myself, to go on an adventure which I was fully open and ready now to experience. Four weeks off. I had never had this before in all my working career of nearly seventeen years. I sincerely hoped the walk would bring me closer to myself and to what I wanted to do with the rest of my life.

I arrived in Saint-Jean-Pied-de-Port late in the afternoon with the light already beginning to fade. It was a beautiful day and so I took a walk into the hills. I watched the sun set with a deep sense of 'beginning to arrive', which was strange, as I was about to depart on a hard 800 km walk the next day.

On the 5th of May I got up with a smile and 'ready to rumble', and before getting on my way I purchased two important items for the walk.

Firstly, I bought my scallop shell, which is the symbol of the walk and which most of the pilgrims have attached to their backpacks. Whilst there are varying explanations as to why the scallop shell became the symbol of the Camino, the

Sunset in Saint-Jean-Pied-de-Port on the 4th of May 2012

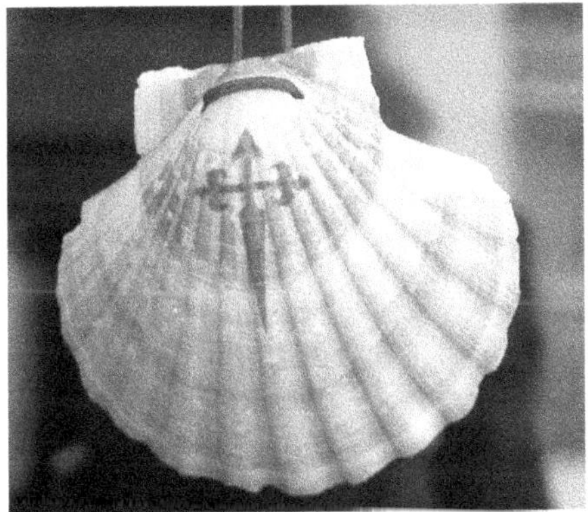

Scallop shell

one I like the most is that, similar to the shell, which has a fine network of grooves pointing towards a centre, the Camino consists of a fine network of pilgrim routes all over Europe finding their end in Santiago de Compostela. The shell is also used on guideposts along the way, together with yellow arrows pointing towards Santiago, and while normally it is a challenge to get lost on the Camino, once or twice it still happened to me, and so I was grateful for those signs.

Secondly, I bought a walking stick, which is something that was recommended to me, as it helps distribute the weight, supports you through difficult passages of the path, and can even be used to keep wild dogs at bay, although fortunately I never had a need for this. But the stick quickly became my companion and its regular click tapping on the ground an integral part of my Camino.

Freezing cold – wearing all clothes available

I was finally ready to go on the first stage of the walk, which is said to be the toughest as it crosses the Pyrenees, with unpredictable weather and an elevation of more than a thousand metres, before descending several hundred metres down into Roncesvalles. Pilgrims, physically exhausted, can get lost in the fog, and there are even reports of some tragically losing their lives on this first leg of the journey.

I was forewarned and put all my efforts into quickly making good progress. The weather was good to begin with, but gradually the Camino began to show its dark side as it became ice-cold, forcing me to literally wear all the clothes I had brought with me.

Having put on layer after layer and finding myself nearly at the top, I got exposed to heavy rain, hail, thunder, and fog. I felt the Camino was throwing me a demanding early gauntlet, but at the same time it also provided help. Out of the blue, a Spanish pilgrim called Xabi appeared, and together we managed this most difficult part, supporting and distracting each other with a friendly conversation.

I arrived in Roncesvalles in the early afternoon, with enough fuel in my tank to walk to the next village, Burguete. Having completed the first day early, I rewarded myself with a little B & B where I had my own room, a hot bath, and a nice snuggly bed. I felt on top of the world, soaking in the hot water with a smile on my face, and the music on my phone playing on shuffle.

All of a sudden, I found myself listening closely: the phone was playing a song which I had never heard before, but which immediately touched me, and which was to become the soundtrack of my walk. The song, by Jason Mraz, is called *Details in the Fabric,* and the lyrics seemed to spell out exactly what I had come here for:

Calm down
Deep breaths
And get yourself dressed
Instead of running around
And pulling on your threads and
Breaking yourself up
If it's a broken part, replace it
If it's a broken arm, then brace it
If it's a broken heart, then face it
And hold your own
Know your name
And go your own way
And everything will be fine

When I heard that song for the first time lying there in my hot bathtub, I had tears in my eyes. Having completed the first and, apparently, most difficult stage of the walk smoothly, I was smiling and 'holding my own, beginning to know my name, and starting to go my own way'. If this was the most difficult stage of the Camino, which I had completed by 3 pm in the afternoon feeling physically fine, I thought nothing could get in the way of my completing this walk with ease.

As you can guess, this was far from the case, and during the following weeks I would get several rude awakenings. Had I known the story of McArthur Wheeler, it might have helped me not become so overconfident, which clearly can be a blind spot of mine. But I did not yet know it, and so I felt completely invincible, just like McArthur Wheeler ...

Are Your Blind Spots Showing?

On the 19th of April 1995, an overweight man called McArthur Wheeler walked into a bank in Pittsburgh, USA, robbed it in broad daylight, wearing no mask, no disguise, or face covering, and walked out again with a lot of money. And then he did the same thing again, that same afternoon. He even smiled at the security cameras on the way out, certain that there would be no way anyone could identify who he was.

The magic ingredient to his scheme was lemon juice. That's right, plain lemon juice. Here's how it worked for McArthur Wheeler: since lemon juice can be used as an invisible ink that will only show up when the paper is heated, all you have to do to make yourself invisible is to rub lemon juice on your face and then stay away from heat sources.

As a competent master criminal leaving nothing to chance, Wheeler of course had to test his method. So, after applying plenty of lemon juice to his face, he took a Polaroid photo of himself to see what he would get, or more to the point, what he would not get. To his unending delight, the camera slowly churned out a picture on which no image was to be seen. Perhaps if he had waited a little longer, he might have had a different outcome, but McArthur Wheeler was a keen man and so he saw his theory confirmed and set off to commit his perfect crime, all the while smelling lemony fresh.

When the police arrested McArthur Wheeler later that evening and showed him the security camera footage, he was astonished: "But I wore the juice!" he exclaimed.

This true story is kind of sad, but also pretty funny, and obviously not exactly about an act of genius. But it inspired David Dunning, a psychology professor at Cornell University to investigate the matter and together with a graduate student of his, Justin Kruger, he conducted some research. In what is now called the Dunning-Kruger effect, the research found that people of low competency in a given area tend to overestimate their abilities, whilst those possessing the greatest competency tend to underestimate their performance.

In the story it is abundantly clear that McArthur Wheeler really thought that he had masterminded the perfect crime. It's a textbook example of a not very capable person overestimating his abilities, to the effect of spending several years in prison.

On the flip side of the same coin, we find the 'imposter syndrome' which has extremely capable people doubting their abilities and feeling as if they were frauds. The good news is that there is a positive message we can take away from all this.

As the Johari window[4] – indirectly named after the psychologists Joseph Luft and Harrington Ingham who developed it – reveals, no matter how smart or capable we are, we all have blind spots when it comes to our abilities, our behaviours, and the way we come across to people. But we don't have to stay blind.

So, how do we discover what our blind spots are? We ask for, and are open to, feedback, such as the anonymous feedback you get from the people who

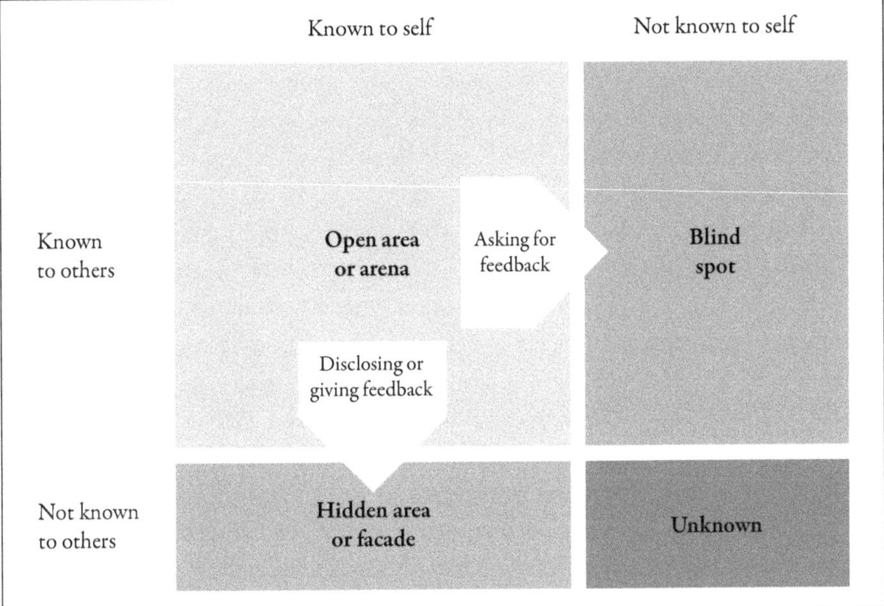

Johari window

you work with in a 360-degree assessment report, or the respectful feedback you can get from your friends, your mentor, or your coach.

We all know that it is not easy to be on the receiving end of targeted feedback and it may even make us feel offended and/or personally attacked. But a good feedback loop can help us to identify our blind spots, our weaknesses, and the less charming aspects of our personality, so that we may become the best person we can be.

Feedback is the key to enriching our lives and enhancing our careers. And it is available to those who ask. So, as you go through your career and life, ask for feedback regularly, and welcome it when it is given to you.

I did not have anyone to ask for feedback on that first evening of the Camino. Similar to McArthur Wheeler, I thought I had it all figured out after one day of walking 30 km. The rest would be a proverbial 'walk in the park'. The police did not come to arrest me, but I would soon realise that I had been sitting on a massive blind spot that first evening on the Camino. The lesson I was about to learn was painful and simple: by no stretch of the imagination was I equipped to walk this walk in an easy way. On the contrary, it was just beginning to slowly break me apart.

Sleepless in 'Lasagne'

I hate to admit it, but I honestly had never walked a longer distance for two days in a row. Even during my fantastic 'prep walks' in Singapore, I had walked only one day and then I had almost a full week to recover. Now, the real Camino was completely different.

Getting up on Day Two was already a bit of a challenge. I could feel the tough kilometres of the first day in every bone and muscle. But off I went, to try and complete the challenging 24 km to Larrosoana, a place whose name I really struggled to pronounce properly. And so, for myself, I simply called it 'Lasagne'.

The actual walk to Lasagne was okay. After my legs had hurt during the first steps in the morning, I found my walking rhythm quite well on that second day and met a 64-year-old pilgrim from Holland, who simply pulled me along with her zest for life, action, and her positive energy.

She spoke of many projects she would tackle after the Camino was completed, such as buying a property and learning how to play the accordion. It was impressive to see Gerda's abundance of dreams, and she shared the following really interesting sentence with me: "If you don't travel first class, your kids will!"

So, progress was good on this second day, but shortly before arriving in Lasagne, I experienced my first real downpour of rain. It was cold, foggy, and suddenly I started to feel low. The 24 km, together with the strain of the previous day still in my bones, had exhausted me. At the same time, I had the bad feeling that I started to develop my first blisters. Even worse though, it was almost dark when I finally arrived in Lasagne, and there was no available accommodation. I was shocked. Would I really have to walk in darkness another 6–7 km to the next village?

Finally, and with a little luck, I found a place to stay for the night, and this was also where I was about to get my first experience of room-sharing – as it turned out, in quite a memorable fashion. Putting my backpack down in the six-bed dormitory, I was greeted with: "*Hola, yo soy Enrique* (Hi I am Enrique)." It came from a very fit Spanish pilgrim, perhaps in his early sixties, who "as a young man had been running with the bulls in Pamplona" and who was now spending time on the Camino every year. He reminded me right away of Karl-Heinz (Karlie) Schulz, a football mate of my father's.

My Spanish was bad, his English non-existent, but I understood from the little we managed to exchange that he was jokingly telling me he would "snore so loud that the lamps will start to sway." True to his word, within a few minutes of wishing each other *"buenas noches,"* Enrique (or Karlie, as I thought of him) started to snore unbelievably loudly.

His snoring-concert began with a massive, seemingly constricted, inhalation effort and it lasted all the way through until 5:30 am. This was when Karlie got up full of energy and, with a big grin on his face, wished me a *"Buen Camino!"* I can recall his wake-up time exactly, as I had witnessed in quiet and growing desperation nearly every minute of his not-so-peaceful sleep. Completely sleep-deprived, I eventually got up, put on my 'Hi-Tec' boots, and tumbled into my third day on the Camino. I had no idea how I was going to walk 30 km in that state.

Sleep deprivation is something that can hit all of us in our busy lives, where we are available non-stop 24/7, always 'on', and seamlessly connected through our many communication channels and social media platforms. The following brief story describes how important sleep can be, and knowing a little more about its importance today, I wish I could have had at least a few hours of sleep during my second night on the Camino ...

Why We Sleep

It was the morning of the 6th of April 2007. Having got home from a long and exhausting trip, Arianna Huffington, creator of the Huffington Post, was up again only four hours later for an interview with CNN. Returning to the office after the interview, she broke down. When she regained her consciousness, she was lying on the floor in a pool of blood, as her head had hit the corner of her desk, cutting her eye and breaking her cheekbone. Arianna had been working eighteen-hour days building the Huffington Post, but this day would change her life. She was diagnosed with exhaustion and a chronic lack of sleep.

That same year, sleep scientist Matthew Walker published one of his many articles, entitled *The Human Emotional Brain Without Sleep*. Both Huffington and Walker have dramatically adjusted their sleeping habits based on personal experiences, as well as a wealth of scientific research, and each went on to write a game-changing book on the subject:

- *The Sleep Revolution: Transforming Your Life, One Night at a Time* by Arianna Huffington, 2016
- *Why We Sleep: Unlocking the Power of Sleep and Dreams* by Dr Matthew Walker, 2017

Both books share the same shocking and alarming message: the catastrophic lack of sleep in modern society is killing us.

In 1942, less than 8% of the population was trying to survive on six hours sleep a night or less. Now, it is nearly every second person. Need proof? Just

Google 'Why am I so …' and Google will conveniently add 'tired' as your top choice.

Aside from the immense cost of sleep deprivation, the list of negative effects on our societies and lives is endless. Here are just three frightening examples [5]:

- Every day approximately 250,000 drivers fall asleep behind the wheel in the US alone.
- In a 2013 study, 50% of UK pilots surveyed admitted having fallen asleep while flying a passenger plane, and 29% of them had awakened to find the other pilot asleep as well.
- Research shows a 24% jump in the number of heart attacks occurring the Monday after we 'spring forward' for daylight saving time.

Sleep deprivation fundamentally impacts our personal health and wellbeing, as those who sleep fewer than seven hours each night are 12% more likely to die prematurely, and adults over 45 who sleep less than six hours a night are 200% more likely to have a heart attack or stroke. Lack of sleep is also linked to the development of cancer, and being chronically sleep-deprived is the cognitive equivalent of coming to work drunk.

But how do we know if we are sleep-deprived? Walker suggests we should trust our instincts. "Those who would continue to sleep if their alarm clock was turned off are simply not getting enough!" You may also not be getting enough if you use caffeine or other stimulants to remain awake or must take drugs to fall asleep. Another clue? If you do not sleep the same number of hours on workdays and non-workdays.

Therefore, my big wish and challenge for you is this: make sleep a priority and carve out at least 7.5 hours every night! Here are some tips on how to get more and better sleep:

1. Maintain regular sleeping/waking hours and keep your bedroom cool (18° Celsius), dark with blackout curtains, and free of electronic devices.
2. Half an hour to an hour before bedtime, dim the lights and turn off all screens and do not cover any more 'heavy topics' for example with your partner or for work.
3. If during the night you wake up and can't sleep for more than 20 minutes, get out of bed, and do something quiet and relaxing like meditating or reading, and stay away from your phone!
4. To reduce anxiety, do a mind dump and write down all your to-dos and worries every night and create a powerful gratitude list.

Zen master Rosie

5. No caffeine after 1 pm and avoid alcohol, which is a sedative, and seda-
   tion is not sleep.
6. Regular exercise, exposure to sunlight, as well as meditation and yoga,
   are wonderful natural 'sleep medicines'.

When Huffington was asked if she would have been so successful had she slept more than 7.5 hours in the beginning of her career, she responded: "My answer is not just a categorical 'Yes'. I also believe that not only would I have achieved whatever I've achieved, but I would have done it with more joy, more aliveness, and less of a cost to my health and my relationships."[6]

My own personal Zen master, cat Rosie, clocks 17 hours of slumber a day and is at zero risk of burnout. We will learn more wisdom from her further on in the book ...

Know Your Destination

After my involuntary and painful observation of Enrique's snoring during my second night on the Camino, I was now not only sleep-deprived, but also smashed by the 54 km I had walked over the last two days. My breakfast that morning did not help, as it consisted of a teabag dipped in heated water from the microwave, together with some terrible cookies. With that I left Lasagne behind and began to walk this third leg of my journey, feeling alone, cold, and scared of what would happen today. I feared that perhaps I would not be able to walk much, that I might face a breakdown, or even had to consider abandoning the walk completely.

All this was exacerbated by my 'Hi-Tec' shoes, which were already slowly falling apart, with little stones beginning to bore through their soles. What did not help matters was a fellow pilgrim showing me pictographic stories about what can happen when someone has bad shoes: massive bloody blisters, followed by inflammation potentially leading to hospitalisation! I was surprised he never mentioned foot amputation, but I started to feel the fear, and with every step I sensed I was already getting more and bigger blisters.

Still, somehow I moved on, making it to Pamplona, and from there, with the help of a woman called Katharina from the Czech Republic and stimulated by good conversation, walked the remaining 10 km to Zariquiegui. This was my goal for the day, but arriving there I had to lie down, completely exhausted. Lying in bed, I felt I could not walk any further. My hips had begun to hurt terribly on the last few kilometres, my shoes were letting through stones, and I felt absolutely exhausted.

But it got worse. I took out the map to understand where I was. What I saw completely devastated me. Whilst I had walked nearly 80 km in three days, I still had more than 700 km to go until Santiago. This fact totally overwhelmed me and lying in bed I slowly started to cry. In that moment I realised that this walk was not in my hands. There were so many things that could happen and go wrong all through this long journey. And sadly, there was a good chance that I might not make it.

This realisation was very humbling, and it made me feel quite hopeless. Then, suddenly, an image appeared in my head. I saw myself sitting in the cathedral in Santiago. In this vivid image I had completed the walk successfully and looked back to this evening of the third day. I was still humbled, but very peaceful and full of gratitude that I had come here and walked all the way to Santiago.

I have to say, this visualisation came out of nowhere. It was incredibly strong and powerful. To this day I struggle to understand where it came from. Maybe it was from the overexertion. Or maybe it was simply fear and worry that I would not be able to complete this walk.

Whatever it was, the image of sitting in the Cathedral in Santiago on that third evening gave me the courage to open up and talk a bit about how I felt with other pilgrims over dinner. They listened and gave me a lot of positive encouragement not to give up here. Just sharing how I felt was good. More significant though, through the visualisation I learnt my first important lesson on the Camino itself: know your destination! Even if on the next day I was only able to walk a few kilometres, I would be going in the right direction and towards my goal.

On the Camino it was very simple to see where I had to go, but in our daily lives this might not always be the case. Going through our busy days, we can lose sight of where we want to go, as we get overwhelmed by life's daily demands and challenges. There are no signposts and mileage information points, and sometimes it can be quite difficult to identify what would be the best direction for us to take.

The following three short stories may perhaps provide a little inspiration and 'food for thought' with regard to finding the right direction in life and knowing your destination:

What Will They Say About You?

"The Merchant of Death is Dead." How would you like it if this were the headline of your obituary? That is exactly what Alfred Nobel saw written about himself in the press one fine morning. You may wonder how he was able to read his own obituary in the first place? It turned out that his brother Ludvig had died in Cannes, and a French newspaper had mixed them up.

This gave Alfred Nobel a quite shocking insight into how he was regarded by many, and he didn't like it one bit, so he set out to do something about it. The mistaken obituary may not have been his only motivation, but it certainly made him keenly aware of the legacy he would leave behind if he did nothing.

He resolved to reform his reputation, and in the process he became a household name associated with something uplifting and good. Today, we know Alfred Nobel as the man who created and funded the Nobel Prize, awarded for outstanding achievements in a variety of fields of human endeavour. But back on the 22nd of April 1888, when the premature announcement of his death was published, he was considered by many an evil man: "Dr Alfred Nobel, who became rich by finding ways to kill more people faster than ever before, died yesterday."

Why such vitriol? Alfred Nobel was no killer. He was an engineer. He made buildings and bridges. But he was also an inventor. And he was curious about how the newly discovered chemical substance nitro-glycerine, which is very volatile in its liquid form, could be tamed for use as a controlled explosive to remove rock from construction sites.

So, he developed a way to mix nitro-glycerine with silica, turning it into a paste – dynamite. And he invented and patented the blasting cap that would detonate the mixture. It was a great discovery, and incredibly useful for peaceful purposes. The problem is that you can use dynamite to blow up a lot of things, not just rock. And as dynamite became associated with death and destruction, so did the name Alfred Nobel.

It wasn't fair, but life is often unfair. The obituary served as a wake-up call for Dr Nobel, causing him to think long and hard about what he wanted his legacy to be and how he wanted to be remembered by the world. And that was not as the 'merchant of death'. So, he endowed the prize that bears his name, and the rest is history.

If a newspaper were to (mistakenly) write *your* obituary today, what would they say about you? Applying this little thought exercise back to your life, you could ask yourself:

- What would you like people to say about your contribution to your family, your community, and the world?
- What do you want to make sure you accomplish in this lifetime?
- What will your legacy be? Your 'Nobel Foundation'?

Think big and know this: whatever it is you want the world to remember, the time to start working on it is now.

The Two Most Important Questions in Life

In the movie *The Bucket List*, a highly intelligent and broadly self-educated car mechanic, Carter Chambers (Morgan Freeman), and an insufferable billionaire hospital magnate, Edward Cole (Jack Nicholson), meet for the first time in a hospital room. Both are diagnosed with terminal cancer.

Without wanting to give away too much about the film, they decide they'd rather truly live their remaining days, than spend them in a hospital, desperately hoping for salvation in the form of one more experimental drug. So, they escape from hospital and set out on an exciting adventure around the world, doing things they'd always wanted to do and going to places they had always wanted to see, ticking things off their eponymous bucket list as they go.

As part of their journey, they visit Egypt and, sitting on top of the gigantic pyramid, Edwards tells his friend Carter, "The ancient Egyptians had a beautiful belief about death: When their souls got to the entrance of Heaven, the guards asked two questions. Their answers determined whether they were able to enter Heaven or not:

1. 'Have you found joy in your life?'
2. 'Has your life brought joy to others?'"

Looking at our own civilisation, I wonder if the 'meaning of life' might not in fact be that simple. What if it is all about joy, not only creating it in our own lives, but also bringing it to others? So perhaps pause for a moment and ask yourself:

- What thoughts, feelings, activities, and people bring you joy?
- Are you actively incorporating them into your daily life?
- Are you actively engaged in bringing joy to others, through your way of being and through your actions?

On the surface, the movie asks what exciting things you would want to do if you were diagnosed with a terminal disease. That's the hook. But the deeper question is, what would you want to clean up that would bring you more peace and joy before you shuffle off this mortal coil?

Joy can come from putting right what hasn't been right for a long time. That's what Edward does. He puts things right. At the request of his friend Carter, he reconnects with his daughter after many years of fights and non-communication. By doing so, he both experiences joy for himself and gives it back to others. The movie has a beautiful ending (and this does come with a small spoiler alert): "Edward Cole died in May. It was a Sunday afternoon and there wasn't a cloud in the sky. He was 81 years old and when he died, his eyes were closed, and his heart was open." We should all live every day with a joyful and open heart. Not just when it comes to the time when we pass, but also, and particularly, while we're still here.

What Do You Regret?

We all have regrets, things we would have done differently if we had another chance. Unfortunately, living with regrets disturbs the soul and makes us unhappy. Bronnie Ware knows more about the subject of regret than most. She is an Australian nurse who worked in palliative care for eight years, caring for people in the final weeks of their lives.

It's natural for people at the end of their days to take stock, evaluating what they are proud of and what they wish they had done differently. Bronnie would listen as they looked back on their lives, confessing their regrets. We humans like to think of ourselves as unique and extraordinary, with minds of our own, free from convention, but it seems we are troubled by a similar set of regrets as just about everybody else, and so as the same ones kept coming up over and over again, Bronnie began to discern certain patterns, to the point where she felt compelled to write a book with the title *The Top Five Regrets of the Dying*.[7]

The top five regrets?
1. I wish I'd had the courage to live a life true to myself, not the life others expected of me.
2. I wish I hadn't worked so hard.
3. I wish I'd had the courage to express my feelings.
4. I wish I had stayed in touch with my friends.
5. I wish I had let myself be happier.

Bronnie's patients undoubtedly wished they could have a 'do-over', a second chance to go back in time and get it right. But that's not how life works. There is no dress rehearsal, or, as they say: "Life is like drawing without an eraser." Living is all about improvisation. You choose your way in the moment, taking your best shot and living with the consequences.

So, what does this mean for us? What could it mean for you personally? Unlike Bronnie's patients, you still have time to make different choices, so when you come to the end of your life, you don't have any serious regrets and you can make your transition with a peaceful mind and an unburdened heart.

The first choice you can make is to forgive yourself for being less than perfect. We're all human. We all come up short of the ideal sometimes. And self-criticism around those things you can't change only makes them worse. You are good enough. You have done enough. And nothing you did that you wish you hadn't can't be forgiven – if you can forgive yourself.

As for the things you can change, notice the word courage comes up twice in these five regrets, because those are the hardest ones to change. They require the willingness to make yourself vulnerable and to behave in different ways, ways that may be emotionally, perhaps also socially and economically, uncomfortable. After all, there is a reason why you haven't done certain things.

Changing behaviour isn't always easy, but without the courage to change, we are likely to have some serious regrets weighing on us throughout life right up to, and especially at, the end. So, let me ask you, right here, right now: what are your regrets? And what do you plan to do about them?

Who Is Walking the Camino

After a good pilgrim dinner with a few glasses of red wine, I was very worried whether I would be able to get any sleep during my third night on the Camino. This time I was sharing a room with seven other pilgrims in a small pilgrim hostel. Besides the noise, I was worried about whether the pain in my body would allow me to get the rest I was desperately in need of. But things turned out better than expected.

Before going to sleep I had put on my life-saver number one: silicone ear plugs. With these little wonders plugged in, there was literally zero disturbing sound to bother me from that night onward. Lying down, my body aches also slowly started to subside, and so I had the astonishing experience of how the body miraculously rebuilds itself during sleep. In fact, in the third night, I slept like a baby, recovering well from the first three straining days of the walk.

On the morning of my fourth day, I woke up with a positive feeling in my heart, and I found some great camaraderie over breakfast. This, together with hot chocolate and zwieback – a rusk-type dry bread that is almost a staple in Germany – gave me the confidence to put on my backpack and start to set one foot in front of another again, inching a little closer towards my destination with each step. At the end of Day Four, I had completed a surprising 35 km and in the evening I suddenly felt like I had 'arrived' on the Camino. I began to settle into my walking rhythm, and I was also starting to cope better with the physical and emotional strains of walking day after day.

But things got even better, because on the next day I found my life-saver number two: shoe inserts. This was probably my best investment along the whole Camino, as in an instant my shoes miraculously started to feel like the 'Hi-Tec' they were supposed to be. No more stones were pushing through. With the new inserts, these boots began to cope and perform, exactly as promised by the competent saleswoman in Singapore. With my shoes not bothering me, at least for a couple of days, I also started to feel a bit more confident and relaxed about my journey.

My body felt better, I got a good rest every night, and all of a sudden, a marvellous inner peace began to settle slowly inside myself. Yes, occasionally I was still thinking about my work or other challenges, but I always reminded myself that I still had more than three weeks off and this in itself was a wonderful feeling. I began to smile, and the weather seemed to smile back, showing me its sunny side. I now started to open myself up to the walk, and more importantly I also began to connect more deeply with other pilgrims.

In doing so, I quickly recognised that everyone seemed to have 'something in their backpack' which needed to be addressed. And here I would like to share with you four short stories of fellow Camino walkers whom I got to know a bit better and whom I valued a lot, as they helped me over many difficult and painful kilometres.

Mr Lionheart

Meeting Helmut was a little bit like the story of the hare and the tortoise. Whenever I saw him during the day, I noticed that he was walking quite a bit slower than me, but in the evening, he miraculously made it to the same village as I did, covering 30 km on average.

It was a remarkable achievement as Helmut was 75 years old. One day I could not hold it in any longer and asked him outright how he covered these distances walking so slowly. In all honesty, I had become highly suspicious of Helmut occasionally taking the bus, which was an absolute no-no amongst serious pilgrims. But Helmut's simple secret was to start two to three hours before everyone else: this allowed him to walk the same distance at his own, slower pace.

His life story was a tough one. Having lived all his life in East Germany, he had worked at a power plant in the Lausitz region, when his wife was diagnosed with terminal cancer in January 1995. Only four months later he had a nurse nonchalantly tell him, while eating an apple, that "there was nothing else that could be done." He took his wife home and was there with her when she peacefully passed away. He did not tell me much more about it, but I could sense that he was still struggling with this, more than sixteen years later.

After his wife's death, he got himself a dog, Senta, and enjoyed the company of this new friend for thirteen long years. It was while walking with Senta that he met his current girlfriend Hertha, in 2000. Hertha was actually afraid of the dog, but somehow she grew very fond of Helmut. Hertha had lost her husband in similarly sad circumstances, and so both moved in with each other, starting a new life together. I got a feeling that Helmut was probably not the easiest of companions, as he held some very strong opinions. But with every day of walking, I could see more and more how his tough exterior softened, making way for a vulnerable and fundamentally good heart to shine through.

Helmut told me that he and Hertha had agreed that he would call her twice a week, every Wednesday and Sunday evening at 7 o'clock on the dot, to share how he was doing. As the walking days went by, I noticed that he seemed to scrap this rule: nearly every evening I saw him happily chatting away to her on his mobile phone.

It was wonderful to see a man in his seventies seemingly grow young again, falling in love one more time – with Hertha. I believe this is the power of the Camino, as it tells us what truly matters in our lives. No regrets! Thank you, Helmut, for the good time and the support. I will especially never forget how we marched together singing our lungs out with East German 'battle songs'.

Helmut Lionheart

The Billionaire

As I was about to settle the bill for my pilgrim dinner and accommodation in the morning of Day Four it turned out that Paul (I am changing his name here for confidentiality reasons) had already kindly paid for it. I did not think too much of it, but later on my journey, I had a chance to walk alone with Paul for several days. During these days I learnt that he was a billionaire. Together with a friend, Paul had flown to Biarritz in his own private jet. Frankly, I was a little intimidated initially to walk with a person who is perceived as so powerful. But the Camino had already done its magic, as everyone here seemed to be the same, stripped of the trappings of wealth or success, 'reduced' to what lies underneath the public life and the mask we might have built up over time.

Paul was easy to get along with, and much like Helmut he had some personal issues that he was trying to get to grips with along the way. He was quite open about it to me, but to respect his privacy, I won't go into further details here. What I can say is that I learnt from his story that money does not make you immune to emotional challenges. If I asked you whether your life would be dramatically different if all of a sudden ten million dollars showed up in our bank account, you would probably say yes, some areas of life would change a great deal, but at the same time others would stay the same.

Paul told me how he had built his impressive business empire, step by step. By the time we met he employed five people just to read and manage his emails, as he did not have the time to do so by himself. I loved that, as it reminded me of my own work and the daily struggle to try and stay on top of the onslaught of emails.

Asking him for some nuggets of wisdom on how I should make my first million (and many more thereafter) he smiled and listed three things. First, he said, make sure that you always have "enough money to repair the washing machine." What he meant was that we should ensure we have sufficient liquidity to sustain our lives even if something goes wrong. Basically, he's saying, have some financial buffers!

Second, he told me about the importance of being able to say 'no'. This for him was the 'pinnacle of simplification'. He was convinced that by saying 'no' more often, "we are able to focus on a few and really important things." With that full attention we substantially increase our chances of getting it right instead of chasing multiple goals half-heartedly.

Third, he shared that it is important "to treat people in the same way you want to be treated." And here he had a remarkable experiment he used occasionally when he met new business partners for the first time. Just before arriving at the venue, he and his driver would swap seats, so that the other party would think he was the driver. He then observed for a little while how they treated him, the perceived driver, against how they treated the 'businessman', his actual driver. Some business deals were immediately off the table if he felt treated badly as 'the driver'.

Walking with Paul made me realise that deep down he was a guy like everyone else, and in his heart, he was looking for something which could not be found in material wealth. I had a strong feeling that the Camino somehow made everyone equal. Everyone had their own problems, their longings and (emotional) 'weights' in their backpack that needed to be solved.

The Magic K&K Duo

Next, I want to share with you a story about a duo I met from the complete opposite end of the financial spectrum. Kyrill, a young man in his early twenties and his dog Kira. They only had a budget of 5–7 euros per day to cover both their needs. I thought that was quite a challenge. The pair had started their walk in Basel, Switzerland, and by the time I met them they had already walked more than 1,300 km together.

Kyrill & Kira

After finishing school, Kyrill had done vocational training as an architectural draughtsman, and he was now considering studying architecture. His plan was to use the walk to get more clarity about whether and how to approach this next stage in his life and education.

His *compadre* Kira was still a very young dog. She was only a few months old when Kyrill got her, days before starting his walk. At the beginning, Kira was clearly not used to the strain of walking miles and miles every day and so she would run ahead for 200 metres, lie down and sleep until Kyrill had caught up. Then she would run ahead again, lie down and sleep. Kyrill told me that she also struggled with all the new and strange smells, sounds, sights, people, and especially the other dogs she met on the walk. It took them a good 100 km until they had found their walking rhythm individually and as a gang.

But when I walked with them, I felt a very deep sense of calm and peacefulness. They were clearly in sync with each other and looked completely at peace with themselves. It was as if Kyrill, in his early twenties, had already reached a remarkable level of inner balance and clarity, which truly impressed me. Not to mention Kira, who was by now an experienced walking dog and of course the darling of all the pilgrims they met.

Kyrill did not have enough money for accommodation, and so I saw both of them on several occasions sleeping in their tent or in a Camino shelter just by the side of the road. But walking side by side with them I felt a level of peace and tranquillity that I had not felt with many others along the way. I believe this further highlights the fact that money may be helpful and important to meet our basic needs, but that there must clearly be something beyond material wealth that allows us to tap into our true inner strengths.

The Brave Dreamer

I had known Marie for only a few minutes when, walking alongside each other, we were starting to introduce each other to our respective life stories and somehow came to the question, what were our biggest dreams? She quickly confided that one of her dreams was to "stand in the midst of a green flowing field and have a picture taken."

"Well," I said, "that is easy!" And so, she quickly ran into the field, and we took the picture below. She liked it so much that she made it her social network profile picture at that time.

Marie had started in France and had already walked 500 km when I met her, with another 650 km to go. But she was not a complete novice: she had in fact walked the final 120 km of the Camino de Santiago together with her father the previous year and like many other pilgrims, she had become 'hooked' and come back to spend more time on it. Since then though, her dad had unfortunately become very ill. She was now doing the walk for him, to remember the time they spent together, but also to find a way to deal with the finiteness of life and the likelihood that his illness could take him away from her.

I asked her what had changed since she went on the walk last year and she told me that the way she looks "at people, nature, and the various situations in [her] life is different. It feels as if the days have become more meaningful, beautiful, and livelier," since her first walk on the Camino. Well, I thought, if the Camino were to have the same effect on me, I would happily take it.

Marie walked the Camino completely by herself and in doing so she to me represented a large constituency of female walkers who embark on this magnificent journey on their own, without any of their friends or as part of a group. I was truly impressed by many of these brave women, some well into their sixties, who take on this difficult physical and emotional journey.

I could probably share at least twenty more tales of people I met on the walk. Each of these individual stories would be different and yet they would all have something in common: everybody comes to the Camino with something they want to clarify, rectify, accomplish, get to grips with, or let go.

Marie

Some got fired from their job or were on the brink of losing their whole livelihood. Some were planning for new chapters in their lives. Some had lost a loved one and wanted to find a way to heal. Some were looking for a new relationship and partner. Some had been diagnosed with a serious illness and went on this walk for new hope. Some, including myself, did perhaps not even know specifically what it was that needed change and attention in their lives when they started to walk, but just followed the calling of their inner voice. Whatever it was, I felt everyone carried something 'heavy' in their backpack. And in its very own way, I strongly believe, the Camino helped most of us somehow.

It was interesting to note that whenever I met new people on the Camino, we talked to each other without the masks that we usually wear when we meet someone in our daily lives for the first time. Perhaps it was the fact that we were walking side by side towards a mutual goal without any commitments or obligations towards each other that created this openness. I do not know what it was, but I think the level of vulnerability created by openly sharing each other's stories made this journey so fascinating, rich, and profound.

Never Walk Alone

For me the vulnerability and the deeply meaningful interactions with other pilgrims were crucial to continue my own walk, not only after the first few challenging days, but on many occasions after, when I was down and on the brink of quitting.

At times our conversations distracted me, at times they carried me, at other times they frustrated me, and many times they made me think about myself and my life. Whatever it was, these interactions helped me to keep going and I am deeply grateful for all the good people I met along the way and for the deep feeling of having 'never walked alone'. So, the second key lesson I learnt on my walk was how important social support has been and probably always will be for me.

Looking at real life, I believe we all need strong bonds to other people to navigate the challenges and the ups and downs that each day can bring, and so here are three short stories which are very close to my heart, and which underline the importance and benefits of these bonds: the ways and reasons why we should never walk alone.

Why Not Walk Alone?

In the early 1960s, the US government decided to fund a study about Roseto, a remarkable small town of Italian immigrants in Pennsylvania. What made the town stand out was the fact that the rate of heart attacks among its population was less than half the US average.

In an attempt to identify the reason for this extraordinarily low risk of heart disease, the researchers first studied nutrition. But it turned out that the Rosetans loved meatballs and sausages, fried in lard with hard and soft cheeses. That could not have been it.

Next, they looked at smoking, but it turned out the people of Roseto loved their cigars. Also not the reason. After that, they analysed their drinking habits, but it turned out they drank wine 'with seeming abandon'. Finally, they investigated the working conditions, but most of the Rosetans were working in the surrounding slate quarries where they breathed dust-filled air. Hardly conducive to your overall health ... So, what reduced the risk of heart attack in Roseto so dramatically?

Its people! The magic of Roseto was the total lack of isolated individuals crushed by the challenges of everyday life. Nobody was left behind or strug-

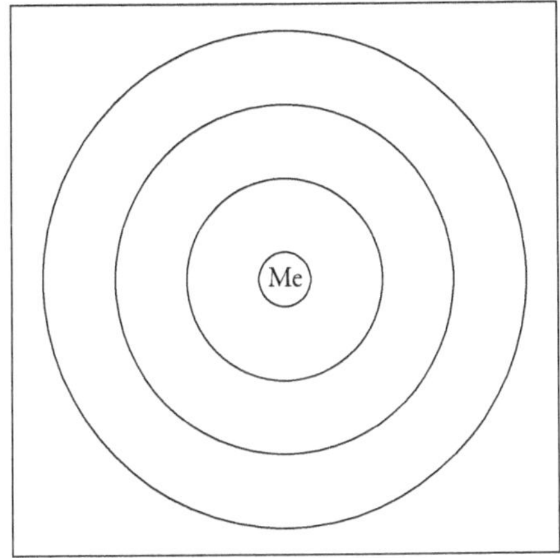

Relationship circles

gled alone with life and its problems. Based on their Italian roots, the Rosetans had replicated a tight-knit and highly supportive community in the US, just as they'd known it in their villages in Italy.

Over the years, these tight social bonds got diluted as people moved in and out of town, and eventually another study, carried out in the 1990s, sadly revealed the same rate of heart disease as the rest of the country.

Looking at other research into what helps people live healthy and fulfilling lives, you may have heard of the Harvard Grant study, which followed more than 250 men and women and their offspring from the 1940s onwards, all the way through their lives.

George Vaillant, the director of the study, summarises its two main findings as to what contributes to happy and healthy lives: "At first love ... and secondly: finding a way of coping with life that does not push love away." I believe the second part is what we struggle with most at times, as we risk treating those closest to us the worst when we are stressed and under pressure.

Overall, and like the Rosetan research, the Grant study highlights the importance to our wellbeing of strong and effective social bonds: friends, mentors, colleagues, and family members who not only help us to adapt to life's challenges, but also support us when the going gets tough in our ever-changing world.

I would like to invite you to do a simple yet powerful exercise that helps you evaluate the effectiveness of your relationships and how they may support or hamper you.

Take a blank sheet of paper and draw four concentric circles (see diagram above). Put 'Me' in the smallest middle circle and then begin to list (with a pencil) all the people that you are interacting with in your life. As an aid, you can use your WhatsApp, email inbox, or friends list on Facebook.

Depending on how close you feel to these people, how much you sense they care for you, and how much you can and usually share with them about what is really going on in your life, add the names of the people to one of the circles. The closer the relationship, the nearer you put them to the 'Me'-circle. There is usually an inner circle of spouses, kids and/or other family members, followed by a circle of friends and a circle of acquaintances.

Once you have completed this exercise, ask yourself how well each of these relationships is working:

- Do you spend enough time with the most important people in your life?
- Are there unresolved conflicts?
- Have you been honestly sharing with them what bothers or concerns you?

Begin with the people closest to you and look at ways to enhance these relationships. Working your way towards the outside circles, ask yourself if you want to reactivate or perhaps wind down some of these relationships?

When doing my own circles, I realised there were some people I simply did not spend enough time with. I also identified two relationships which required more work, as well as some clarification. But in general, I was quite happy and grateful, as I felt I had a strong and good support structure in place in my life.

So, spend ten minutes to evaluate your own social network. By doing so, you will not only make sure you never walk alone, but quite probably reduce your risk of a heart attack.

How Not to Walk Alone?

Twenty-year-old Jonny Benjamin was not well. He had been diagnosed with a mental illness which caused him to slide into severe depression, and on a cold January morning in 2008 he decided to end his life. Wearing only a T-shirt against the cutting winter air, he walked up to Waterloo Bridge in London, stepped over the railing, and prepared to let go.

But out of the blue, a stranger came up and started talking to him: "Hi mate, can you tell me why you're sitting on the bridge?" Gloomily and hopelessly, Jonny replied he was going to take his own life. But the stranger would not give up and kept talking to him. "Please don't do this mate. Please don't

Jonny Benjamin (left) and 'the stranger from the bridge', Neil Laybourne

do this. Let's just go for a coffee. Let's just talk it over." The stranger kept talking to Jonny in tones full of compassion, kindness, and genuine concern. Eventually Jonny climbed back over the railing. He was taken to a hospital and went through a rehab programme. The man had saved Jonny's life.

During his recovery, Jonny regretted never having had the chance to thank the stranger from the bridge. He couldn't because he did not even know his name. And so, six years later, on 14th January 2014, Jonny decided to change that and launched the #FindMike campaign – using the name Mike as a best guess, with a short video clip of himself standing on Waterloo Bridge.

Within 24 hours, the clip was shared 43,000 times and viewed more than a million times. By the next morning, the campaign was picked up by ITV's breakfast show, propelling the story across the UK. It gained further momentum with celebrities like Stephen Fry, Boy George, and the Prime Minister David Cameron getting involved in the search. But the story didn't just go viral in the UK, it began to appear on TV shows around the world.

Soon messages started to come in from people who thought they knew someone who might be 'Mike', and two weeks after the campaign started, with several false leads ruled out, the real 'Mike' was found. His actual name was Neil Laybourne, and his fiancée had seen the post. She called her future husband right away. Soon after, in an emotional and touching moment, Jonny and Neil were reunited, and Jonny finally got the chance to hug the man who saved his life and say thank you to 'the stranger from the bridge'.

Sadly, many suicide attempts are not prevented. Nearly 6,000 people end their life in England and Wales every year, with 75% percent of them being men. It is how TV presenter Roman Kemp lost his producer and best mate, Joe Lyons, who took his own life in August 2020. Kemp has since made a moving BBC documentary, *Our Silent Emergency,* in which he talks to health professionals and young men who have lost friends through suicide.

What touches me most in this film is when he speaks to a group of teenagers from Belfast about their friend Carl, 'the class clown', who killed himself in May 2020 at the age of only fifteen. None of the boys knew Carl was suffering until he was suddenly gone. Discussing their feelings and working through their grief, they all agreed the only way to prevent such tragedies is to open up with each other in conversations and share what's really going on.

Another group of teenagers in Reading, who had lost their friend Ashley to suicide in 2017, has come up with a remarkable rule among themselves, which they call the 'two okays'. When asking each other how things are going, they always ask twice. It goes like this: "Hey man, how are you doing?" "I'm okay." "How are you really doing?"

By using this simple practice, they create the opportunity for the friend to share what's really going on and not suffer through the 'silent emergency' – feeling alone and bereft of hope.

As we walk through our lives, some of our friends, colleagues, or family members may be going through dark times. My challenge and wish for you is to reach out to a friend (or a stranger) today and check in with him or her, using the two okays. Ask them how they're doing, and then ask them how they're really doing?

The same is of course valid if you are struggling yourself with something in your own life. "A problem shared is a problem halved." This really holds true: simply talking to a friend or a trusted colleague can make such a big difference.

Men, especially, often feel and think they can't share their thoughts, so it's hard to see a way out, which results in so many taking their own lives. It is a great and still widely unnoticed tragedy that takes place in our midst every single day. But the simple key to never walking alone is the act of opening the lines of communication.

Rupture and repair

'Rupture and Repair' to Never Walk Alone

Relationships are not easy to maintain, as our lives and we ourselves are going through constant changes, impacting the way we feel and interact with each other. A trainer of mine once said, "Relationships are the fast track to enlightenment, they constantly challenge us to grow."

Dr Alan Shore developed the powerful concept of 'rupture and repair' in which he describes building relationships in a similar way to how we build muscles in the gym. There, we strain our muscles by exercising, and then allow them to repair themselves and grow stronger through recovery.

A very profound, longstanding Polynesian tradition does exactly that for relationships: helping to repair them after they get ruptured. The name of this lovely tradition might sound a bit weird to us: *Ho'oponopono*. But, in this case, weird really is also wonderful.

Ho'oponopono is an ancient Hawaiian practice of forgiveness and, literally translated, means to make *(ho'o)* right *(pono)* right *(pono)*. The double use of the word *pono* is at the magical centre of this practice, as we are 'making things right' with ourselves and with others.

In the Hawaiian tradition, a *kahuna* or doctor would be called in if members of the family were not *pono* with each other. The facilitator would allow family members time to express themselves to get whatever the issue was off their chests, let it go, and then move forward together, thereby making it *pono*. Hawaiians believe conflicts and grudges eventually can cause illnesses and diseases, so they work proactively to resolve them.

In 1976, Morrnah Simeona, who is regarded as a healing priest or *kahuna,* adapted the traditional *ho'oponopono* to the social realities of our modern times. She extended it to become a process which not only helps solve problems within families and other groups, but also aids individuals to find peace, happiness, and forgiveness within themselves.

A condensed version of Morrnah Simeona's process features the following four steps, which I would encourage you to practise whenever you are struggling with a relationship. It has the power to make your life less stressful, to help you gain more control over your emotions, and to maintain calm and composure, even in the most difficult situations.

Say the four phrases to yourself and put them out into the universe. If you want to say them to someone else, that's fine, but that's not at all necessary to obtain the benefits. Speaking to yourself, in a way that is not specifically focused on another person or a particular instance, will allow you to find peace already. That said, you can personalise the practice and apply it to specific circumstances.

1. "I'm sorry." If you have negatively impacted someone, saying "I am sorry," even if it is just in your own mind and not to the actual person, can help significantly when it comes to reconciling that relationship. If someone has treated you badly, you could say, "I am sorry for the resentment and anger this has triggered inside myself." Saying "I am sorry" is a wonderful opportunity to release negative emotions by accepting the actual situation as it is, rather than adding further 'fuel to the fire'.

2. "Please forgive me." If you have made a mistake, saying to yourself "please forgive me" provides an amazing opportunity to make things right *(pono)*. It's liberating, even if you never actually say it to the other person directly. And it is not just forgiveness you ask from others. You may want to forgive yourself for a mistake you have made or for how harsh you have been with yourself. In any case, asking for forgiveness will have an immediate calming and soothing effect on how you feel. Just try it and see.

3. "Thank you." To thank is to create happiness. Thank the other person for teaching you a good lesson, for forgiving you, for working through this difficult time with you. Or thank yourself for doing the best you could under the circumstances. Just being grateful for the simple things can make a big difference to how you feel, even in the gloomiest moments.

4. "I love you." This is the one that clearly can transform relationships not only with others, but with ourselves. Try it out and feel the impact this sentence can have on yourself and your loved ones. As odd as it might sound, please appreciate this key insight: saying "I love you" in your mind – it doesn't have to be to anyone else – can have the most uplifting effect, especially on relationships with the most 'difficult' people, including yourself. Just say it quietly and peacefully to yourself and watch how relationships, including the one with yourself, begin to blossom.

Repeat the magic four phrases as often as possible to yourself and, if you wish, to others. It is a real gift that will grow the relationship muscles within yourself and with others stronger and stronger, making life more peaceful, relaxed, and joyful. The power in those few phrases is limitless and will help you to 'never walk alone' again. Try it out.

The Going Gets Tough!

After my initial struggle walking the Camino de Santiago, Days Four to Seven felt really good. I started to get a better feeling for the walk, and especially for how to pace myself, taking sufficient breaks, drinking enough water, and eating at the right times. At the same time my body began to adjust to the daily strain of walking 30 km.

The weather was good and the interactions with the many other pilgrims along the way were very friendly and positive. With this I truly began to settle into my own rhythm, making good progress towards Santiago. By the end of Day Seven, I had completed 206 km and arrived in a small village called Ciruena.

I still remember that evening, as we climbed into our beds very early, in a small pilgrim hostel after an interesting dinner with a spooky hostel warden. It was a Friday evening, the first week of the walk was completed, and in contrast to other Fridays in my life, when I was eager to go out and meet friends, here I was ready to go to bed at 9 pm. But I felt very fulfilled, calm, and full of inner peace. It was fascinating to me how simply walking from A to B every day seemed to reduce the noise and the distractions, but also the sheer amount of 'wants', while telling me more about 'what I really needed' in my life. Falling asleep that evening I smiled to myself about the progress I had made, the people I had met, and the good lessons I had learnt already.

But after every high there comes a low and for me this next low began to seep in rather gradually. Having never walked 200 km in a row before, I now felt physically up for the task, my shoes were 'so far so good', and the weather was manageable despite some cold mornings and short spells of rain. All seemed fine.

There was only one downside, and that was that I still had to walk another whopping 574 km to Santiago. For the last few days, I had not looked at the map too much and focused more on the present moment, but I had a clear deadline to catch a flight to Singapore and be back in the office by the 4th of June. Hence, there was pressure that I absolutely had to maintain my average of 30 km per day for more than another two weeks to make it on time. Even though Singapore and my work at Procter & Gamble were very far away, these thoughts brought up strange feelings of uneasiness and even slight fear.

Once it registered, this nagging little thought seemed to not leave the back of my mind, and it completely changed how I experienced the walk in my second week. I probably should not say this, but to a certain extent it started to feel a bit like going to work, as every day was almost a copy of the previous one: my days began to stretch out before me in an endless, monotonous flow.

Each morning started with breakfast, usually in the hostel or at a café along the way, together with a big cup of *café con leche* (white coffee). At that point I declared my goal for the day and decided where I wanted to spend the night, usually around the required 30 km mark from where I was. I normally started to walk between 7 and 8 o'clock and tended to make good progress at the start.

About midmorning it was time for a break, to have a small bite to eat or another coffee, and to refill the water bottle in one of the many little villages along the way. This was followed by another period of walking before the lunch break, which ideally was a big plate of spaghetti or anything else with a massive amount of calories, because walking the whole day burned roughly 3,000 calories on top of the normal 2,000 for a man of my size and age. After lunch it was usually tough for me to find my way back into the walking rhythm, but still, on I went until I took a short break in the early afternoon, followed by another stint of walking.

When, hopefully, I made my destination for the day by 4–5 pm, I had to look for accommodation, which sometimes could be a challenge, because although May is not the busiest month on the Camino, some hostels were fully occupied. So, it was essential to leave sufficient fuel in the 'walking tank' to continue to the next village to find a bed for the night there if necessary. After arrival at the hostel, it was time to wash my clothes and cream my feet, followed by a bit of rest and chat with other walkers, before we then usually had a pilgrim dinner together and went off to bed between 9 and 10 pm.

The next day this sequence started all over again: get up, breakfast, walk, break, lunch, walk, break, walk, wash clothes, dinner, sleep, and repeat. In Week Two the

Me and the Meseta

days started to drag on, making me feel a bit bored, whilst at the same time feeling the pressure of having to complete my compulsory 30 km. Yes, this basically was my 'job' now and I went to work diligently, but what I did not realise was that the physical strain of it was massive. With the deadline occupying my mind, I very slowly started to spin into negative thoughts. They not only made it more difficult to get up in the morning, but together with my now slowly and steadily growing blisters and a substantial number of worries, these thoughts grew bigger and bigger.

What did not help was that after Day Twelve I started to enter an area called the Meseta, a desert-like strip of many kilometres without any villages. It is one of the few stretches along the Camino that can be a danger to pilgrims if they don't carry enough drinking water.

The walk through the Meseta feels like walking in an endless, straight, dusty line. I recall a cyclist overtaking me on that stretch. When I looked up much later, I could still see him on the horizon, highlighting to me not only how far I still had to go, but also that there was no village, no tree, no shadow, no water, *nada* for the foreseeable distance.

To make matters worse, I was faced with a massive headwind and the curious fact that, as if by conspiracy, all the other pilgrims seemed to have disappeared. I was alone and there seemed no hope of meeting anyone whom I could talk to and make the time go by a little faster. It was just me alone, struggling against the wind, feeling my blisters growing, and worrying, as the magic insoles in my shoes now also started to give way to little stones. All this whilst constantly reminding myself that I absolutely had to keep up my 30 km per day. In those moments I began to question and eventually even hate myself. Why on earth had I made this stupid decision to go on this walk? It was really tough and started to feel grim and hopeless, as the destination for the day seemed not to come any closer during hours and hours of walking.

Eventually though I made it and arrived in Calzadilla de la Cueza, which I knew had only two pilgrim hostels, with the next village another 10 km away. This caused further anxiety: I would not have been able to make it the extra stretch that day. Fortunately, there was room at the hostel, but when I arrived, I felt even more devastated: some older ladies whom I thought I had passed several days ago had already arrived before me and were happily chatting away about the great progress they were making and the "absolutely magnificent time" they were having on the Camino.

I wanted to hear nothing of this. I just wanted to be alone. Taking off my socks, I was shocked by the size of my blisters and especially one blister at the back of my heel.

But even more concerning was the discovery of a sizeable cut under one of my toes, which had gone completely numb. And now I started to really worry. Looking at the map, I was staring at the fact that the following day I would only just cross the halfway point. That meant I still had 400 km to walk to Santiago. How was I supposed to do this? In my physical state, with my blisters growing, my toes going numb, my shoes falling apart ...? I felt like crying, and despite sharing a room with probably 50 other pilgrims I felt utterly alone. It was as if I had not learnt anything during my time on the Camino. I was completely stuck in self-doubt, pessimism, and negativity.

After dinner I went out to sit quietly by myself in the grass, watching a beautiful sunset, but full of worry about what would happen the next day. Back in the hostel I made myself ready for bed and got another big shock: I could not find my phone. I'd still had it at dinner, but now it was gone. Losing my phone was a big tragedy because not only had I taken a lot of pictures with it, but it also saved my journalling notes and of course a lot of other important information. In a panic, I ran out to the dinner place and then to the field where I had watched the sunset. Phew: a big weight fell of my shoulders when I found the phone lying there peacefully in the grass. I made it back with five minutes to spare before the hostel locked its doors at 10 pm. Any later than that, and I would have had to spend the night out in the open ...

With lights off, I was lying in my bed alone, forlorn, and hopeless, trying to get some sleep alongside 50 other pilgrims. My bed was not far from the toilets and

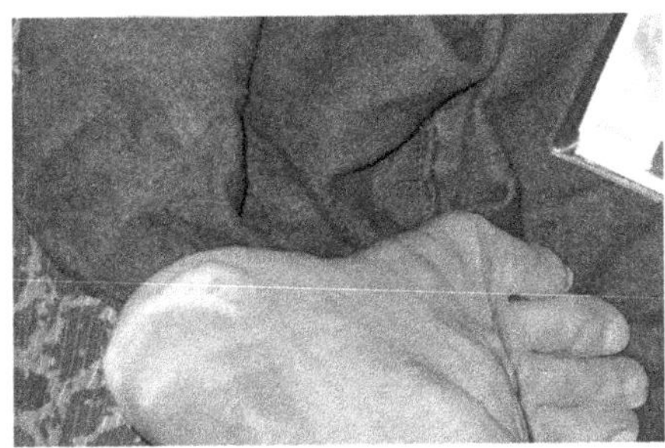

Blister mid-way through

during night every few minutes someone opened and closed the creaking door, accompanied with a beam of bright light streaming in. Restful sleep, which I would have needed desperately, was not an option and the worrying thoughts kept spinning around in my head. What will happen tomorrow? Will I be able to walk the distance? Will I break down? What will happen to my blisters, the cut under my toe, and to my shoes? How on earth will I be able to walk 400 km in the state I am in? How can I maintain an absolute minimum of 30 km a day to meet my 'deadline'?

That night was horrible. If ever there was a night when I would have needed resilience, that was it. But I felt far from resilient: I felt small, lonely, and scared. The word 'resiliens' can be traced back to the 1620s. It's derived from the Latin word *resiliens*, describing 'the act of rebounding', 'bouncing back', or also 'springing back' into shape after being 'deformed'. My coaching supervisor Steve describes it as 'bouncebackability'.

Resilience is a life skill we all need as we go through our daily lives, when we are faced with change, challenges, and sometimes even unbearable adversities, especially in our VUCA (Volatile, Uncertain, Complex, Ambiguous) world. The following two short stories capture examples and ways of how to develop resilience. I wish I had known some of these tricks during my desperate and lonely thirteenth night on the Camino!

Is it a Threat or a Challenge to You?

"The test you will take today is designed to help us identify people who are exceptionally weak in their problem-solving reasoning abilities. Your performance on this test will not be scored like most normal tests, but rather will be classified as either above or below a predetermined cut-off score. If you score below that cut-off, this suggests that you are exceptionally weak – in other words, well below average in your problem-solving reasoning abilities. Thus, this test and the scoring method used are designed only to separate those who are especially weak from everyone else."

This is how Dr Chalabajev and her team introduced a test to participants of Group 1 in their study about how people deal with performance anxiety.[8] Group 2 was introduced differently, with words replaced as follows: *weak* by *strong* and *below* by *above:*

"The test you will take today is designed to help us identify people who are exceptionally strong in their problem-solving reasoning abilities. Your performance on this test will not be scored like most normal tests, but rather will be classified as either above or below a predetermined cut-off score. If you score above that cut-off, this suggests that you are exceptionally strong – in other words, well above average in your problem-solving reasoning abilities. Thus, this test and the scoring method used are designed only to separate those who are especially strong from everyone else."

The intention was to trigger fear in Group 1, making participants feeling under threat, by being at risk of getting classified as *'especially weak'*, whereas Group 2 was helped to see the test as a *challenge* where they could potentially be identified as *'especially strong'* problem solvers with not much else to lose. In scientific terms, Group 1 was targeted to become 'goal-avoidant' and Group 2 'goal-approaching'. The study results are mind boggling:

Group 2 performed approximately 40% better, pumping more blood through their bodies and brains, with blood vessels widened compared to their normal state, while Group 1 in contrast pumped less blood, with blood vessels more constricted than normal. Perceiving a situation as a threat versus a challenge makes us likely to perform worse, and it risks damaging our bodies due to higher blood pressure and similar effects it has on us. Several other studies have confirmed these findings, and so the million-dollar question is: how can we switch from threat to challenge when we are under pressure?

Sports psychologist Dr Martin Turner has successfully applied a simplified version of the ABC model from Rational Emotive Behavioural Therapy (REBT) with his athletes.[9] The ABC concept starts from understanding that *Activating* events alone do not cause unhealthy emotional and behavioural *Consequences,* but that the real cause behind these are irrational *Beliefs.*

Once we start to analyse and understand what irrational beliefs may be causing our reaction to an event, we then can begin to challenge them and thus change our behavioural consequences. Dr Turner classifies four faulty belief categories:

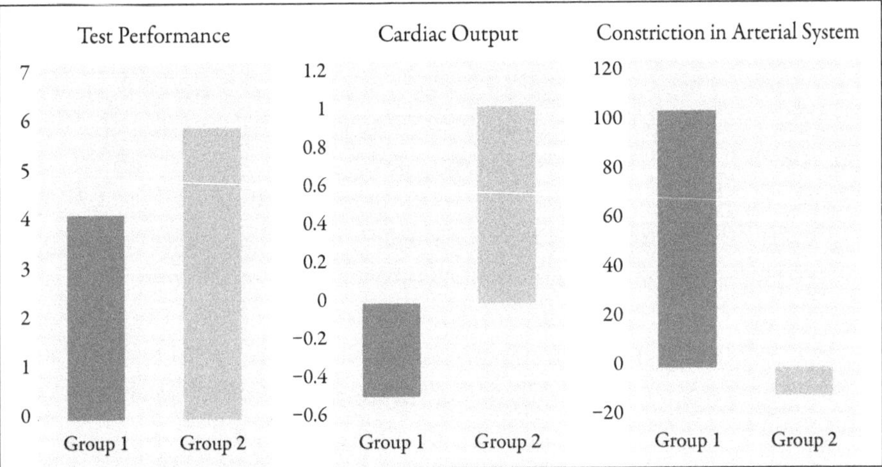

Study results on performance anxiety

1. Rigid demands: "I must succeed in this situation" or "I must be treated fairly"
2. 'Awfulising': "Failure is awful/terrible" or "Being treated disrespectfully is awful/terrible"
3. Low frustration tolerance: "I can't stand being treated with disrespect" or "I cannot tolerate unfairness"
4. 'Downing': "Failing here makes me a failure" or "If I fail, it shows what an idiot I am"

Once we have identified such faulty beliefs we can challenge and amend them according to Dr Turner:

1. Flex your thinking: "I want to succeed in this important situation"
2. Challenge awfulness: "Being treated unfairly is bad, but not awful/terrible"
3. Increase frustration tolerance: "Just because I don't like unfairness, does not mean I should be treated fairly all the time"
4. Big picture view: "Failing here does neither make me a failure nor an idiot"

When things get tough and you need resilience, check if you feel under threat, and try to find a way to change this from threat into challenge. Perhaps you don't have to 'succeed by all means' or can learn to accept that 'others are not perfect', whilst life at times is 'unfair'. Whatever it is, challenging and amending beliefs from threat to challenge will make you perform better, stay healthier, and certainly become more resilient.

Think Straight and Keep Making Decisions

In 1985, Joe Simpson, then aged 25, and Simon Yates, 21, went to Peru with the aim of doing something that had never been done before: climb the west face of a 6,200 m mountain known as Siula Grande, high up in the Peruvian Andes.

The two Brits were planning to do this in what mountaineers call 'alpine style', which means carrying all their equipment, food, and sleeping kits with them, rather than relying on sherpas or porters. But climbing in this way meant carrying minimal equipment, and so on the way up they did not fix ropes and thus establish clear routes they could use to get back down in a hurry if needed.

They reached the peak after two and a half days and things looked to be on track. But on the way down everything changed dramatically. Joe slipped, fell, and broke his right leg in a very bad way, crushing his tibia into his knee joint.

They were still at high altitude with no chance of calling for help. Nobody even knew where they were. Joe thought Simon had no choice but to leave him behind to die. Instead, Simon came up with an idea for how they could descend the mountain together, by connecting single ropes to create a 300-yard rope. Simon would lower Joe down and then Joe would have to stand on his good leg to give Simon enough slack to unclip the rope and move down to join him. Then they would repeat the process. This was the theory. The practice was much harder.

They made good initial progress despite Joe's leg occasionally getting painfully stuck. But then, Simon lowered Joe over a hidden cliff edge. Joe was hanging in mid-air above a deep crevasse with only Simon's strength holding him and preventing him from falling.

Joe tried to climb up the rope, but to no avail. Both screamed their lungs out, but they could not communicate with each other. In the meantime, the weather had turned, and the storm now raging was too strong. Simon held Joe for several hours while slowly sliding towards the overhang and beginning to lose his grip.

Simon had to make the most difficult decision of his life: after much agonising and wrestling with his conscience as much as with the increasingly untenable strain on his body, he cut the rope. To avoid being pulled off the cliff himself, Simon severed the thin piece of material that attached him to his friend, and Joe plummeted 20 metres into the deep crevasse. This surely was

Brendan Mackey as Joe Simpson in *Touching the Void,* directed by Kevin Macdonald (2003)

the end, Simon knew. Without a doubt he had let his climbing partner fall to his death. He had cut the rope. Something you never, ever do, as a climber.

But this wasn't the end. Joe was knocked out by the fall, but miraculously he survived and regained consciousness. In the light of the following morning, Simon saw the deep and deadly crevasse. He called out but got no answer from Joe. Simon drew the only possible conclusion, that his friend had been killed by the fall. Devasted and with no other option than to try and save his own life, he continued his lonely descent in despair.

Joe was stuck with his badly broken leg deep inside the crevasse. He was about to give up and die when an inner voice told him: "You must think straight. You must think straight and keep making decisions."

Thinking creatively despite the harrowing circumstances he found himself in, he decided to do the opposite of what would be the instinct. Rather than trying to climb back up, which he already knew was impossible, he lowered himself deeper into the crevasse. And against all odds, it offered a way out. Several hours later, and after incredible physical exertion, he was lying on the white snow, enjoying the sunlight like he had never seen it before.

But he was still in grave danger. He faced a 9 km downhill crawl, dragging himself backwards on his backside through terrain strewn with boulders and boobytrapped with more crevasses. He was dehydrated, in agony, hungry, and doubtful whether Simon would still be at the base camp.

But he kept telling himself, "Think straight, think straight and keep making decisions." He began to set tiny targets for where he wanted to be in twenty minutes' time. Sometimes, this was only a few metres away. But he kept setting these small, achievable goals. And over and over, he was able to reach them.

After three agonising and horrendous days of setting and reaching tiny goals with no food, nearly no water, and having lost almost a third of his body weight, he arrived near the camp site where they had started their climb seven days earlier. He was not able to move any further. Delirious and with his last bit of energy, he screamed Simon's name.

Simon couldn't believe his ears, ran out of the tent, and found Joe in an extremely weakened physical condition with excruciating pain because of his broken leg. With all his heart, full of astonishment and joy, he hugged his friend with the feeling that he suddenly had a second chance to save him. Joe himself lacked the strength to understand that this hug meant that he was no longer alone. It meant that he would be saved.

Simon, who had planned to leave that morning, quickly collected all the things and got Joe ready for transport into the nearest hospital. This was not an easy journey either. Barely conscious, Joe was strapped on a mule for two days and then spent twenty-three hours in a pick-up truck. It was eleven days after he had broken his leg, that he finally reached the hospital. Joe had six surgeries over the next two years, and despite the doctors saying he would never climb again, he did.

Why am I telling this story? In our lives we sometimes face situations where there seems to be 'surely no way out'. Such chastening adversity has Joe's mantra ringing in my ears: "Think straight and keep making decisions!"

When we face difficult times, as we move through uncertain and unchartered terrain, how about setting some simple, tiny goals like Joe did? When you are stuck, think about what you can accomplish, or how you can improve your situation, over the next hour, by tomorrow morning, over the coming week, or the next month.

It doesn't matter how modest the goals are, as long as you keep reaching them and creating new ones. Keep heading in the right direction and keep going. That's all that really matters. Think straight and, above all, keep making decisions: that's what makes us resilient.

Simon and Joe's story is told in the book, film, and play *Touching the Void*. Their experience is regarded by mountaineers as one of the most remarkable instances of survival against the odds ever recorded.

For me, lying in bed during the night after that thirteenth day of my Camino walk, I unfortunately did not look at my situation as a challenge. I was completely overwhelmed by the fear of what would happen and whether I would be able to make it (and even more so by when) to Santiago. With that I was also not open to consider thinking straight and setting small goals. I was just dreading the morning which then came. By that time I was not yet aware that this day would change everything.

The Day That Changed My Life

Friday the 18th of May 2012. It was 4:45 am when I was woken up by pilgrims who were putting their gear on to start their walk for the day. I was appalled. Why would you start that early? But apparently it was so they could find accommodation for the night at their next stop early. Some were wearing head lamps as it was still dark outside. After a night of very bad sleep due to all my worries and the constant opening and closing of the toilet door, I finally got up at 6 am, completely shattered.

I was alone and I hated those early-morning pilgrims, but more than that I hated myself. Today was 'half-time' on the Camino, but looking at the map I felt helpless and completely hopeless. How would I be able to walk 30 km, with my growing blisters, the cut under my toe, the disintegrating shoes? Even more troubling, how would I be able to walk another 400 km in this state? I felt scared and angry at the same time.

Without looking left or right, I was out on the Camino by 6:30 am. Although the sun was already coming up, I felt cold. Something was not right. I could feel deep inside that something was going to happen today that would change the course of my Camino. I did not feel like talking to anyone but just wanted to walk as fast as I could. Ideally, I wanted to run to prove that I can do it and finish this walk, but I knew this was completely ridiculous. My head was imploding with doubts, fears, negative thoughts, and ever-growing worries.

In that state I walked a brief distance with a fellow German pilgrim, who told me that the Camino teaches us to deal with our internal conflicts and problems. "It provides us with the ideal opportunity to learn to accept the external circumstances, whatever they are, and to learn to work on our inner reaction to them." He called it the 90/10 principle, because according to him, only 10% of our happiness and wellbeing is impacted by the circumstances, whereas 90% is impacted by how we react to them.

I was clearly not reacting well to my own circumstances on that day. Full of anger and fear, and boiling inside, I left the German pilgrim behind. I could not talk further but had to just get away from everything and everyone as quickly as possible. I probably walked the fastest I ever had and by late morning I arrived in Sahagún, nearly 20 km of walking having just flown by.

There I bumped into Peter and Gabi, German pilgrims whom I had walked with in the past and whom I valued greatly. Gabi was sad. She would have to take the train from there because she just did not have enough time to walk the whole distance. Peter on the other hand had injured his ankle and had to take the train to Leon to see a doctor and get some rest. He was as devastated about his circumstances as was Gabi about hers.

As we parted, Peter gave me a big hug and said: "Now you are on your own. Now you must walk your own Camino!" His hug and these words triggered something deep inside me. I put my backpack on. My legs suddenly heavy as lead. And out of the blue there were tears. Embarrassed and lonely I walked out of Sahagún.

Something was different and the walk now felt even more daunting. The weight on my shoulders and the pressure to keep walking 'my own Camino', as Peter had called it, seemed to put me in an unbearable situation. I was alone and felt the 400 km I still had to walk building up as a huge, towering wall in front of me. "What if I don't make it? What if I have to give up like Peter and Gabi? What do I tell my friends, my parents, my colleagues when I come back home?" All this effort, only to give in after all: I am a failure.

This sentence was the final straw. I started to cry uncontrollably. Tears were streaming down my face as if they had been waiting for years to come out. I just could not stop. I kept walking and crying. All of a sudden, I saw in my mind very clearly the picture of myself as a little boy. Everything seemed to be still in that moment. That little boy with blond hair, shorts, and a cute smile looked at me and said: "You have proved so much in your life. You do not have to prove anything to anyone!" With tears flowing, I gave that little version of myself a big hug. In that moment it was as if all the pressure, all the fear, all the anger, all the doubts were just falling off my shoulders. Just like that.

I began to understand the source of my distress. I was not walking my own walk. I was walking to prove myself to others. To learn this was shocking, but also extremely liberating. Reflecting further, I realised that all my life I had been trying to meet other people's expectations – the expectations at school, the expectations at university, and of course the expectations at work, with all its scorecards and Key Performance Indicators (KPIs).

But here and now on the Camino, I had already walked 400 km and that was a huge achievement. And looking at my life there were so many things I could be proud of. I said out loud: "I am not a failure and I do not have to prove anything to anyone." With that I could feel deep inside that it did not matter if I finished this walk, but that "I can be proud to just be here and walk as far as I can!"

I do not remember anymore how long the tears lasted, but I reckon it was probably after 2–3 km of walking when I passed a traffic sign where someone had scribbled something in very small capital letters on the back. For whatever reason I paused my walk, went closer, and read what it said: "You are very very special!"

In that moment I dropped my backpack and sat down just behind that traffic sign. The angst was gone, and in its place came strong inner calm and self-belief. I felt I had arrived at the destination 'Me'. Nothing else mattered. There was peace, gratitude, and a deep sense of joy.

I did not have to finish this walk. I could just enjoy another two weeks of wonderful walking holiday through magnificent landscape, meeting interesting people, and basically celebrating life. I will not forget this feeling, and I wish I could conserve it forever. In hindsight, this experience on the Camino changed my life. It gave me the courage to look for and find my own path. Not the path that was expected by others. Same as the lyrics go in my Camino soundtrack: I would now "hold my own, know my name, and go my own way."

After resting there for probably half an hour at the traffic sign in complete bliss and peacefulness, I stood up and began to walk on – without any pressure, fear, or anger. But with my eyes wide open to the beauty around me.

Soon after, I met a German pilgrim called Evelyn who had lost her husband a few years back. Immediately, we were in a deep conversation about life's beautiful and difficult aspects. I told her what had happened to me, and I felt a deep connection as Evelyn understood me so well. We did not notice how, but we walked another 15 km together, chatting away, and so in the evening I arrived in El Burgo Ranero, having set a new personal record for the furthest distance I had ever walked in a day: 42 km.

We found a beautiful little pilgrim hostel, and after a wonderful dinner with other pilgrims I fell asleep blissfully happy and full of inner peace. The Camino had spoken to me and told me that I am okay the way I am. Nothing to prove, nothing to reach, just to be there.

The next morning was cold and rainy, but I woke up with a smile on my face. The blisters were the same, the cut was still there, the shoes were still taking on stones, but I had completely changed how I looked at all of this. Now the 10/90 principle was working for me. I had regained my faith. The trust that someone would help me with the blisters, that my shoes would carry me just as far as they needed to, and that I would be protected and okay on this walk. I walked the first 12 km together with Evelyn and then, as if something was carrying me, I walked

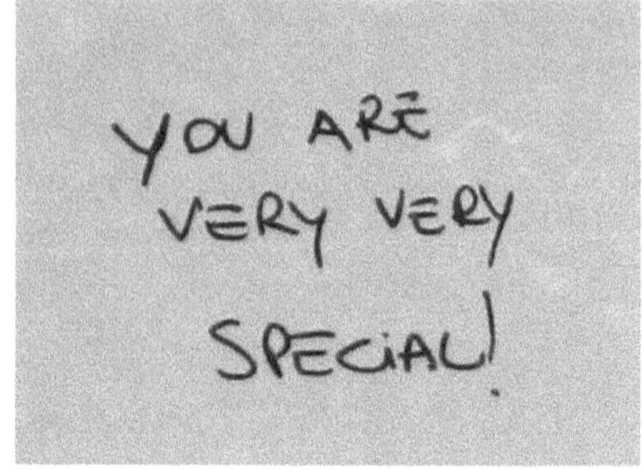

'You are very very special' on the back of a traffic sign

Sitting at the traffic sign and at peace

With Helmut and Evelyn in El Burgo Ranero

another 26 km, 'flying' to make it my second longest distance covered in a day, 38 km, all the way to Leon.

Here I treated myself to a proper hotel room with a bathtub. I had a couple of beers and some schnapps with two other pilgrims, Peter and Herbert. I had arrived. Nothing else mattered. I was okay the way I was, and I had changed the Camino from being a 'threat' where I could fail, into a marvellous 'challenge' which I would ride as far as I could without having to have to complete it 'by all means'. That was freedom! I was finally on my way.

Many years later I came across a wonderful little story, which I think summarises how I felt on that so important day for me on the Camino, and I hope it can also provide you with a little of that deep inner peace and calmness.

There Is a Crack in Everything – for a Reason!

A long, long time ago, there was an old woman who was living all by herself. Every morning, she would get up, leave her little house, and walk to the river to get fresh water for the day. To carry the water, she took with her a long wooden carrying pole, from which hung an old bucket on the left side and another bucket on the right side. Always the same buckets on the same sides of the pole.

The walk down the dirt path from her house wasn't very long. At the river, she would take the pole with the buckets off her shoulders and carefully dip each bucket in the river, filling it with cold, fresh water. Then, just as carefully, she would place each bucket back on the pole, lift the pole up onto her shoulders, and slowly make her way back.

As she walked home, the right-hand bucket held the water perfectly, whereas the left-hand bucket had a small crack in the bottom, from which leaked out a persistent drip of water. By the time the woman reached home, the bucket would be half empty. This happened day after day, week after week, year after year.

Nothing changed until one day, just as they arrived at the river, the left-hand bucket sighed a deep sigh. This surprised the old woman. In all her many years, she had never heard a bucket sigh before.

Then the bucket spoke. "I am so sorry. I am so sorry."

"What are you sorry about?" the woman asked the bucket.

"That I keep leaking. You work so hard bringing water to the house, and I am half empty when we arrive home. A bucket has only one job, and I can't even do that well. I am useless."

"Well, you do bring home half a bucket full of water."

"Don't mock me. I know what I am. I'm a failure. I was made to carry water. I can't do it. I have this crack, this defect. I'm a failure at the one thing I am meant to do."

The old woman looked at the bucket, which had been with her on her left side all these years. With sadness and compassion in her eyes, she began to speak: "My good friend. I am so, so sorry. I had no idea you felt this way. You've been suffering all this time, and it is entirely my fault. You have no idea at all, do you?"

"What do you mean? No idea about what?" asked the bucket. "Let me show you." She filled the buckets and gently picked up the pole and, as they walked home, she asked the right-hand bucket, "what do you see?"

"I see the path. I see dirt. I see the same as I do every day," said the right-hand bucket. "That's right," said the woman. "Now, what do you see?" she asked the left-hand bucket.

The left-hand bucket looked down for the first time ever and was amazed. All along the edge of the dirt path were flowers, blooming beautifully in a

The leaky bucket

splash of colours. While the right side was bare, the left side, its side, was lush and lovely. Through the crack in the bucket, water dripped out and fell right onto the flowers, giving moisture to each plant.

"I planted those flowers," said the woman. "They're lovely, but they need a lot of care. And they need daily watering. So, when I found you, I knew I'd found exactly what I needed. Every morning, I fill you with water. And every morning, as I walk back up this hill, you sprinkle it out, so carefully, so precisely, drop by drop, exactly the right amount of water to keep these flowers flourishing so beautifully. This path is a wonderful place, and it's all because of you. I'm so sorry you never knew this and thought you were a broken failure. You're not a failure, and you're not broken. You're perfect."

The bucket was stunned and smiled a silent smile. The woman looked at it and, with a wise twinkle in her eyes, said: "The crack that you thought made you a failure was exactly what was needed to make our world a more beautiful place. Thank you for this!"

Just like the old bucket, we all have our cracks, our weaknesses, and things that sometimes make us think we are failures. But what if that's not true? What if these perceived shortcomings just make us whole and perfect and useful to the world and those around us just the way we are, no fixing required? What if they actually mean that as 'buckets' we aren't 'half-empty' in any real sense after all?

Looking back, that is exactly what I learnt during that wonderful halfway day on the Camino. I recognised my cracks and saw that they were okay. I saw that I was okay the way I am. I saw that I was even more than okay and suddenly understood what had previously seemed like a deficit (the crack), that I had to meet the expectations of others, was simply not true! It is true that the expectations of others have given me a lot of energy, drive, and strength, but now I could use all this energy for things that are meaningful and important to me and that are not represented by the expectations of others.

I want to encourage you to pause for a moment, open your eyes, and look at the flowers that you create along your way. Look for even the tiniest little shoots with which you make this world a better place and let yourself be awed by the many glorious blossoms that appear when you allow yourself to really and fully acknowledge your own value, your worth. Perfection: it's a nice concept, but who would trade lovable or generous or kind or happy for perfect? Who would choose to grind out the job of 'carrying water' perfectly if it meant a path – a life – with no flowers?

In the words of songwriter Leonard Cohen: "Ring the bells that still can ring, forget your perfect offering. There is a crack, a crack in everything. That's how the light gets in."

The Journey Is the Destination

I woke up in Leon with a slight hangover, after a great night out on Saturday evening. But somehow that did not matter, as I could still feel that deep inner calm from what had happened to me on Friday. It might sound very strange, but it felt as if I had found my peace. I was smiling from the inside. I felt a lot of strength, confidence, and energy to move on, with all the pressure gone.

The weather was cold and rainy. Somehow, I ended up walking together with The Billionaire for the next full couple of days. It was just the two of us. At times we followed our own thoughts walking in silence, at other times we were deeply engaged in conversation. Everything felt natural, positive, and in a wonderful flowing rhythm.

We walked nearly 70 km in those two days. But my blisters were now at a stage where I had to decide whether I should see a doctor or do something else about them. And almost as if I had foretold it, someone came to help me.

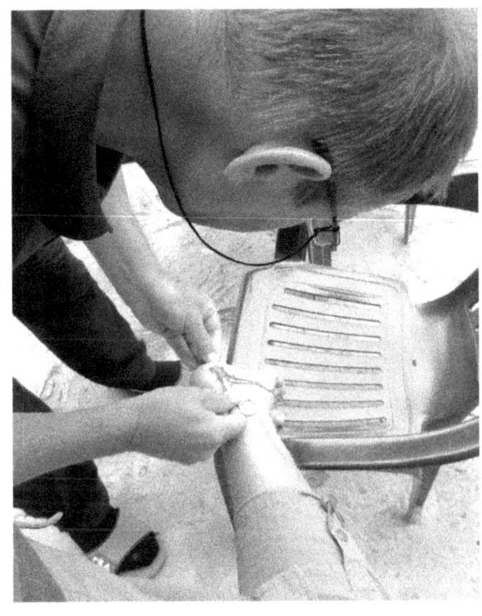

Getting help with the blisters

Peter, who had given me that fateful hug and told me that I now needed to walk my own Camino, was spending the night at the same hostel as I that evening. His injury had improved, and he had caught up by bus and train. It was very nice to see him again and of course I told him about my experiences after we had said goodbye.

Peter was an expert on blisters, as he had walked the Camino the year before. I showed him mine and without further ado, he pulled out some scissors, disinfected the blisters, and pierced them open. Then he poured a generous amount of disinfectant on them while using his full weight to hold me down, as I was trying to jump up in agony. But he only smiled and said, "Leave them open for the night; in the morning we'll see if there is still liquid inside. If not, we just tape them up and let them heal."

It sounded almost too simple, but it worked. With the liquid drained and the tape on, the blisters began to heal and soon a massive worry was sliding off my shoulders. My faith that someone would help me had proved well-founded. Thank you, Peter!

With this I was able to walk on and the next day we passed a place called Cruz de Ferro, about 230 km from Santiago. This has a remarkable tradition: for hundreds of years pilgrims have been bringing little stones from their homes, leaving them here at the Cruz de Ferro, as a symbol of something they would like to leave behind in their lives. In many cases pilgrims not only carry their own stones, but also the wishes and prayers of others who cannot make the pilgrimage themselves.

Blister-saviour Peter

Cruz de Ferro – leaving self-doubt and jealousy behind

I had not known about this beautiful tradition when I started my walk. But it was probably on my fourth day when someone told me about it and so I had picked up two small pebbles which I had carried with me since then. One of these little stones represented 'jealousy' and the other represented 'self-doubt'. These two feelings I had felt too much in my life and I wanted to leave them behind here and now, forever. It was very moving when I kissed my little pebbles and put them to rest with the millions of other stones pilgrims have brought and left here.

Today, more than ten years later, I of course still have the occasional self-doubt and I also experience the odd jealous episode, but they hardly begin to impact and hamper my life in the way they did before I went on my walk. The walk has helped me tremendously. It was the trigger point of my self-development journey about which I will share more in Part Two.

For now, I kept walking with a smile on my face. It was so wonderful to be able to enjoy the glorious landscape, hear the birds, and just be there. With my mind open, relaxed, and friendly, I started to connect deeper with other pilgrims who were equally open, supportive, and kind to me. With this, the second half of my Camino was pure joy. The weather, the people, my feet, and even my shoes were all good! Everything seemed to come together. I was in a complete flow. Nothing was missing.

The only question I had to ask myself was this: how come I could feel such a deep sense of peace and fulfilment with only my three pairs of underwear and a couple of shirts in my backpack? And, more importantly, how would I be able to take this calm and peace with me to my life back in Singapore? The short answer would be: "I just could not!" But more about this later …

With this amazing flow, the kilometre count to Santiago went down steadily and almost a bit too fast now. I had crossed the milestone of 100 km to go on Day 22 of walking and soon I found myself on Day 25 walking with Helmut, towards our final overnight stop in Monte Gozzo, which was only about 6 km from Santiago.

We bought a couple of beers to celebrate, but it almost felt as if the Camino lifted its finger one more time before the end, saying to us: "You have not done it yet. Stay humble!"

The last kilometres to Monte Gozzo seemed to stretch out endlessly. Eventually we made it and for the first time we could see in the distance the silhouette of the Cathedral of Santiago de Compostela. This was a feeling that I cannot describe in words.

Sipping our beers we sat in the comfortable grass looking at the cathedral. On the one hand there was pride, joy, gratitude, and deep inner satisfaction to reach Santiago on the next day. On the other hand, there were also already a few thoughts about what would happen afterwards. How would my life go on? How

Beers at Monte Gozzo – only 6 km from Santiago

would I find my way back into my everyday walk of life? What would remain of this important life journey?

In the evening we enjoyed a delicious pilgrim dinner and even though this was a very large hostel, and I was sharing a room with many other pilgrims, I did not feel lonely this time, but rather wonderfully connected and safe.

On the morning of the 30th of May, twenty-six long days after I had started walking in Saint-Jean-Pied-de-Port, I was lying in bed and could not sleep. There was just too much going through my mind. I sent a text message to my good friend Denis whose T-shirt I was wearing proudly: "It's 4 am here. I'm lying in bed. 6 km from Santiago, which we saw last night after a long, hard walk. Tears of joy, of pride, of gratitude are flowing without break. Amazing! Soon I will be entering the cathedral with my faithful friend's T-shirt! I cannot fathom in words how I feel but wanted to send you a *'Buen Camino!'* and a big hug from far away!"

Within a minute Denis replied: "Wow! I am proud of you. F*@k man, what an experience! It rocks and you just did it. Until next week. A big hug back!"

After a lovely breakfast we got going and it was as if we were sailing these remaining 6 km to Santiago. We arrived and I simply cannot express how I felt. A deep feeling of ease, the feeling of achievement, but also the feeling of humility and humbleness. We had a hearty brunch with some celebratory beers and then joined the service at the cathedral, which was very moving.

Arrival in Santiago

When I looked around the church, I saw many familiar faces of pilgrims I had met along the way. Everyone seemed to have their own moving thoughts. Many had tears in their eyes. Many just looked peaceful and happy in the festive and contemplative setting of the cathedral. As an old tradition, a massive pot of incense is swayed here on a long rope all through the cathedral, pulled manually by a group of monks. In the past this was done to mask the odours of the pilgrims, who were not able to wash themselves a lot. Today it is a touching event. It brought tears to my eyes. I was sitting there and thinking back to the evening of Day Three when I had imagined myself sitting in the cathedral. Here I was and I had done it. Absolutely amazing.

Suddenly there was deep gratitude for having made my way and not given up. At the same time, I was amazed at how exactly this image had appeared in my mind on the evening of the third day. Admittedly, it looked and smelled a little different in reality, but I felt like I had come full circle. I was okay the way I am and that was a very touching feeling!

I rewarded myself with a beautiful hotel room, took a long, soothing bath and then met up with a group of other pilgrims for a dinner with loads of laughter, joy, and drinks. When the bells rang out for midnight, it was my 42nd birthday. We lay down on the plaza in front of the cathedral, looking up into the starry night. I had arrived in Santiago and deep down I also felt I had arrived at myself.

My birthday was a sunny day, and I spent it strolling through the city, meeting other pilgrims with hugs, and enjoying wonderful, light-hearted conversa-

The Birthday Gang

tions. Everyone seemed to have a smile on their face. In the afternoon I walked a little outside of town and took in the lovely view of the cathedral, writing down thoughts of gratefulness in my journal.

They say, "Happiness is only real when shared," and so in the evening of that 31st of May, we met up for a little birthday dinner. It was amazing to see that most of the people I had walked with and shared many meaningful conversations with had come. We enjoyed the evening together and then after many hugs said goodbye to each other.

With a bit of a hangover but a big smile on my face, I left Spain early in the morning on 1st June 2012, now on my way back, via Berlin and my hometown Hartmannsdorf, to 'real life' in Singapore. Little did I know what would await me there.

I want to close Part One with another walking story, one that has truly touched me. This story represents to me exactly what I felt when flying back to Singapore.

The Power of Gratitude

"You have seven days to vacate your property!" That's what the judge told Moth and Raynor Winn in the spring of 2013 after a three-year court battle. They had made an investment with a close friend of Moth's. It had turned

Raynor and Moth

bad, and creditors were now claiming their small farmhouse in Wales. Moth and Raynor could not believe the judge's order. Together, they had built up the house and farm from a ruin over the last twenty years. It was the place where their two children had grown up and still came back to on university breaks. It was a place where families came to stay for the summer as a countryside holiday. And most importantly, it was their home.

Now, within seven days, they would be homeless. There are times you think things can't get any gloomier, but they can. Within the same seven days, they also had a doctor's appointment and Moth was diagnosed with a rare brain disease. The doctors gave him two to three years to live.

Moth and Raynor Winn had met when they were still teenagers, a 'love at first sight' fairy tale. They had raised two children, lived a modest and honest life on their farm, building and shaping it with their own hands. Now, suddenly, this was all falling apart. How much more misery can you endure in a week? Can you imagine becoming homeless and facing a terminal prognosis for yourself or your loved one at the same time?

When the bailiffs knocked on their door, Moth and Raynor were hiding under the stairs. They did not want to leave. They had nowhere to go. It was in that moment that Raynor happened to look at one of the many boxes of books stored there and saw *Five Hundred Mile Walkies,* written by a man who had walked the 630-mile Southwest Coast Path in England with his dog.[10]

As they needed a lifeline, a goal, and somewhere to go, both literally and figuratively, Raynor decided, in that instant, to try and convince Moth to walk the path together. It would "give them something to do." It would give them a reason to face the next day. It would simply give them hope. Moth agreed.

Based on tax reliefs, they had £48 per week between the two of them to live on. They camped wild in a small tent. They walked and slept in wet clothes, drenched by the regular torrential rains. They struggled with the physical strain of walking. They shivered through cold nights, and they were hungry. But through walking, they also started to find their feet, their voice, and their hope in the close bond with nature.

Here's how Raynor describes the transformation of her mindset: "As we were walking, I started to realise that home is a state of mind. It's what makes you feel safe – and you don't need walls for that. You can define home in a different way, and for me that would always be my family, whether they were 100 miles away or there with a rucksack next to me."

Walking set them free and gave them a new identity. Two days before reaching their final destination, a stranger offered to rent them out a small place on the path for a very reasonable price. They were able to finance it with a study loan. During the walk Moth had miraculously got stronger and fitter, completely defying the odds. And now, after 630 tough miles, they had found a new home and the chance of a fresh start.

Raynor, whose childhood dream was to be a novelist, wrote an article about their walk for the UK homeless magazine, *The Big Issue*. And she went on to write a book for Moth. "A gift to him: a big fat love letter, and maybe a reminder for when his memory began to fade."

As their daughter read the book, she was deeply touched and suggested they try to do something with it. In 2018, it was published and became short-listed for a book award. It has sold thousands of copies since then, inspiring people all around the world with the couple's transformation from losing everything to finding hope and starting over again.

Appreciating the bleakness of Moth and Raynor's fate humbled me and made me deeply grateful for the life I live. Despite having to go through my own challeng-es, I have a roof over my head every night, sufficient funds to eat, and I am bless-ed with a wonderful supportive social network of family and friends. I am very grateful for that. I am telling their story because, like Raynor and Moth, I felt a tremendous sense of gratitude at the end of my Camino journey. Gratitude that I had completed it, gratitude that people had helped me, and above all gratitude that I had set out on my journey in the first place. I was very grateful that I had listened to my inner voice for the first time in my life.

It was with this uplifting feeling of gratitude that I got on the plane back home to Singapore. On the flight, I made a list of all the things I was grateful for in my life during the Camino and beyond. It was a lot! And it felt good. I was happy, joyful, and full of inner peace.

With this, at the end of the first part of this book and if you are up for it, I would like to invite you here and now to do the same exercise: just write down all the things for which you are grateful. It's not an easy task. Don't worry, just write whatever comes to your mind and have the list handy if you think of anything to add later. Maybe that makes you a little bit more content and happier. Just as I felt, when I was on top of the world, returning to Singapore – not knowing what would await me there and how difficult it would be.

Part Two
The Walk of Change

Welcome Back to Reality!

After a wonderful birthday celebration in Santiago de Compostela, I was then on my way back to Asia. I first flew to Berlin, where I met up with my good friend Martin, whose daughter Mascha had just been born a few days earlier, and then I went to see my family in Hartmannsdorf, from where I began the long journey back to Singapore.

The flight was excellent, and I could not stop smiling. Having just successfully completed the 'walk of my life', I looked like Jesus and perhaps also felt like Jesus. I thought my experience on the Camino had provided me with an invincible enlightenment. I felt from now on everything would be fine and life would be a gentle stroll. Little did I know what was to come …

The first few days in the office still felt a bit like a honeymoon. It was great to see all my team members and colleagues again. There was a lot to share and to talk about, and so the first week back at work just flew by. But then, after the second week, I started to notice that my calm and inner peace began to fade away very quickly. I got fully absorbed back into the daily grind of running the supply chain operations of a fast-moving half-billion-dollar consumer goods business: the wave of 'busyness' swept over me, and gradually I began to drown.

The daily emails – 150 to 200 on average – with all their various demands and problems needed attention. But how to do this, when the diary is completely blocked with back-to-back meetings from 7:30 in the morning through to the evening? Answering emails and doing any actual strategic thinking was only possible very early in the morning or late at night.

At the same time, the work to be done was not very pleasant. We went through the challenging organisational restructuring my boss had already mentioned to me back in March. This meant we had to reduce head counts and that entailed having some very difficult conversations.

After two weeks 'back to reality', it felt as if the Camino had never happened. There was no more calmness and clarity of mind. In the evenings when I came back after a long day at the office, I missed the simplicity of knowing whether I had met my 'walking target' for the day or not. Life was much more complex away from the Camino and with this also came the distractions of social media as well as many other things that can overwhelm us in our daily lives. I felt like the son asking for advice from his father in the song by East German songwriter Gerhard Schoene …

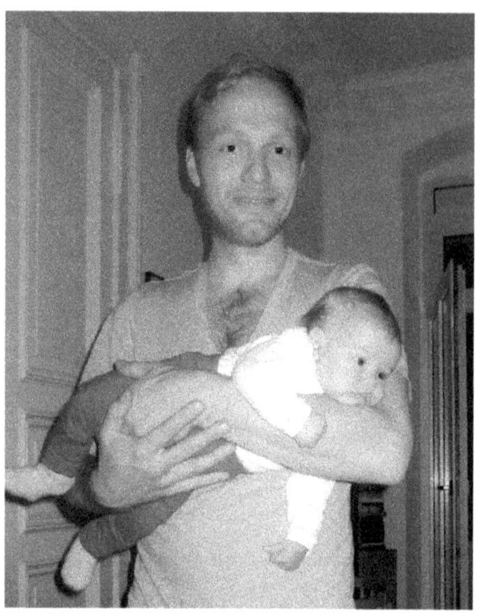

Martin & Mascha

The Simple Magic of a Peaceful Life

Gerhard Schoene wrote a song in 1988 called *Ganz einfach,* which translates as 'very simple'. It tells the following story:

A very stressed-out man pays a quick visit to his father out in the village where he grew up. When he arrives, the old man is just about to feed his cats. The young man says to the father: "Hello Dad, I will not stay long. I actually do not have time to be here at all, because I do not really know where my head is at the moment! I rush all day long, and, in the end, I feel I get nothing done. I'm just a nervous wreck. Can you explain to me how you are so calm and relaxed?"

The old man scratches his left ear and says:

"My dear, listen well. I do it this way. It is very simple: When I sleep, I sleep. When I get up, I get up. When I eat, I eat. When I plan, I plan. When I go, I go. When I work, I work. When I speak, I speak. When I listen, I listen."

The young man responds, "What is this nonsense? I do all of that, and yet I find no peace."

The old man scratches his left ear once again and says: "My dear, listen well, you do it all a little differently: When you sleep, you get up already. When you get up, you eat already. When you eat, you plan already. When you plan, you go already. When you go, you work already. When you work, you speak already. When you speak, you listen already. When you listen ... – you sleep."

Psychologists at Harvard University did a study about the daily activities, thoughts, and feelings of 2,250 volunteers to find out how often they were focused on what they were doing and how happy they were.[11]

The results were stunning. During 46.9% of their waking time, the participants were not really there. They were engaging in certain activities, but their minds were actually somewhere else, wandering, or focusing on other things. Tellingly, the study concluded that the people who were most distracted from the task in hand were most likely to report feelings of unhappiness.

Looking at this, we begin to understand why the old man seems to have found the simple solution to a happy and contented life: being present. Still, the million-dollar question remains: how can we live more in the moment without constantly having our attention spirited away by the multifarious 'weapons of mass distraction' around us? How do we live the present without the urge to plan our next move or the need to worry about the future?

How cool it would be if we had a tool that could remind us daily, regularly, of the importance of living in the present moment and focusing on the very activities at hand?

Here is the good news: you do not need to download another app, because you already have access to such a powerful personal tool right now. It is available to you any time, any place, and it is highly effective at bringing you back to the present moment wherever you are and whatever you are doing: your breath!

Let's try it out right now. Take a deeeeeeeep breath in and, with a deeeeeeep breath out, slow everything down and let your mind and body settle into a more relaxed state.

Let's repeat that: take a deeeeeeeep breath in and a deeeeeeeep breath out. Feel the release, the calm. Feel the stillness. Feel the connection to the here and now.

What are you doing in this moment besides reading? What is going on in your head? What sounds can you hear and what smells do you notice? What do you feel? Isn't it pleasant to simply be more present?

The more you can remind yourself of taking regular breathing breaks during the day, the more you will create these small oases of peace, calm, and true presence. Our breath is a wonderful tool, always available, and highly reliable: it works every time, helping you to become less stressed and happier, as it focuses you on the here and now, so that:

When you sleep, you sleep.
When you get up, you get up.
When you eat, you eat.
When you plan, you plan.
When you go, you go.
When you work, you work.
When you speak, you speak.
When you listen, you listen.

Beautiful Flowers Wither, the Seed Lives!

I wish I had reminded myself of this insight and taken these regular breathers, as 'coming back to reality' from my exhilarating Camino experience I slowly began to drift into a downward spiral. It felt as if I had to catch up on the four weeks I had not been working, now trying to squeeze even more meetings into my already busy days.

The result was that we started to make progress in our many projects and deliverables at work and got the organisational restructuring done in a way that minimised the impact on my team, but on a personal front my inner calm was replaced by exactly the same hectic rhythm as I had been living before the Camino.

During the week it was full-on work, and on the weekends I then went out with my friends, 'celebrating life' with quantities of beer. This was fun, but it did not help at all to bring the peace from the Camino into my daily life. By the end of the weekend, I'd be feeling the Sunday blues, and worrying about all the demands of the week ahead, together with quite frequent hangovers and lack of sleep from partying.

It was dreadful and I was stunned and shocked to realise this. I had created so many good and productive ideas during the walk, especially about what I wanted to do with my life, but it all seemed to go haywire during the months after I returned 'back to reality', and sadly it felt as if there was not much I could do about it, as I just 'got swept away'.

Not everything was gone though. There were some fleeting positive feelings of the Camino inside myself: seeds of change sown deep inside, which were waiting to be watered, nurtured, and cared for so that they could spring to life and begin to show their beauty, helping me to change my life.

About ten weeks after I had come back from the Camino, I finally got a breather. I went to visit some beautiful volcanoes in Indonesia. This extended weekend trip not only gave me a break from the relentless onslaught of work and parties, but more

At the Indonesian volcanoes in August 2012

importantly it allowed me to take a step back and look at where my life was going. It gave me the opportunity to suddenly see very clearly how the past ten weeks seemed to have taken away completely the serenity that I had treasured so much.

Sitting on top of the Indonesian mountains and watching a magnificent sunrise reminded me of the Camino: it was that same sense of being in nature and being one with life. Fully in sync and deeply connected.

When looking ahead I realised that I needed to begin to take things into my own hands now and to shape what I wanted to do with my life. If I didn't do that, life would continue to 'happen to me' as it had done for the past twenty years, when – I realised with hindsight – I was riding waves of professional opportunities which had opened up in front of me, but which probably were not truly what I wanted to do with my life.

I had to take the steering wheel firmly into my own hands. And this meant change. I had to change what I was doing and how I was living my life. I was still a long way from making my Wheel of Life run smoother and in a more efficient fashion. I still had not found a fulfilling long-term relationship with a woman, and I still ground through my days as a cheerless supply chain director. And during that whole weekend in Indonesia, one specific situation popped up again and again in my memory, trying to tell me something.

Change Before You Have to!

By the end of the 1980s, the world was deeply divided. This division was especially felt in Germany, which had been split into West and East Germany for nearly three decades. By the autumn of 1989, the situation in East Germany was becoming incredibly tense.

Hundreds of people had escaped from behind the 'Iron Curtain' to the West, via Hungary and the West German embassy in Prague. Tens of thousands were on the streets, demonstrating for freedom and against the rule of the Communist party. The government was intent on pushing back and staying in power, by all means necessary.

During this time, I was doing my compulsory 18-month national service in the East German army. As I was tall and quite handsome – see for yourself in the next image – I ended up being selected as an honour guard, parading in front of the *Neue Wache* in Berlin. As a soldier, I was under the orders of the government. And I was afraid. I was afraid I might end up in the same position as soldiers had been in China where, earlier in June 1989, they were ordered to use their weapons to shoot at demonstrators.

As hundreds of thousands of people were marching the streets in Dresden, Karl-Marx-Stadt, Leipzig, Berlin, and other cities, the East German army was on alert. In my army barracks in central Berlin there were alarm drills almost every night. Each time the alarm bell rang, I was absolutely terrified, scared we would be told to get our guns.

But instead of guns, they usually gave us batons, and we spent many nights on trucks, ready to go out and beat up demonstrators. These were some of the most difficult hours of my life. I knew that my family, friends, and school-mates were out there demonstrating, and I wished I could be as well. In all honesty, I was not sure how I would react if I received the order to beat up those demonstrators or, even worse, to shoot them. It was horrendous.

On the 6th of October 1989, the Soviet prime minister and most powerful figure in the Eastern Bloc, Mikhail Gorbachev, visited Berlin to celebrate the 40th anniversary of East Germany. In 1985, Gorbachev had instituted a policy of perestroika and glasnost, which stands for restructuring and openness, to change the political and economic system in the USSR.

Together with three other soldiers, I was asked to perform in a special memorial service as Gorbachev remembered the victims of World War II during his visit. We carried wreaths ahead of Gorbachev and his delegation, and, by the end of our drill, he stood about four metres ahead of us and bowed.

In the army now – 1988

As he left the building, I could hear thousands of people outside, chanting his nickname: "Gorbi! Gorbi! Gorbi!" Then, something strange happened. Gorbachev was supposed to go back to his car and drive off. The protocols for these events were extremely rigid, and those who had planned everything out to the smallest detail did not want to see any changes. But Gorbachev changed the protocol.

He did not go back to his car. Instead, he turned to his right to talk to the people and the Western journalists. That's when the picture on the next page was taken.

In those few moments, he said something so profound that it would eventually end the Cold War. Asked by the journalists how he saw the East German government handling the crisis, he (literally translated) said: "I think life is only dangerous for those who don't adjust to its changes adequately." Two journalists present picked up the sentence and paraphrased it into a compelling catchphrase, which Gorbachev liked and later even used in his own biography: "Change before you have to."

After only four weeks, on 9th November 1989, one of the biggest miracles in modern times occurred when the Berlin Wall came down without a single shot being fired. It was absolutely amazing and not something anyone would have predicted only five years earlier.

Gorbachev's crucial words on 6th October 1989

Today, more than 30 years after these events, I believe Gorbachev's insight is more valid than ever. The world we are living in keeps changing at an astonishing pace every day, and this triggers fundamental stress and tensions within us. Each change creates its own discomfort and often takes a lot of personal effort to deal with. But deal with it we must. If we refuse to make the necessary changes now, we may face even bigger problems and more wrenching change in the future.

When you look at your own personal and professional life, is there an area where you know that you have to change, but you keep resisting that necessary first little step forward? An area where perhaps you struggle to accept, on a deep personal level, that this change is required of you and that it is for your own good and further development?

Embrace the change, and who knows, you may feel the same kind of relief and joy the millions of people around the world felt when the Berlin Wall came down, and our world became more closely connected than ever before. By actively and courageously dealing with change, millions became free. You too can become free from the tyranny of difficult circumstances, indecision, and inaction. The key? "Change before you have to!"

Enjoying my tranquil time in the Indonesian mountains reminded me of what Gorbachev had said. Listening quietly and closely to my inner voice once more, I felt something had changed inside myself. That 'something' was a very vague but still present feeling I had taken back from the Camino. A feeling that I can go my own way, and that now was the time to do something about it. It was exactly that powerful message the Camino had told me on that fateful 18th of May 2012, when it broke me apart and whispered to me, "Stop proving yourself to others, and begin to go your own way now!"

Sitting in Indonesia and writing down my thoughts, I began to take stock of the changes I had to make in my life. First of all, there was my work. I felt strongly that it could not be my life's purpose to make a billion-dollar money making machine a little richer every day. Being honest with myself, I did not enjoy the industry of beauty care I was working in. Despite putting in so much effort, I struggled to find a connection to the products. It may sound harsh when I say that I was 'selling a lie' to consumers, telling them that they could stop their ageing if only they were to use our remarkable creams and lotions, but clearly, I lacked passion or even a sense of purpose: my job felt meaningless.

Still, looking at my work from a different angle, I also realised that there were parts of it which I absolutely loved. Those were the moments when I was in one-to-one meetings or working with my team, when I felt I could help to develop and grow others. These occasions, when I saw someone learning something new about themselves, giving them a chance to progress in their professional or personal life, were so fulfilling and gratifying that I wanted to have more of them.

Understanding what I loved about my work was a light bulb moment for me. Whilst it was perhaps only 20% of my job, I truly enjoyed it. And I would have done this personal development work even without getting paid. With this realisation I suddenly knew very clearly what I had to do. I had to increase the share of people development work from 20% to 80% of my working time, whilst eliminating the hardcore KPI-driven supply chain improvement work and politics.

I had to replace that 80% with the meaningful work of helping others grow. Yes, that was an eye-opener. And I also already knew through previous experiences how to do that: coaching! All of a sudden, I had discovered my potential dream job.

To be honest, in retrospect, it sounds pretty straightforward, and I really struggle to understand why I had not thought of that much earlier, especially since for many years I had been contemplating what exactly I could do with my career. I had even participated in the occasional coach training course, but never had the courage to really think this career option through to the end with all the consequences. But suddenly, and above all with the courage from the Camino to go my own way, this was now a real option to consider. The clarity, the excitement, the motivation this brought was something I could feel everywhere in my body, and with this also returned the peacefulness and clarity. It was crystal clear what I wanted to do: qualify as a coach.

Coming back from Indonesia I started to do some research. One of the major associations offering coaching qualifications was the International Coaching Federation (ICF). Looking through their website, I found out what was necessary to certify myself as a coach and what coach training organisations would be on offer. I also looked around my personal network for people who had already completed such a training. I quickly found what I was looking for and in a very good conversation with my P&G colleague, Carol Fusek, the American coaching institute Coach U was recommended to me.

I contacted them, signed up, and started my official coach training at the beginning of 2013. But before I became a coach, there was something else I wanted to experience. Another 'crazy thing' which my inner voice had been telling me to pursue: I wanted to become a monk.

The Fired Part-Time Monk

Soon after my return from the volcanoes, I began to drown again in my hectic working life. Whilst my inner direction of what I wanted to do was clearer, I still had to grind through the days with ten hours of back-to-back meetings and hundreds of emails to answer either before, after, or in-between. Whilst the volcanoes had reminded me of the peacefulness and tranquillity of the Camino, in these next months I was again swept away by the daily priorities. And I somehow felt like a donkey.

What's Your Carrot?

Donkeys are very strong animals and can pull a cart or carry someone over long distances. They are also quite stubborn. To make a donkey move, some people whack them with a stick, but that usually does not work too well. Other people tie the stick to the donkey's neck, so it pokes out two to three feet in front of the donkey's mouth, and then dangle a carrot from it.

That works. The donkey moves to get to the carrot, but, of course, he never reaches it. Even if he starts galloping, the carrot still dangles just a tiny bit in front of him.

I feel that this is sometimes so similar to what we do. We chase after the best job, the perfect partner, the most vibrant health, and all round fulfilment in our life and work, but just as it is with our friend the donkey, the more we struggle to reach the prize and the harder we try to close the gap between what we want and what's just out of reach, the more frustrated we get and the more unobtainable the carrot seems to become: whatever the carrot may be, it seems forever out of reach.

Yet there is a way the donkey can catch the carrot, and once you understand how he does it, we can apply this to your own life as well. After the donkey's been running towards the carrot for a long time, he decides to stop and let go of the chase. As he comes to a stop, the carrot swings further away, because of the momentum: it's never been so far away before as in that moment. But then, suddenly, and all of its own, the carrot swings back and moves towards the donkey's mouth at high speed, and now, with one skilful snap, the donkey finally enjoys a bite of the long-desired, juicy carrot.

And the moral of the story? Sometimes, you might find yourself chasing your 'carrots' for too long, and too intensely. But the moment you stop, let go, and trust yourself to wait a bit, it will move toward you. That's the moment when you can catch your 'carrot'.

Yes, it's important to have 'carrots' (goals) as they provide us with a strong motivation and determination to move forward. But I think it is absolutely crucial to select the right 'carrots' to chase in our personal and professional lives. And once you have defined your personal 'carrots' well, the secret is to go after them in a focused but also balanced way, which sometimes may mean to 'let them come to us'.

When you look at your life now, is there a carrot which you have been chasing with so much effort that it always seems to be just a couple of inches out of reach? If so, perhaps stop for a bit, observe what happens, and who knows, maybe by letting it go for just a little while, you may find it 'coming back to you', because the momentum is there, you have put in the energy, it just needs time to rebound? Or it could even be a case of just finding a whole new approach that simply didn't occur to you beforehand. Either way: giving it a rest can do wonders for your chase.

At the beginning of 2013, I definitely needed some time to stop everything, to allow the 'carrot to swing back to me'. So, it felt amazing when, on the 10th of February, I boarded a plane in Singapore to go on my first ever silent retreat. My destination was the Wat Ram Poeng monastery on the outskirts of Chiang Mai in North Thailand.

The day before my departure I had celebrated my temporary disappearance into 'monkhood' in style with all my football mates. In a tradition that went back many years, we met on the evening of Chinese New Year in Singapore's Chinatown and welcomed the 'Year of the Snake' with many Tiger beers. As a result, this 'monk to be' was still a little hungover when I arrived, but I made my way safely to a small hotel near the temple. The next day everything would change, at least for ten days, so I thought; but in hindsight the retreat would change my whole life.

Walking into the monastery in the morning, I was conscious that I would now completely disconnect from the world and just be alone with my mind. I felt excited, but at the same time also a little apprehensive: how on earth would I be able to cope with not talking for ten long days? Mahatma Gandhi once said, "There are more important things in life than to continuously increase its speed." Well, I was certainly ready to decelerate and let the carrot come my way.

In good German mechanical engineering tradition, I had prepared myself well for this Vipassana meditation retreat, which is attended by thousands of people every year. The rules were clear, stark, and sternly emphasised and enforced by Phra Chaibodin, whom I would call the 'warden monk' of the monastery:

- No talking/socialising.
- No eye contact with others.
- No books, music, pens or writing material.
- No phones or computers or tablets.
- There are two meals a day, at 6:30 am and at 10:30 am, then no more food can be eaten after midday.
- Everyone must wear white clothes including white underwear.

Phra Chaibodin gave us all a booklet to read and then made it clear that our flow for the coming days would be very similar to the daily routine of the Buddhist monks:

- 4 am: wake up with the monastery bell and start meditation.
- 6:30 am: the bell rings for breakfast followed by cleaning of our rooms and work in the garden.
- Back to meditation practice.
- 10:30 am: the bell rings for lunch. Then back to meditate.
- 4–5 pm: report daily practice to the teachers.
- 6 pm: a hot drink is served in the common area.
- Back to meditation.
- 10 pm: lights out.

After we had moved into our simple but clean rooms, Phra Chaibodin met us near the pagoda and gave us a quick run-down on how to meditate, handing us a mat, a pillow, and a timer. He spent probably half an hour explaining to us how we could reach a more peaceful way of life by creating present awareness. Many of his simple

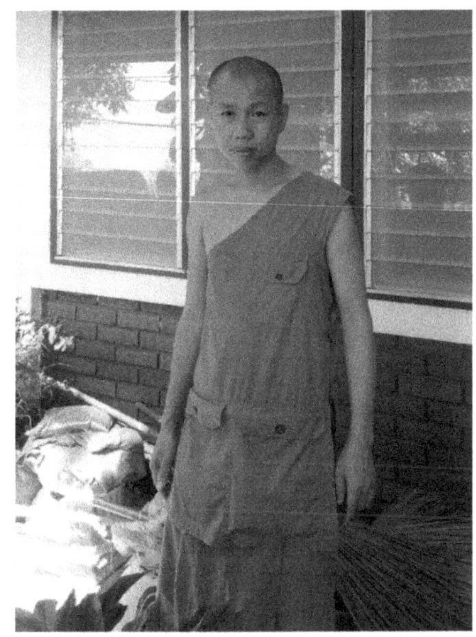

Phra Chaibodin

messages I would never forget as they were brought home, occasionally very painfully, during the coming ten days.

We would start out with fifteen minutes intervals of sitting followed by walking meditation. Phra Chaibodin told us to "just focus on rising and falling" of the breath when sitting and "left foot thus, right foot thus" when walking at a turtle speed of about twenty metres per hour (no joke).

He made it clear that we had come here to "learn suffering." According to the Buddhist philosophy, life is suffering triggered by the "cravings and aversions" we have developed due to our attachments to almost everything in our lives.

The golden rule for meditation and a peaceful life therefore, according to Phra Chaibodin, had only three words: "Accept, accept, accept." Whenever we are confronted with difficulty, whenever something is triggering us, whenever something is painful, say out loudly or just quietly in your mind the words: "Accept, accept, accept."

One evening though, I saw the monk walking frantically in circles in front of his office and loudly saying to himself "accept, accept, accept." It made me realise that accepting whatever it is without judgement seems to be an ongoing learning process, even for a monk with decades of meditation experience.

Another one of Phra Chaibodin's golden rules was: "Don't cry before you hurt." I could not really relate to it much at that point, but he would later emphasise this rule to me in a way that I would never forget. He finished his instructions by telling

Meditation in Wat Ram Poeng

us that with everything we did in our time in the monastery we should be "mindful, mindful." Then he walked away, and we started to meditate.

The first day was alright. Fifteen minutes sitting and fifteen minutes walking – which I clearly preferred – were a good pattern to help us settle into the new rhythm. I found some peaceful spots within the monastery grounds and truly enjoyed the stillness of my first eight hours of mediation. Our practice was only interrupted by breakfast, lunch, and some tea in the late afternoon. Similar to the Camino, by the end of Day One I thought, perhaps this is not so bad! But things were about to change ...

From the second day onward, we began to increase the meditation intervals gradually every day until we were sitting and walking 45 minutes each time. And on Day Two it already started to get tough. The afternoon especially dragged on and on forever, also in the light of knowing that my next meal would not be before 6:30 am the next morning.

From Day Three onward I began to "learn suffering." Not being very flexible and having to sit cross-legged for hours started to wear me down. Whilst we were not supposed to look at the timer, I could not help but do so frequently. Only a few minutes into a sitting meditation I started to peep at the clock and realised there was still an 'infinity' of time and pain to go.

On the fourth day it all came to a head. My inner voice began to run riot. "What am I doing here? This is damaging my knees and spine! I hate this! Why have I

98

come here?" With these thoughts in my head, I limped into Phra Chaibodin's office and asked him whether I could have another pillow please, as I could not stand the pain.

His response was straightforward: "Do you have operation?" Somewhat puzzled I replied "No." With that he made a hand movement as if he was trying to swat away a fly. I got angry and asked whether there was nothing that could be done to ease my pain. Now almost smiling he looked at me and said, "Meditation is the best medication! Don't cry before you hurt!" And that was the end of the conversation. I think the following little story conveys Phra Chaibodin's teaching of that moment in a light-hearted but also very graphic way.

A Crucial Learning from Transcend-Dental Medication

Did you read the headline as 'transcendental meditation'? Have another look ... This story is about how to pull out your own teeth, by yourself, with a pair of pliers, with no anaesthetic, and almost no pain at all. Not what you expected? Stay with me.

Let us start with a question: How would you feel if you got the message that in two hours, you were going to have two teeth extracted without the benefit of an anaesthetic? Miserable? Panicked? Mortified? All of the above?

That's probably how most of us would feel. But what if we didn't? What if we treated this prospect as if it really were no big deal? Could the experience be different? Apparently, it just might and so I want to share the following story, which my favourite Buddhist monk, Ajahn Brahm, related in one of his talks:

"A member of our community has very bad teeth. He needed to have many teeth pulled out, but he'd rather not have the anaesthetic. Eventually, he found a dental surgeon in Perth who would extract his teeth without anaesthetic. He has been there several times. He finds it no problem.

Allowing a tooth to be extracted by a dentist without anaesthetic might seem impressive enough, but this character went one better. He pulled out his own tooth without anaesthetic. We saw him one day outside the monastery workshop, holding a freshly pulled tooth smeared with blood, in the claws of an ordinary pair of pliers. I asked him how he had managed to do such a thing. What he said exemplifies why fear is the major ingredient of pain.

'When I decided to pull out my own tooth, because it was such a hassle going all the way to the dentist, it didn't hurt. When I walked to the workshop, that didn't hurt. When I picked up the pair of pliers, it didn't hurt. When I held the tooth in the grip of the pliers, it still didn't hurt. When I wiggled the pliers and pulled, it hurt then, but only for a couple of seconds.

Once the tooth was out, it didn't hurt much at all. It was only five seconds of pain, that's all.'"

You probably grimaced when you read this true story of 'transcend-dental medication'. Because of fear, you probably felt more pain than that monk did! If you were to try the same feat, it would probably hurt terribly, even before you reached the workshop to get the pliers. Anticipation – fear – is the major ingredient of pain. Anticipation and the fear that you create is the problem. Not the pain itself.

What a lesson in life that is. I'm not suggesting you pull your own teeth (with or without anaesthetic), but how many times have you worried, and agonised, and worked yourself into a frenzy over something that turned out to be no big deal, or absolutely nothing at all?

In the words of the famed American author, Mark Twain, "I have had a lot of worries in my life, most of which never happened." [12]

So, imagine for a moment the power you could gain from not being afraid, from not being consumed by concern and doubt.

- How much time and energy do you lose by just simply worrying?
- How many of the things you've worried about in your mind happened to you? And when they happened, how bad was it really?
- What would you do if you could not fail?

Probably a lot more, and this might include things more impactful to your life and your work than being able to pull a tooth. You would be able to do truly extraordinary things, things I know you are capable of, and which genuinely matter to you, things that could qualitatively change your experience of life and the lives of others. And I believe that's something worth giving up the fear of pain for.

When Phra Chaibodin dismissed me without an additional pillow, I went back to the painful sitting, now completely frustrated, angry, sad, and also hopeless. But sitting down, I began to let go. I stopped looking at the timer so often. I just sat, experiencing the pain. Breathing. Rising. Falling. Rising. Falling. I realised that I could sit. I realised what had made it so painful: the timer! Looking at it repeatedly and with increasing frequency had made it much worse. Almost similar to picking up some pliers to remove a tooth. Each time I looked at the clock, it reminded me painfully of how long I still had to sit and in doing so vastly amplified my pain.

I decided to ignore the timer completely and just sit into the pain. It was tough. I was sweating, breathing heavily, struggling. But gradually something began to happen. The pain seemed to be getting less and less intense. And by not focusing on the pain, I realised I had followed Chaibodin's golden rule: "Accept, accept, accept." Wow! It began to work. Gradually, I could sit still with the pain. Profound inner calm and peacefulness started to settle in at last.

The days that followed were not easy, but much better. I had found a way to work through the pain and accept deeply. To be truthful, there were times when I missed talking to someone, or when I wished I was on one of the many planes we could hear from the nearby airport. But the monastic rhythm of waking up at 4 am, eating in silence twice a day, meditating, sweeping the monastery, and cleaning our rooms really started to quieten my mind. And yes, when unobserved I here and there also exchanged some words with other fellow meditators ...

Thus, the days passed and on the evening of Day Nine I started to feel a tremendous level of happiness, accomplishment, peacefulness, and stillness. I was so overwhelmed by this feeling that I could not stop talking to my fellow student Ethan about it whilst sweeping the monastery. Not a good idea. Phra 'Controlbodin' seemed to be everywhere, watching us. He caught me. Almost aggressively he shouted at me: "Stop talking!"

The next day was my last, and in the afternoon I would fly back to civilisation, back to 'real' life. My taster of life as a monk had been tough but extremely enriching. Sweeping the floor in the morning, I must have been completely 'out of my mind' when I quietly told Ethan my concerns: How on earth could I take this tranquillity into my hectic existence back in Singapore?

I had not really said much yet when I was screamed at from behind. Chaibodin had caught me. Again! And this time round, he was far away from "accept, accept, accept." Also, the "learning suffering," as well as the "don't cry before you hurt" wisdom seemed to have gone completely out of the window. He shouted at me: "You! Yooou! You are not ready! Your mind too loose! You go home now! Come back when you ready!" And then he walked off.

That was it. For the first time in my life, I got fired! Very disturbed and sad, I went to my room, collected all my stuff, and made my donation. Walking out of the monastery I felt pity for myself, but more importantly I felt really, really stupid that my first silent retreat had ended that way. In hindsight I think this was perhaps Phra Chaibodin's final teaching: reinforcing to me the need to be disciplined and keep learning to let go. Even if it was very difficult, near impossible. He reminded me to "accept, accept, accept" that I had been fired, and with this gave me a wonderful opportunity to practise "learning suffering!"

Despite this inglorious ending, I left Wat Ram Poeng content, as I felt I had learnt a new technique, which I could take back into my hectic life as a way to cleanse my mind on a daily basis. With this I hoped I could live a more connected and fulfilled life, staying the course even when things started to overwhelm me.

One of the monks, Phra Soopan, had told me during a consultation that "every day when you learn something about yourself is a good day." And by implementing a regular daily meditation routine I was beginning to learn a little more about myself every day. I think the following brief story encapsulates what I had learnt during those challenging days in the Northern Thailand monastery where I got fired as a part-time monk.

The Power of Equanimity

Once upon a time, in China, there was a poor farmer who worked on his modest farm together with his son and their horse. One day, inexplicably, the horse ran off, and the neighbours came around to him to express their sympathy: "How unfortunate for you!" The farmer replied: "Maybe yes, maybe no."

And indeed, a few days later the horse returned, followed by a herd of wild horses, and the neighbours gathered around and exclaimed: "What good luck for you!" The farmer stayed calm and replied: "Maybe yes, maybe no." While taming one of the wild horses, the farmer's son fell and broke his leg. He had to rest up and couldn't do any of the work on the farm. "How sad for you," the neighbours cried. "Maybe yes, maybe no," said the farmer.

Shortly thereafter, an enemy army threatened the country and all the young men in the village were drafted to fight the invaders. Many died. But the farmer's son had been left out of the fighting because of his broken leg. People said to the farmer: "What a good thing your son couldn't fight!" "Maybe yes, maybe no," was all the farmer said in reply.

We often ask ourselves when something is happening to us, "is that a good thing or a bad thing?" But how do we know? Like the farmer in our story, we can't know what comes next that might change everything: good fortune may turn awry, and a calamity may be a blessing in disguise.

Whether we see an event or a condition as good or bad is always and forever a matter of perspective. To know this is equanimity: A "calm mental state, especially after a shock or disappointment or in a difficult situation," as the Cambridge dictionary defines it.[13]

The great challenge in life is not to get so wrapped up in our perceived good fortune or bad luck that we lose sight of the fact that the future is and must be uncertain. No one knows how the story will turn out, so maybe it's best to do as our level-headed 'hero' does and maintain a degree of equanimity throughout the perceived ups and downs of life.

One of the things I have learnt about myself is that I am a slave to my circumstances. My happiness depends a lot on things 'going right'. And when they don't go well, I feel lost. Smart people celebrate the ups and brush off the smaller downs. But what do you do when your world is rocked to the core by 'bad' news? Maintaining your equanimity becomes much harder. What if the farmer's son had died in his fall? Game over. No more opportunity for the tables to turn. But even then, we can grow: much as any change is a form of bereavement, so any loss is an opportunity for change. And even painful change is simply part of life. Any time we experience a change we perceive as seriously negative, it forces us to adjust and adapt mentally and emotionally to the new circumstances, and that process can throw us for a loop.

You may be familiar with the Kübler-Ross Stages of Grief model.[14] It really applies to anyone going through significant unwanted change of any kind. Here's a simplified version, which shows the four phases of change as:

1. Denial – "This can't be happening; life like this is impossible, I am at a loss."
2. Resistance – "I cannot accept this. If only this or that hadn't happened, then this wouldn't be the case now. Who is to blame?"
3. Exploration – "The situation has not reverted back to what it was before. What does being me now mean?"
4. Commitment – "I need to move forward. Here is what I am going to do: this is the next stage of my life now."

Living in our VUCA world we are asked to deal with an immense and ever-increasing amount of change. Sometimes those changes trigger substantial personal disruptions, sadness, anger, or frustration, and they may even lead to burnout and depression.

The farmer teaches us a very important lesson on how to effectively deal with change: by not judging, debating, questioning, or denying it, but embracing it. His lesson is exactly the same as Phra Chaibodin taught us: "Accept, accept, accept."

Whenever we are confronted with change, we need to take a step back and stop ourselves from judging and going into an emotional meltdown, which more often than not simply triggers a destructive downward spiral. Instead, we should accept the situation as quickly as possible and commit to dealing with the change. That will allow us to dramatically short-cut the change cycle and live more content and happy lives. Try it out for yourself by starting to accept, accept, accept, and then moving on quickly.

Becoming a Coach

Returning from the monastery I was very grateful for the experience and the teachings of Phra Chaibodin. Sitting with 70 people and eating in complete silence was something to remember, as was observing the villagers who came to do good deeds by 'sponsoring' the food we ate. It had been a tough ten days and without a happy ending, but I learnt a lot!

Coming 'back to reality' from the monastery was slightly different than my return from the Camino. I now had my daily meditation routine to help me process emotional turmoil and to create daily spaces of calm and awareness which provided me with more clarity about my situation and what I could or should do next. But of course, it was not all plain sailing.

At the end of February 2013, I started my training with Coach U, the US based coach training organisation accredited by the International Coaching Federation (ICF). My goal was to qualify as an Associate Certified Coach (ACC), and just for that, there was quite a bit of work to do:
- At least 60 hours of coach-specific education or training (Coach U)
- A minimum of 100 hours of client coaching experience (with 75% paid hours)
- 10 hours of mentor coaching
- Pass a performance assessment of a recorded coaching session
- Computer-based written exam delivered by ICF Credentials and Standards

Diving into the training with Coach U, I truly enjoyed the lessons it was offering me, especially on my own personal development. I participated in various online courses, like for example:
- Foundation of coaching
- Effective listening
- Coaching language
- Effective questioning
- Coaching mindset
- Fundamentals of coaching ethics
- Personal foundation

For me, particularly the latter, 'Personal Foundation Program' contained incredibly interesting learning elements, such as:
- 'Clean Sweep Program' to create space and declutter my life
- 'Need Less Program' to understand what my personal needs are and how to get them met
- 'Zap Tolerations Program' looking at all the things I am tolerating in my life which require change
- 'Life Values Program' together with a
- Comprehensive 360-degree feedback from friends and colleagues

It was a lot to take in, but I absolutely loved it, especially when I had 'aha' moments, like for example in the 'Life Values Program' when I realised how coaching could provide me with my life purpose.

When working on my personal values I came across a coincidental quote in the daily inspirational calendar I had received from my good friends Steffi and Juergen: "If you want to be happy for one hour, get drunk; if you want to be happy for a week, get married; if you want to be happy for ever, get a garden."

Pondering on this quote and on my own personal values and purpose, I suddenly had a remarkable visualisation and an epiphany. Working with coaching clients is like supporting flowers in a beautiful garden. Instead of plants I would work with 'human flowers', supporting them, caring for them, and nurturing them. With this I could be 'happy forever'.

This realisation did not only make me smile, but to this day it gives me a clear reason for getting up in the morning. I work in my garden and see which 'human flower' needs a bit of 'watering' or 'caring' to help them bloom or to get through a challenging 'drought' in their life. Even now I still smile about how clearly and easily this metaphor helped me to define my purpose and gave me the clarity to live a more meaningful and fulfilled life.

Working on my personal foundation was not easy, but very insightful at the same time. And besides understanding and developing myself further, I also had a lot of other skills to learn to become a coach. Most importantly, I needed to learn the 'number one hostage negotiation skill'.

Why You Should Master the Number One Hostage Negotiation Skill

Chris Voss had been with the FBI's Joint Terrorism Task Force for several years when he became intrigued by the idea of becoming a hostage negotiator. To try his luck, he went to see Amy Bonderow, who ran the FBI's crisis negotiation team in New York at the time. "I want to be a hostage negotiator," Voss said.

Amy replied: "Well, everyone does. Do you have any training, experience, credentials, or a degree in psychology/sociology?" Chris had none of these, but he did not give up: "Come on, there must be something I can do?" Amy's reply came as a big surprise: "Yes, volunteer at a suicide hotline."

Voss was puzzled, but he took her advice and went to volunteer at Help-Line, founded by Norman Vincent Peale. The basic rule there was to not give advice to the callers but to get them to a better place within a maximum twenty-minute phone call by "fully listening and being with them."

After working at HelpLine for several weeks, Voss had his first performance review by his supervisor, Jim, who listened in on a caller conversation. The call came from a cab driver, Daryl, who was afraid to go outside as he did not feel safe anymore. This would be a problem for anyone, but for Daryl, not leaving the house meant not working and that would lead to not being able to pay the mortgage and risk losing his home and family. Daryl was in deep despair.

Chris got to work and asked him: "When was the last time someone tried to hurt you on the streets?" "Well, I mean it's been a long time," Daryl said. "Like?" Chris asked. "I can't really remember a date, Chris. Maybe a year I guess."

"So, it's safe to say that the outside world has not been too hard on you?" "Yes," Daryl said. "I suppose so." The conversation from there flowed well and Chris even managed to make Daryl laugh a couple of times. By the end, Daryl could not give one more reason not to go outside and ended the call with: "Thank you Chris for doing such a great job."

Chris felt he had absolutely nailed it and went for his performance review. "Jim, did you hear Daryl congratulate me? I talked him down, man. I killed it!" Jim replied, "I don't want to be harsh, but you were horrible! By the end of our calls, the callers should congratulate themselves and not you. They should have found a way forward which they really plan to act on. Daryl had none of this."

Voss realised that the whole call had been about himself, his ego, his thinking, his solutions, and not about Daryl. He had received a vague, "yes, I suppose so," but had not enabled Daryl to talk about what was really going on emotionally, with the likely result being that Daryl would continue to feel not heard and be miserable.

Why am I telling this story? As we go through our daily lives and connect with other people, how often do we take the time to truly listen to the other person? Research suggests that we usually focus on the 7% of communication that is conveyed in words, while we're busy developing our own solutions and responses. But how much do we pay attention to the 38% that is communicated by tone of voice or the 55% that is made up by body language? [15]

We all have this natural ability to mirror others, and when we truly listen to someone, we get a chance to understand their inner emotional landscape in that moment. This creates the opportunity to move them into a more positive frame of mind as they feel heard and respected, which often leads to feeling more in control.

Meeting these basic human needs creates a positive mindset, which again, according to research, can increase the productivity of our brains by a whopping 31%.[16] It opens the window to work constructively on finding solutions together. That's when we get a chance to work with the other person and perhaps also influence their outcome.

So the next time your co-worker comes to you with a problem or your child tries to speak to you, resist the natural urge to immediately switch into 'solution mode'. Instead, listen for how they are saying things. Hear from the sound what is really going on, and then make use of the golden ingredients of active listening:

- Effective pauses
- Minimal encouragers (like 'yes', 'okay', or 'I see')
- Mirroring (repeating their last 3–4 words)
- Labelling ("it seems this makes you very upset")
- Paraphrasing and summarising

Observe how they begin to open up as they feel heard, respected, and more in control.

You may wonder what happened to Chris Voss. Five months after volunteering at HelpLine, he came back to Amy and told her what he'd learnt. She was impressed. He got into the FBI's negotiator program and eventually became the FBI's chief international hostage and kidnapping negotiator. In his book *Never Split the Difference: Negotiating as if Your Life Depended on it*, co-authored with Tahl Raz, he explains how active listening has revolutionised the FBI's hostage negotiation approach, helping him and his colleagues successfully resolve numerous hostage cases.

If it works in crisis situations and for kidnappers, why would it not work for the people we are interacting with in our everyday lives, especially those closest to us? Try it out. Maybe we have two ears and one mouth for a reason …

I personally had a lot to learn and practise to become an active listener, but gradually I became more familiar and more used to the technique, and I also found out that it is part of my nature to let others speak first, since I do have a genuine interest in trying to learn more about them and their ideas.

As I was progressing through my coach training, attending the online lessons, doing all the exercises, as well as beginning to link up with other fellow students for coaching sessions, I had one big issue to solve: How to collect 100 coaching hours, of which 75 hours had to be paid by clients?

For the first time in my life, I was very passionate about what I was doing, but if I could not get clients, it was basically irrelevant. Thanks to the work with my mentor coach and the 'practice-building course', I found a way to get over that hurdle. I put together a simple short letter about my coach certification programme, and let it be known that I needed 'trial clients' to get started towards becoming a coach.

Writing this letter was easy. But to press 'enter' and send it out with a personalised note was another thing. For the first time ever, I had to sell myself. And that was very uncomfortable, as all my life I had been the mechanical engineer who never had to do any marketing for himself. But eventually the letters went out to about 30 colleagues and friends. And I was surprised by the positive responses I received. From April 2013 onward, step by step, I started to provide coaching, and I can happily say I have never stopped since.

Collecting my first coaching hours was still a steep learning process. The focus of these sessions was of course on the client, on what he or she wanted to get out of them, but I had to keep an eye on the time, take notes, ask questions, and most importantly I had to deeply connect with the other person. I am very grateful to my friends and colleagues who volunteered to allow me to practise and start my learning journey.

As I got more sessions under my belt, I gradually began to ease into these coaching conversations, which was great, but there was now another big issue looming: I was beginning to 'burn the candle from both ends'!

I loved my coach training and I loved practising coaching. At the same time there was a lot to study, and not to forget, I was still working full time at Procter & Gamble. After only a couple of weeks, I reached a point of near burnout. Fortunately, my mentor coach taught me an extremely valuable lesson for which I am grateful to this day. I am sharing it here, as at times life can get a little overwhelming and stressful for all of us.

Are You Ready for Your Forrest Gump Challenge?

It was the 9th of June 2013 when I came down with a high fever that forced me to stay in bed. Looking back at how I was pushing myself, it is surprising that this had not happened earlier.

In my highly demanding day job, I was still managing the Asia supply chain of Procter & Gamble's complex skin care business whilst attending online classes for my coaching certification in the US time zone at odd hours, such as 5 am or 11 pm. The coaching qualification also entailed substantial homework and a requirement to clock up more than 100 coaching hours. Trying to juggle it all, my body had said: "Stop." As I shared the 'breakdown' experience with my mentor coach, she listened attentively and then asked whether she could give me a challenge. I took a deep sigh, expecting another item to be added to my lengthy to-do list and said, "okay." "Do you know the movie, Forrest Gump?" My astonished confirmation was met with her next question: "What do you recall from the movie?"

Digging deep, I remembered that Forrest Gump had been a runner, a table tennis champion, a hero of the Vietnam War, and a shrimp boat captain. I also recalled that Forrest's 'momma' always said, "Life is like a box of chocolates – you never know what you're gonna get."

Whilst discussing this with my coach, I was expecting her to tell me that I fully deserved my 'health collapse', as I had put far too many things into my 'box of chocolates'. Instead, she started to describe the beginning and the end scenes of the film, which show a white feather floating through the blue sky, accompanied by an inspiring piano theme.

My coach continued to explain: "To me the feather represents the successful mindset of genuine acceptance and positive determination, with which Forrest Gump approached each of his highly demanding and occasionally heart-breaking circumstances. That's what I'd like to see you do, so I want to challenge you to schedule one Forrest Gump day per week."

I was puzzled. "What is a Forrest Gump day?" I asked. "On a Forrest Gump day, you wake up in the morning whenever you wake up and then you 'float' through the day like a feather. There are no schedules allowed, no obligations, no to-do lists, and no commitments. Try it out and we'll see whether your health gets back on track." What an awkward challenge, I thought, but I started to free up the next Sunday from work emails, study homework, coaching sessions, and all my other normal Sunday commitments, like buying groceries.

I woke up with an initial uncomfortable feeling of 'not having a plan'. But I bravely began to 'float' by enjoying a wonderful breakfast with my favourite football newspaper, followed by a refreshing long walk, a nap, and some reading in the afternoon. And I closed out the day by watching an inspiring movie with a very good friend.

Waking up on the Monday was different from the normal 'blues', as I felt more rested, recharged, and ready to rumble. During the subsequent weeks, I religiously stuck with my Forrest Gump days and was surprised that I was not only progressing well ahead of schedule with my coaching certification but felt less stressed and much more positive and in control at work.

Numerous studies show that taking regular breaks helps us to get more done to a higher standard in a shorter time. Being self-employed, for me, every day now is a 'working day', and it is at times unrealistic to free up a whole day, but I still take those two to three hours on some days when I leave the house, grab a coffee, and go for a long walk, making up the route as I go. It still feels as if I am a bit 'floating like the feather', and each time, I come back refreshed, rested, and recharged with new ideas.

Just as my coach challenged me years ago, I want to challenge you to schedule some 'Forrest Gump time' for yourself, time when you float and just do the things you enjoy without any obligations or pressure on your shoulders.

Be it ten minutes a day, several hours a week, or even a full day every month. Try this out in the coming thirty days, and maybe with that little tweak, you will become as successful as Forrest, who not only did well as a shrimp boat captain and got an invitation to the White House by the president, but also became a millionaire by investing in a little startup company that made computers which were named after the founder's favourite apple ... – happy floating!

By sticking to my regular Forrest Gump days, I was now progressing well and healthily through my coaching certification, whilst also keeping the work stress at bay. It clearly helped me to stay focused and sane, starting to 'help human flowers grow', whilst not dropping any balls at P&G. Working with my coach, I also defined the following 'Deceleration Strategy' to ensure I continued to juggle studying, coaching, and working well:

- Work no more than 8 hours per day at P&G.
- Get 8 hours of sleep each night.
- Do not start the day before 6 am.
- Have 3 priorities for each day and do them first.
- Never check emails first thing in the morning.
- Read emails rigorously only 3 times a day.
- Duck out of as many meetings as possible (meetings are there to make decisions not define the problem).

- The most important actions are never comfortable – do one uncomfortable action each day.
- Do not multitask – be aware and go one step at a time – remember "it's very simple."
- Keep doing daily yoga and meditation.
- Remember: doing something unimportant well does not make it important.

With this I was getting along fine, but there was one area I still struggled with, after coming back from the monastery, and that was alcohol. Back there, when sitting in stillness and going through the tough lessons taught by my own pain and by Phra Chaibodin, I had realised that all these years alcohol had played a big role in my life. It was the social glue that connected me to my football community and across various networks of friends. Whilst I was never an everyday drinker, I had to concede that during weekends I could go overboard quite a bit, bingeing the stress of the week away.

Coming back from the monastery I wanted to change that, and I began to reduce my alcohol intake quite drastically. This helped me a lot in staying focused and getting through my work, study, and coaching commitments, but overall, I also felt it took me away from the 'fun of life', the deep philosophical discussions, as well as the laughter and enjoyment from being slightly tipsy together. As the year went by, I gradually moved back into my old habits of weekend drinking. It looked like I just was not yet ready to make a change regarding my relationship with alcohol. It would take another five years and many hangovers to find a new way there, of which more later ...

By the end of 2013 I was about to finish my coaching course work and complete the 100 coaching hours, when during a peer coaching session, my coach brought up the million-dollar question: "As you are about to complete your coach certification, what is next for you? Do you want to quit your job and move into full-time coaching?"

This question – though hardly unreasonable – hit me like a rocket, but I knew I had to deal with it. During the coaching session my coach would not give me any advice, but skilfully played the questions back and made me explore, think, and feel what was right for me. It was difficult, and whilst by the end of the session I was leaning towards leaving my secure corporate career, I was far from making a decision.

The coaching session triggered further thoughts on what I wanted to do next with my working life, but it was not until I formulated the question for myself in a different way, together with a simple yet powerful questionnaire, that I would get the clarity I needed.

Why Not Quit My Job?

It was the 24th of November 2013. I was just about to complete my coach certification with the International Coaching Federation (ICF), and I was totally confused. I knew I had to make a difficult and life-changing decision. Should I become self-employed, moving into coaching, where my passion clearly was, or should I keep the security of a well-paid senior job in a large global corporation and pursue coaching part-time at best? I was scared and at a loss as to what to do. I was constantly making two different lists:

- Why I should quit my job!
- Why I should not quit my job!

I was getting nowhere until I came across the following questionnaire by Tim Ferris.[17] So, on the evening of 24th November, I sat down quietly and put my thoughts on paper in answer to his five key questions. I could not have known how much this would change my life.

1. Why do I want to leave my job?
What I wrote down completely shocked me: "In the last 3–4 months, there hasn't been a single day I looked forward to going to work. Expectations just keep increasing. I am tired. I've lost my passion, energy, and drive for the job. I sit in back-to-back meetings without a lunch break, wondering what I'm doing here? I'm grinding through the days, rather than living."

2. What are my biggest nightmare and worst-case scenarios when it comes to quitting my job? Answering this question was easier and cathartic. My biggest concern was "not being able to make sufficient money as a full-time coach." This could lead to "depleting my savings. Eventually, I could end up bankrupt, homeless and hopeless, hating myself for being stupid enough to give up a successful career" with people around me saying, "we told you so!"

But there were three important follow up questions:

- On a scale of 1–10, what is the permanent impact of these scenarios on my life? I rated it 2, as I felt that I would somehow be able to make a living and find my way back.
- How likely are these scenarios to happen? "Not very likely."
- What can I do to minimise and/or repair the damage of these worst-case scenario(s)? I came up with lots of corrective actions, like "cutting down spending, moving to a smaller place, pulling the emergency break early, applying for a stable job, working part-time …"

3. What are the probable outcomes of the more likely scenarios? On the financial side, there was the likely scenario that I would cover at least part of my costs.

Together with reduced spending, I realised that I would be able to go on for quite some time. There was also the optimal scenario, where I could make sufficient money or even save some, assuming I would get enough coaching or training engagements.

Imagining my emotional state in these likely scenarios was the breakthrough I needed. "I wake up in the morning and look forward to what I do. I make a difference in the world. I live my purpose. I know every day what I have achieved and whom I have helped!"

The sub-questions I answered as follows:

– What would be the impact of those more likely scenarios on a scale of 1–10? "10+"
– How likely is it I could produce at least a moderately positive outcome? "It's definitely possible!"
– Have less intelligent people done this before and pulled it off? "Yes."
– If I quit my job, could I get back onto the same career if really needed to? "Yes."

4. What is it costing me to postpone action, and if I do not pursue what I want, where will I be in 1, 5, and 10 years? The answer to this question was very clear: "If I allow circumstances and fears to impose themselves on me, I will waste 1, 5, or 10 years of my life doing something I know does not fulfil me!"

5. What am I waiting for? In the beginning of 2014, there was another potential restructuring on the horizon for my organisation at Procter & Gamble. So, I gave myself three months to see if there was a chance of a severance package. If not, I would quit.

The questionnaire had brought me a great deal more clarity during a time of substantial confusion about my next steps. Many years later I sense more and more people are asking themselves the question of whether they could transition to better work arrangements. They're considering taking a plunge into something new.

If that's you, I hope this questionnaire can perhaps provide a little inspiration for you to look at your own situation and consider what you would like to do next. And if you ever need a good coach to serve as a sounding board, I guess you know where you can find one ... :-)!

Answering Tim Ferris's questionnaire made it very obvious to me that I had all the necessary cards in my own hands to give it a go and become a full-time coach. If things did not go well, I could still return and find a job in the supply chain area I had been working in. That would be sad, but clearly not the end of the world, and it would definitely enable me to say by the end of my life that at least I had given my dream a really good run for the money.

With the decision made that I wanted to leave P&G sooner rather than later, miraculously, things started to happen. It was very similar to when I had asked my boss the second time whether I could get four weeks off to walk the Camino: the universe began to conspire! And how magically it worked will be revealed shortly, but before we get there, I need to describe another absolutely life-changing event that happened to me on the 18th of October 2013.

Whilst I had spent time in a monastery in early 2013, my plan was definitely not to keep living alone 'like a monk'. And so I had participated somewhat in the dating scene in Singapore, using one of these wonderful 'matchmaker' apps. But given I was working full-time, studying, and clocking hours for my coach certification, there was really not much room for anything else.

So, my dating and love life was more or less lying idle, when out of the blue I received a contact request on the dating platform Singapore Expats. The request came from a stunning looking woman. She had curly hair and looked very kind, and also a little mischievous. I really liked that!

We met for a dinner in Chinatown, and I think both of us felt a little bit awkward and stiff in the beginning, searching for topics to talk about, whilst eating our Chinese food. At that time, I had no idea what a great and positive influence this date would have on my life.

The Year That Changed Everything

The year 2013 came to a very good close as I had completed all my class work and clocked up the necessary 100 coaching hours together with a recorded coaching session. With that I was ready for my online exam to then graduate as an Associate Certified Coach with the International Coaching Federation.

Similar to my 'breakdown situation' on 18th of May 2012 halfway through the Camino, I felt at the beginning of the new year 2014 that something, if not everything, was about to change. I had made the decision to leave my job, I was awaiting my official coach certification to be issued, and with that was ready to move into a completely new chapter of my life by becoming self-employed as a full-time coach.

But doing so would trigger a lot of new demands and necessary next steps, as I would have to set up a company, create a business and marketing plan, establish a website, and most importantly find a way to either become a Singapore Permanent Resident (PR) or get an Employment Pass (EP) to be able to open a coaching practice in Singapore. Working for Procter & Gamble it had not been a problem at all to get an Employment Pass in Singapore, but as an independent coach it was a completely different matter, as I was to painfully discover soon after.

By the end of 2013 I had also met that cute lady again since our initial date in October, but after our first date and a lovely dinner a few weeks later, things went a bit quiet between us, which was partly due to my traditional Christmas trip to Germany, but also to the fact that we were both not really sure whether and how we wanted to take things forward.

It felt as if there were millions of open questions at the beginning of 2014 and little did I know how completely different my life would be by the time this year would draw to a close.

Anne

All my life I had been looking for women who were probably a little on the 'flashy side' and whom one could perhaps describe to some extent as 'party girls'. This was mainly triggered by the fact that all my life I had been a strong party animal myself, but also that I wanted someone with me who was seen as fun and engaging by all the party people around me.

Anne was a little different. She had wonderful curly hair and was rather on the quiet side. She was clearly no party animal, even though she later emphasised to me that she had been through a "hard-core clubbing phase of probably two weeks, 'regularly' visiting the Zouk nightclub." But there was something about her that was drawing me towards her.

She was a very smart person, having completed a bachelor's and master's with Second Upper Class (Honours) at the London School of Economics (LSE). She had worked in large banks like Morgan Stanley, Deutsche Bank, and JP Morgan in London and Hong Kong, and after all of this she had recently made her own lifestyle switch by leaving the banking industry altogether.

Having lost three friends in her direct network in Hong Kong to cancer within only a very short period of time, she felt that there must be something more to life than working crazy hours in this soulless banking industry. So, she quit her job, used all her good sense, and invested in a property. This worked out so well that she had further funds available, which she invested together with her mum in a very smart way.

At the same time, she moved in with her mum in Singapore and substantially cut back on her spending, and so she had reached the remarkable achievement of living a humble and quiet semi-retired life at the age of only 36.

I absolutely admired her courage, clarity, and decisiveness in taking this step. Her life had not been easy, as she had suffered a horrific, near-fatal car accident at the age of twenty, after which the doctors doubted that she would ever be able to walk again, let alone finish her degree at LSE or work in a bank. But with extraordinary effort and determination she had made it through the tough studies and worked her way up in the banking world. This showed me she was a fighter.

Sometimes in our lives we get those moments where suddenly everything changes from one minute to the next. Anne visited me in Tiong Bahru early in 2014 and we had a good chat about life in general but also about a presentation that I had to prepare, for which I had asked her whether she could give me some feedback. Anne sat on the couch on my balcony, and I was sitting on the floor taking her through my slides. When I was done, I could feel Anne's hand gently touching my hair. This was the electrifying moment when I felt the connection to her deep, kind, and caring soul. That moment changed something inside myself which gave me the courage to open up and gradually begin to establish a new relationship with this wonderful woman.

In most of my previous relationships I seemed to have yearned for and missed this caring side of my partner. With Anne it felt different, and I really liked that. But at the same time, I was very scared, wondering how to move forward and whether it would end once again in a similar disaster as most of my previous relationships had done.

We both agreed to take it easy and step by step. I had to sort out a couple of things within me first by working through my own indecisiveness and uncertainty. For this I decided to embark on some deep personal work with my psychotherapist, Maria.

But before describing how this impacted myself and my relationship with Anne, I would like to share a little story very close to my heart, which describes what Anne has become to me since then. It clearly was not an easy journey, but today I look back with tremendous gratitude. I am clear I could not have made my transformation and become who I am today, if it were not for Anne's love, care, and support.

Who Is Your 'Lieutenant'?

Anybody who is successful in their life and career needs someone at their side. Someone who acts as a right-hand man or woman, a person who is there, supporting and helping. Someone who can be fully trusted to carry out aspects of a mission which the successful person has neither the time, skill, or personality to handle on his or her own. The following story describes such a person who made it possible for an epic adventure to find a happy end – Frank Wild.

You may never have heard of him. Almost certainly, though, you have heard of Ernest Shackleton, who mounted an expedition to cross the continent of Antarctica on foot in 1914. Here's the ad Shackleton put in the newspaper to recruit men for the trip. He didn't sugar-coat the challenge ahead: "Men wanted for hazardous journey. Small wages. Bitter cold. Long months of complete darkness. Constant danger. Safe return doubtful. Honour and recognition in case of success."

Fascinated by this, Frank Wild applied. He brought to the table not only a lot of relevant experience but most importantly the type of honest, humble, yet strong character that was needed for the role, and Shackleton hired him right away, as his right-hand man and lieutenant.

True to the warning in the ad, things didn't go so well on the expedition. In fact, they never made it to Antarctica: the ship got locked in ice. They couldn't move and had no way to contact anyone for help, and so ended up spending the whole winter trapped on the stranded ship.

There were plenty of supplies, but the challenge for Shackleton and Wild was how to keep up morale. Then, in the spring, as the ice started to melt, the ice floes began to shift back and forth, battering and eventually crushing the ship.

They spent another five months camping on an ice floe hoping for it to move close enough to land, until finally, after 15 long months at sea and on ice, the crew was able to reach open water in three small lifeboats. After seven days on the treacherous ocean, they made it to Elephant Island, a small, ice-covered rock on the edge of Antarctica. With no hope of rescue and no way to sustain themselves indefinitely, Shackleton left Wild in command of twenty-one men who would stay on the island while he and a crew of five took one of the lifeboats to search for help.

By some miracle, using primitive navigational aids, and under tremendous strain, Shackleton and his team made it the 800 miles to South Georgia Island which they then astonishingly crossed on foot with almost no equipment to get to the whaling harbour on the other side.

There, Shackleton borrowed a ship and sailed all the way back to Elephant Island to rescue their mates left behind there. It took five months. The crew had survived on seals and penguins and seaweed, and fully assumed that Shackleton and his five men had been lost at sea.

You would think that Frank Wild might have had the mother of all morale and discipline problems. But not so. Leading the group, he got them to stick together and work through impossible circumstances with very little hope of rescue.

As one of the survivors explained: "When the end was in sight, we all realised the debt of gratitude we owed to our splendid, capable leader, Frank Wild, who by his buoyant optimism, dogged determination, unrivalled experience as well as calm demeanour, had pulled us through these trying months of waiting. If ever a man worked hard and conscientiously to keep up the spirits and maintain the general peace and welfare of a community containing one or two 'difficult' members, that man was Frank Wild."

Shackleton has a well-deserved reputation as a courageous man and an extraordinary leader, but what would his reputation be had he not been able to leave his trusted lieutenant, Frank Wild, in charge of these twenty-one men in a nearly hopeless situation? As the account of the journey reads, "It is said that Shackleton never made a decision without first consulting Wild."

May I ask you: when you look at your own life, who is your trusted lieutenant? Who looks out for your interests when you can't?

In my life, I am glad to say Anne has become my Frank Wild. She is always there to help and support me with her calm, friendly, and loving way. She frees me from administrative burdens while being both my biggest critic and my best cheerleader. She is there when I need someone to talk to and she always gives me her smart and honest opinion. Before I make any big decision, I always consult with my beautiful lieutenant. I could not do what I do today and be who I am today without Anne. And the best thing: she is much, much better-looking than Frank. Thank you, my love!

Maria Therapy

At the same time as starting my relationship with Anne in the beginning of 2014, there were all these other changes on the horizon for me. Whilst I had made the decision to leave my job, I clearly had a long way to go before I would actually become a full-time coach. There was still a lot of inner turmoil, confusion, and fear. There were many considerations on how to start such a transition successfully. All these fundamental decisions and thoughts were beginning to weigh heavily on me, to the point where I made the life-changing decision to sign up for a coaching and therapy programme with Maria Micha.

Walking the Camino in 2012, I had started to listen more to my inner voice and intuition. Coming back from the monastery I had kept up my daily meditations, which gave me a space of calmness but also connected me more to this inner voice. And so I felt that there must be an immense power in my subconscious, providing answers and further guidance for my life.

Maria is a very experienced psychotherapist and hypnotherapist, and in all honesty, it was the hypnosis part which intrigued me most. After I had met Maria during a BBQ, I went for a trial session in the autumn of 2013, and I was really impressed by how much I learnt in just one session about my past, myself, and especially my very own 'inner matrix'.

Still, I had been a bit hesitant to sign up and engage in a full therapy programme, as this could mean up to a whole year of weekly sessions, which would require capacity, energy, and attention, quite apart from a considerable financial investment. But at the start of 2014 I felt the time was right and I decided to give it a go: in hindsight an absolute blessing, key enabler, and worth every single dollar invested.

As we began our work, I was initially a bit uncomfortable since all the focus was on me. I had done a couple of coaching sessions myself and worked with a mentor coach before, but working with Maria was different. She provided a calm, open, and safe space for me to explore where I was and where I wanted to go. More importantly though, she opened my eyes to look backwards in my life so that I could live it better forward.

This was not always an easy task, as I realised that my life had not been the 'plain sailing' I had always thought it was. There were challenging experiences in my past, losses as well as belief systems which on the one hand had brought me a long way in my life, but which at the same time and on the other hand had also held me back in some areas, such as for example being able to find a relationship where I felt truly happy and myself. Not to mention starting my own family, becoming a father, and raising children. As I began my therapy, I felt far from ready for that, but working with Maria gradually helped me to open my eyes, my mind, my heart, and my soul.

One of the first exercises she asked me to do was called Morning Pages, a concept developed by Julia Cameron as part of *The Artist's Way* to reconnect and link back to our creative inner voice. The task sounds simple but is tough to do: as the first thing in the morning, write three pages by hand on whatever comes to your mind. Beginning to write my Morning Pages taught me a very important lesson, which is illustrated by the following story.

The Answers Are Inside, Not Outside

It was the 3rd of September 2003 when Medical Manager and CEO Michael Singer received a panic call from his division's attorney. The FBI was raiding his R&D facility, along with several other locations across WebMD, a publicly listed company in the field of health information services. The FBI confiscated 1.2 million email messages, more than 3 million pages of documents, and 830,000 computer files.

The reason for the inquiry became clear a few weeks later. It turned out that an employee who was being internally investigated for taking customer kickbacks had informed the authorities about his dealings, alleging the company board was fully aware of these illegal affairs: he was hoping to cut a deal for himself.

Despite Michael Singer's career as the CEO of a division with more than 2,500 employees, he lived a withdrawn, spiritual life in 'the woods' where he had moved in his early twenties to learn 'how to quiet the voice in his head'.

All his life, he had been practising 'how to surrender' and create 'inner peace'. This federal investigation now offered a massive challenge to his inner peace. If things turned out badly, he might end up in prison.

As the investigation began in July 2004, Singer stepped down as CEO and then resigned from the company completely in February 2005. How would you feel if, suddenly, through false accusations, all you had built up in your life was taken away from you?

I'm sure most of us would be asking questions like: "How could this happen? Why me? Will I lose everything? What will happen to my family?" Instead, Singer did something remarkable. He began to write a book, *The Untethered Soul,* about how to quieten down our 'constantly nagging inner voice'. The book changed the course of millions of lives all around the world. It is the kind of writing someone could only do after extensive spiritual growth gained from years of regular mindfulness practice. The key lessons?

Anything that happens to us on the outside is an opportunity to develop ourselves by working on the inside. Situations that bother us, that make us anxious, angry, fearful, or sad – basically anything that causes an internal reaction – are triggered by what Singer calls "past experiences you either liked and tried to keep or could not handle and pushed away."

The way to overcome that constant mind chatter is simple, and yet so hard to do. "Be with the good and the bad inside, then ... let it go." Remain as an independent inner observer. Sense the emotion that floods up and acknowledge it the way a good friend who consoles another would, but "do not get caught in it." Singer describes it as "leaning back from the actual emotion."

The big wake-up call from Singer's book for me was the idea of resolving external problems by dealing with the inner turmoil first. "If you resist this inner turmoil in the slightest, you will struggle with these emotions. If you do not resist and welcome them with an open heart, you will provide them the room needed to be released."

If you struggle with something that you seem unable to get on top of, I encourage you to give it a go and write every morning whatever comes to your mind over three pages. Very soon, you will find out that all the answers are inside.

You might wonder what happened to Michael Singer? He was cleared of all allegations, but during the nearly seven years of investigation and court trials, he "had to let go a lot of stuff which had been holding me back." He worked through it. His first book became a New York Times bestseller. A few years later he wrote another bestseller: *The Surrender Experiment*. "Surrender is not surrendering to somebody; it is the act of letting go of what is holding you back. Surrender is not weakness; it is the ultimate strength." Letting go – that's where true freedom and peace ultimately comes from: the inside.

When writing out my Morning Pages there were so many external triggers coming up, for which my inner voice either gave me an answer or guided me towards further questions. Some of them I brought to my sessions with Maria. Step by step I started to realise that the answers were indeed inside myself and not on the outside. With every page I wrote, my connection to my inner voice grew stronger, and gradually the frustration, anxiety, and confusion began to slowly lift. Writing every morning, I started to get guidance – from the inside.

Whilst I had put together quite a successful career, there were lots of moments when I felt uncomfortable or anxious. Working with Maria, I began to establish the links to my past, realising why certain situations made me so uncomfortable. This in turn helped me to process some of the fear and to begin to better manage these challenging situations. It was especially valid for conflicts, which was something I had been struggling with in my life, as I wanted to please people so that I would not be left behind.

Some of the sessions with Maria were tough, but they also revealed to me another revolutionary new insight: I tend to think a lot! Sometimes these thoughts could get out of control and make me feel stuck and lost. Like a dog chewing on a bone,

I kept putting thoughts from left to right and upside down, trying desperately to understand what they meant and how to interpret or work with them.

Talking through some of these situations with Maria, it became clear that not everything I was thinking in my mind was true! That was an absolute game changer for me, and the following 'scary' story about a young monk, acid, bones, and skeletons perfectly illustrates the mistake I had made over and over again.

Don't Believe Everything You Think!

My favourite Buddhist monk, Ajahn Brahm, tells a memorable story about a novice monk named Little Grasshopper from the 1970s TV-series *Kung Fu*. One day, Little Grasshopper was brought to a room by his blind teacher who asked: "What do you see in this room?" The young monk looked around and answered: "Dear teacher, I see a big swimming pool." His teacher said: "Good, listen to me. This is not a swimming pool. This pool is not filled with water. It's filled with acid." A chill of fear shot down the spine of Little Grasshopper. Sensing his fear, the teacher continued: "See those bones at the bottom of the pool? These are the bones of novice monks like you who fell in the pond during their test." Little Grasshopper wanted to run away, as he could almost guess his teacher's next words: "Do you see that narrow plank across the pool? Your test in seven days shall be to walk across the pool on that plank." The teacher then brought Little Grasshopper outside to the courtyard. There, laid out on the grass, was a plank of exactly the same shape and length. The teacher said: "This plank is for you to practise on. Remember your test in seven days."

Little Grasshopper was filled with fear and despair but started his practice immediately. The plank was about 10 cm wide and probably 8 m long. It was actually not all that difficult to balance on, and with diligent practice he got to the point where he could walk across the plank with complete ease. But then came the seventh day and the crucial test of life-and-death.

As he entered the room, Little Grasshopper panicked. He saw the bones and his mind started racing with fear. "Go ahead," said the teacher. Stiffened with anxiety, Little Grasshopper made his first careful steps on the plank. Five or six steps in, he noticed his entire body was shaking. As he took more steps and reached the middle of the pool, he trembled even harder. But by now he was committed – too far in to turn back and still a long way from the other side. The acid graveyard seemed to grow bigger. Overwhelmed with panic, he tried to run, but quickly lost his balance and plunged into the pool.

Little Grasshopper had expected he would feel an intense burning sensation as his flesh dissolved in the acid. Instead, he felt a rush of cold and wet, and he heard his teacher roaring with laughter: "Ha ha ha! This is just a pool of water, and those bones are thrown in for effect."

Why did Little Grasshopper fall in the pool even though he had proved he could cross the plank with ease? It was not the size of the plank, but the thoughts in his head that made Little Grasshopper fall. It was the constant thought of the dangerous acid and the bones of past victims, which made him lose all the skills he had mastered during the seven days of intense practice.

So, what was the crucial lesson taught by the wise monk to Little Grasshopper?

1. Not every thought you think is true, and
2. You are well advised to focus diligently on what you want, rather than what you fear and think you can't do.

So, what do we do with this knowledge? As you go through your day, I would like to challenge you to pause, take a breather, and observe your thoughts. Then pick a specific negative and daunting thought and ask yourself the following question: would I say this out loud? Even to myself? And if I did, would it pass the most basic and also most effective test: is the thought True, Helpful, Inspiring, Necessary, and Kind (THINK)? If any of these are not the case, you should not say it, and if you can't say it, you shouldn't think it, because it doesn't stand up to scrutiny.

More positive beliefs open up a world of possibility. And sometimes the mere absence of negative thoughts will do the trick. You might surprise yourself at how many of 'life's planks' you can cross with ease without falling into a single 'acid-filled pool', if you simply stop believing everything you think.

Digging into the flood of my own thoughts and reflecting backwards through my life in my sessions with Maria, certain patterns and key themes began to emerge. On the one hand there was this area of nagging self-doubt, whether I will be good enough and able to accomplish what I wanted to. A key mountain towering ahead of me in this regard was the planned transition into becoming a self-employed coach. At times I still felt very doubtful whether I would have the right and sufficient skills, the knowledge, as well as the resilience to move from a very well-paid stable job into the uncertainty of basically zero guaranteed income.

Working with Maria on these elements took an interesting turn, as instead of drawing from the logical and rational mind she drew my attention further inside. Helping me to connect with that little inner 'Jogi' – my nickname as a child –

whom I had met on the Camino. With that, I gradually started to feel more at ease with myself and the daunting changes ahead. I began to feel things would be alright and, similar to when I was on the Camino, I began to remind myself of the mountains I had already climbed and the challenges I had overcome in my life before.

Part of this work with the inner child was also related to regaining respect for myself. Now this may sound weird as we all would expect to have a lot of respect for ourselves. In my case Maria uncovered that there were several friendships where, most likely due to my underlying fear of being left behind, I had lent money to friends, with these friends then making no move or attempt to pay that money back.

Maria identified this as an area where I was letting myself down, and if I were to grow and heal my respect for myself, she challenged me to collect these outstanding debts. As homework I had some uncomfortable calls to make, but in the end, I realised it was indeed beneficial for myself to have this sorted. Looking back, I still felt somewhat appalled that these friends had not taken the initiative to pay that money back proactively. But of course, one can argue that I had allowed this and therefore had only myself to blame. Be that as it may, things were now resolved, and the air was clear.

As part of my inner healing journey, Maria made me develop an HTLM (How To Love Myself) programme. Like the German mechanical engineer I had started out as, I created a meticulous spreadsheet of daily and weekly activities, reminders, and exercises, teaching me how to love myself more. It sounds weird that I needed a 'user manual' on how to learn to love myself, but looking back I absolutely treasured these exercises and learnt so much through them. Together with Maria we developed the following items as part of my HTLM programme:

- Daily morning meditation followed by emotional journalling, being truthful to myself and my emotions.
- Practise receiving love; for example, when I get praise, I say, "Thank you" and allow myself to feel proud ("I deserve it!").
- Practise saying "no" to requests I am not up for.
- My Body = My Temple → delicious nutrition, regular exercise, and good quality sleep.
- Attitude of Gratitude – list three things I am grateful for in the evening.
- Mirror Exercise – standing in front of the mirror and telling myself that I loved myself (to be honest I could not do this one).
- Thoughts-Feelings-Behaviours Worksheet – awareness of negativity, anxiety, fear, and not being 'worthy'.
- Sharing how I feel and telling my fears and joys to friends brings congruence.

- Have fun and take neither life nor myself too seriously.
- Pamper and invest in myself.

As I was gradually making progress in feeling more comfortable in my own skin, I also realised that conflicts were something I was trying to avoid at all cost. I had always felt I needed to be the 'harmoniser'. In Germany there is a saying: *Der Klügere gibt nach* – The one who is more clever gives in. This may be true for some situations, but it has its own inherent dangers, whence perhaps the numerous 'alternative' versions, such as: *Der Klügere gibt so lange nach bis er selbst der Dumme ist,* which translates to something like: The one who is more clever gives in until he ends up being the stupid one himself.

Because I was avoiding conflicts, I was not honestly communicating my own true wants and needs to others at times. Still, I can be quite selfish and strong-willed. Hence inside myself these needs and wants are loudly expressed whilst they are not being met by the outside world, as I do not communicate them clearly and promptly. When the discrepancy between my inner needs and reality grew bigger and bigger, there could be a point when I would explode.

Working with Maria helped me a lot in this area, which I think was crucial to get my relationship with Anne off on the right foot. What I had learnt from my past was that in some situations my reactions could be either passive-aggressive or even actively aggressive. Many who know me probably have not seen this impatient and impulsive side of mine, but my closest friends and especially my girlfriends certainly have. Working with Maria made me realise that perhaps I was not the easiest person to live with and could be quite self-centred and strong-willed.

Sadly, in the past, by bottling up my inner thoughts and feelings for too long without communicating them, I had become 'poisoned'. Occasionally this inner poison then seeped – or more often burst – out into 'poisoning' my environment, which I clearly wanted to change. I hope that my explosions never went as far as the following story of Ignaz Semmelweiss, which I believe teaches a remarkable inter-personal lesson.

Danger – Risk of Infection!

In the early 1800s, between 15–25% of mothers who gave birth in hospitals died of childbed fever. In 1844, the Hungarian physician Ignaz Semmelweis became an assistant lecturer at the Vienna General Hospital. Only a short time into his tenure, he noticed something strange. The mortality rate in the ward run by doctors was 18% while in the ward run by midwives, it was only 2%.

Semmelweis tried to discern the difference between the two wards, but the changes he instituted, such as correcting the position in which women gave birth and even altering the way a priest walked through the wards, did not improve the situation.

Not giving up, Semmelweis eventually discovered the key difference. Doctors performed autopsies on dead bodies. Midwives did not. And they delivered babies directly after dissecting cadavers, without washing their hands.

Semmelweis wondered whether the doctors were carrying 'cadaveric particles' to the mothers and were themselves the cause of the childbed fever and high mortality rates? He immediately started experimenting with various disinfectant solutions, and offered an answer considered radical and ridiculous by many at that time: he advised doctors to wash their hands with a chlorine-lime solution after autopsies and before assisting with childbirth.

The doctors in the maternity ward complied. The mortality rate dropped to 2–3% almost immediately.

What can we learn from this? For me, the handwashing and disinfecting serves as a metaphor for how we build and manage relationships. When we move from one stressful meeting or exchange to the next, do we 'infect' the next conversation with anger, aggressiveness, or even rudeness just like the doctors infected the next patients they saw? I'm afraid so.

And who usually bears the brunt of our negative behaviour? The people who are closest and most important to us: our friends, our spouses, our children. Maybe we believe that we do not need to be as 'careful' or 'polite' with them as we are when talking to our bosses or peers. Not so.

Taking a step back and being honest with ourselves, might we sometimes poison some of our closest relationships with the toxins we carry over into their world? What if we took the time to experience a bit of stillness and just breathe before we connect with others when feeling highly strung and stressed ourselves? With this we can ensure there is no unnecessary 'contamination'. The likely result? Open, healthy, and constructive conversations as opposed to defensive, dysfunctional, and negative exchanges.

You may wonder what happened to Doctor Semmelweis? Surely his breakthrough turned him into a feted physician, showered with praise, awards, and recognition? Sadly, not quite.

He had identified the doctors as the ones responsible for causing all those deaths. They felt they were being labelled 'dirty'. And those doctors were like the rest of us. They didn't want to admit they were unwittingly at fault. They had reputations to uphold and large egos to protect. And so, the doctors fired back in publications and in public debate, accusing Semmelweis of not being able to truly explain the specific mechanism behind his findings.

And to a certain extent they were even right, as Louis Pasteur and Robert Koch wouldn't develop the germ theory of disease until later in the century. Though Semmelweis was correct with his hunch, and the mortality rate plummeted, they savaged him for not being able to explain why. They brought poison and prejudice, rather than open minds, to the debate.

Semmelweis was no diplomat either. His own reaction to his critics was very emotional and venomous. He did not 'disinfect' or calm himself down before responding. He called his opponents 'irresponsible murderers' and 'ignoramuses'. During the bitter conflict, he started to develop a mental illness, characterised by severe depression and 'absentmindedness'.

Things got so bad he had to be taken to a mental asylum. He tried to escape and was severely beaten by the guards. He sustained an injury during the beating, which later got infected, and he died shortly thereafter of the same disease he had managed to prevent in new mothers – blood poisoning. He was 47.

Things could have been so different. If only Semmelweis and the doctors in question had approached the issue with open and compassionate minds, and actively listened to each other and worked together to put a stop to childbed fever. If only they had left the poison behind.

For me, this remarkable though sad story is a good reminder of how we can become 'toxic' and not only poison important relationships, but also prevent ourselves from having the full impact on the world we could have otherwise had.

Working with Maria I created more awareness of when I was becoming 'poisonous' and used my daily meditation practice together with powerful breathing techniques and anchors to 'keep calm and carry on'. It clearly is not working all the time, but I definitely believe it made me a better human being and partner, by creating regular stillness and quiet reflection to detoxify myself from negativity and stress. With that I think I began to show up more consistently, a skill that would be essential when I moved into coaching and later therapeutic work.

I left each therapy session with Maria with a good list of actions and homework to be completed before the next one. This disciplined approach was helpful as it provided me with a structure, and step by step I was healing and working towards becoming a more whole human being.

One of the many changes I implemented during that time was to stop drinking coffee, which initially was tough, as I had to wean myself off with headaches and sleepiness for nearly two weeks. But eventually it helped me reduce my overall anxiety levels quite a bit.

The other area I was still somewhat indecisive and struggling with was alcohol, for which it would take another three and a half years before I implemented a step-change. Maria observed that in my case alcohol played the role of ensuring I 'belonged'. Not drinking would cause me the challenge of feeling alone and left behind. Of course, I struggled with that insight and therefore still delayed a change.

Another one of Maria's many revelations was that I was trying by all means to control life instead of going with its flow. I had already painfully experienced this on the Camino and so it was an area we did a lot of work on, especially with regard to my burgeoning relationship with Anne, together with the upcoming career transition.

Working with Maria I gradually shifted my inner state of desperation with this urge of being in control into a more relaxed and calm state. This allowed me to let go of some of the external events, and I began to slot better into the natural flow of life's ups and especially downs.

When it came to establishing and developing my relationship with Anne, Maria's support was invaluable. In one of the sessions, we had reviewed my previous relationships and it became obvious that in the bigger picture I was "attracting rejections" as an unconscious behaviour. In doing so, I had diminished my own worth and violated my own values for the sake of not being alone. I had unfortunately been through several spectacularly failed relationships and I will share a little more about one of them soon.

With Anne this began to feel completely different. After the electrifying situation on my balcony in early 2014 and the time I had spent together with her since then, I felt I could be more myself in being with her. Through the course of 2014 we grew closer and closer.

But even so, I think we were still a little unsure about whether to take the next steps as a couple together. I had the advantage that I was able to sort my thoughts in the sessions with Maria and thus gradually gained more clarity about what I wanted. Above all, it became clearer and clearer that I could very well imagine a relationship with Anne, despite all the past experiences and possible risks associated.

Then, in September 2014, I plucked up the courage to ask Anne if she would be willing to move in with me. Fortunately, she said yes and thus a completely new chapter in my life began. My days of being single were over, and we began to build a deep partnership and a new life together. Anne moving in brought another roommate into my home, a cat named Sebastian, who taught me several valuable lessons. But more about him later.

New roommate Sebastian

After all the work with Maria was done, I felt for the first time in my life ready not only to set up a long-lasting relationship with Anne, but even to start my own family and become a father. We began to try for children, something that would turn out to be a very enriching but also heart-breaking experience. And about this, too, more a little later.

Taking the Plunge

I had started the year 2014 with the clear intention that at some point after receiving my coaching certification, I would try my luck as a self-employed executive coach. Interestingly enough, and in a similar way to my situation two years earlier when a workshop had come up in London enabling me to walk the Camino, the universe must have heard about my career-shifting plan, and it conspired in spectacular fashion.

The job situation in large Multi-National Companies (MNCs) can change relatively quickly, and so did mine. The company had to look for synergies (again), trying to optimise the organisational setup and with this reduce costs. There were suddenly rumours about a plan to fold the haircare and personal beauty care businesses together. I immediately sensed the chance to potentially be able to use this opportunity and leave P&G with a severance package. After nearly 15 years of tenure, this would be an unbelievably helpful financial start-up blessing before moving into coaching.

My P&G Supply Chain Dream Team

But I had to be cautious and work through the process carefully. I fully trusted my boss, and as conversations began, I put my cards on the table, sharing that I would be okay to leave P&G when the two businesses got merged. My boss was truly brilliant, and to this day I am still grateful to him for how professionally and effectively he managed the situation. Soon it became clear that I would indeed be able to leave P&G by the end of the fiscal year. With a package.

That was exhilarating! Similar to the news I had received on the 1st of April 2012 about getting the green light to take four weeks off to walk the Camino, now, two years later, I received the news that in another three months' time in July 2014 a completely new chapter in my life could start. I was taking the plunge to become a coach. Exciting and scary at the same time.

The last few weeks at P&G were wonderful and I will never forget how my team bid me farewell. Not only did they create a video and organised a surprise party, but they also gave me a book as a memento, with personal greetings and wishes from each team member. To this day I sometimes take out the book or watch the video, which ends with: "Follow your heart to pursue your dreams and from all of us we wish your dreams come true." Watching it gives me goosebumps and makes me teary. Thank you so much guys!

And then the last day at P&G came. I still remember the moment when I took the office elevator for the last time, went down to the IT floor, handed in my computer and my P&G badge. That was it. Fourteen and a half very rich and sometimes tough years were behind me, I was now embarking on a new journey. Much like on that fateful day in Spain when I broke down, I was now 'walking my own Camino'!

Becoming an Entrepreneur

Once it was clear that I would move out of P&G by mid 2014, there was a lot to consider getting started as a self-employed coach. One thing I learnt very early on: I was now really on my own. When I had a computer problem in the past, I called the help desk and things got sorted. My salary came punctually every end of the month, and when I went travelling someone booked my flights and hotels.

Now all this comfort was gone, and I would quickly have to learn the hard way that becoming an entrepreneur is far from the romantic perception of 'rolling up your sleeves and thriving in your calling'. It's hard work, it requires self-discipline, and a massive portion of being able to work through setbacks without doubting yourself.

With the help of a football mate, Rolf, the company JK Executive Coaching Pte Ltd was born very quickly in April 2014. And with the support of Steve, a good friend of Maria's, the website and logo were ready soon too. Theoretically, the 'shop was open' by the end of June 2014. But there was one massive problem: I was not allowed to work!

I had done my Employment Pass (EP) applications with the Ministry Of Manpower (MOM) in Singapore in May 2014 and was hoping to receive a positive result, but learnt that it was declined at the end of June. By that time, I was already on a well-deserved holiday break in Germany.

Flying there I had felt on top of the world, as I was soon to follow my passion by coaching people and helping them to improve their lives. That felt so good! I still remember sitting in a café in Berlin with my good friend Juergen who was also on a career break. Together we enjoyed the sunshine by the waterside, with boats floating by, sipping our coffees, and drinking in the beautiful holiday atmosphere.

But when the news of the declined EP began to sink in, anxiety started to take over, and that only got worse when, a month later, the MOM rejected my EP application for a second time. Suddenly, my dream began to crumble. Arriving back in Singapore I was now a tourist. The paradoxical truth was that as a tourist I was not allowed to work, but at the same time MOM was asking for 'contracts and actual clients' which could prove that I had a clear intention and chance of success in setting up my coaching business.

I absolutely panicked and went into a crisis meeting with Rolf and a consultant who had managed the applications. Fortunately, my network rallied to my assistance, and so I signed some first contracts with Nick and others, which I could show to MOM. After a long and desperate wait, finally, in September 2014, I got the EP granted. Phew, now I could officially start and grow my business.

Curiously though, getting my EP almost had a detrimental effect on my state of mind. I felt I had overcome a massive hurdle and thought now everything would be plain sailing. With some financial reserves in place, I felt I could start slowly and enjoy gradually commencing the life of being self-employed.

But whilst I absolutely love being a coach, the stark reality kicked in that there were no clients to be coached. It surely sounds a bit stupid that I really only started to think about this fundamental question now, but to get new customers I had to go out and sell myself. This made me feel very, very uncomfortable. I was procrastinating, until Maria spelt it out for me in one of our sessions: no clients would come my way until I got my act together and did something about it. Fortunately, there was help at hand ...

Home Far Away From Home

Back on the 21st of July 1999, I had put an ad in the German *Frankfurter Allgemeine* newspaper: I advertised myself as a young engineer with four years of working experience who was looking for 'a new challenge abroad' and offered to be 'mobile worldwide'.

At that time, two of my best friends were living in South America, so I had started to learn Spanish, thinking I might join them. But life had different plans. I got offered a job with the German haircare company Wella, based in Bangkok. My role was to closely link Wella's six manufacturing plants in Asia with their headquarters, which were in Germany at the time.

On the 3rd of June 2000, after a five-month onboarding period in Hünfeld, Germany, and a tearful and beer-ful farewell, I hopped on a plane to Bangkok and into a completely new life in Asia.

The start was tough, but within only two weeks, I was 'at home far away from home'. All it took was one phone call to 'Ralf – The Legend', who warmly welcomed me to join the German All Stars Bangkok football team. Two days after the call, I was at my first football practice session, not only playing the sport I loved, but also instantly becoming a member of a friendly, open, and longstanding German community in Bangkok.

I made friends for life. Friends who helped me through culture shocks and difficult times at work; friends I could enjoy the fun and beauty of life in Thailand with. Regular practice sessions followed by ice-cold beers, games on weekends, as well as trips upcountry made the time unforgettable and literally gave me the feeling of belonging.

My advertisement in the newspaper *Frankfurter Allgemeine*

German All Stars Bangkok

German All Stars Singapore

After Procter & Gamble acquired Wella, I moved to Singapore in mid-2005 and, surprisingly, the same wonderful story repeated itself. Within only one week I got in touch with 'Magic Marcus Z' and joined in the activities of the German football club in Singapore. New and deep friendships were built quickly with amazing ease during training sessions, trips, games, and 'occasional' parties ...

My friends not only helped me through challenging job situations, but supported me in various personal crises and transformations. I felt as if I was part of one big, wonderful family. And this was exactly the family that came to my rescue in 2014 when I was drifting along somewhat naively in what Maria called 'La-La Land'.

This trying time showed me that 'a friend in need is a friend indeed'. Scrambling to find coaching clients, in September 2014 I reached out to my football network asking for help. And my friends came to support me far beyond my biggest hopes. They recommended me to people they knew, and some also hired me as a coach for their companies or themselves. Without them, I would not have been able to survive, much less start up my business successfully. I was rescued by 'vitamin F', F standing for Football.

The results have been amazing, and many years later, I look back with gratitude at a wonderful journey, during which I not only learnt a lot but was able to touch and improve peoples' lives as a coach.

This would not have been possible if it were not for my friends who helped me when I needed them most in autumn 2014, and I hereby want to officially say a big "Thank you" to Rob, Airplane Roland, Warm-Water Roland, Denis, Markus D, Katze Klaus, Big Mike, MC, Christian, Nayantara, Tommy, Swati, Jai, Madse, Maria, Denise, and many, many more who helped me get my feet on the ground as a coach. I could not have done it without you guys!

In East Germany we called good relationships 'vitamin B', where B stands for *'Beziehungen'*: the English equivalent would be 'vitamin C', with C standing for 'connections'. And connections were absolutely crucial to survival in the East German 'shortage economy', triggering a rich shadow trade: bartering.

Going to the shops in East Germany, you often found that many shelves were empty and so you could not just buy the things you wanted. But we still got what we needed, through our connections. As an example, my father was a gifted electronic engineer and able to repair radios and TVs. In exchange for his work, he could get us all manner of things, from sausages and beer to clothing and spare parts for the car. The people in our networks in East Germany were all in the same boat and we took care of each other, relying on the power of 'vitamin C'. And we got by quite well.

Our ancestors were all part of multi-generation households and tight-knit communities, whether they liked it or not. Nowadays, it is common for family members to be dispersed across the globe and for your 'community' to be the people you choose to associate with. You might have more in common and feel a greater affinity to a friend living in Angola who shares an interest in Chinese art than you would for someone you grew up next door to.

Our support networks may be more diverse and dispersed these days, but we still have just as great a need for them as we did during the bartering days in East Germany. For me in autumn 2014, 'vitamin C' and 'vitamin F' were absolutely crucial, and with this I began step by step to establish myself as a coach. It was not easy and there were months when I had to dip into my savings with only a very moderate income. But by 2015 I was slowly beginning to make a living with my passion. And that was cool!

I learnt that close and personal connections help us through difficult situations, make us enjoy the good times even more, and give us a home when we need it. They are remarkable, precious, and you cannot buy them for any money in the world. Yet, they give you back so much more than many of the material things we are chasing today. A very good friend of mine recently called friends our "true human capital."

My wish and challenge to you is to reach out today to one friend or family member and rekindle and strengthen your connection with him or her. Ask yourself, if you found yourself in need tomorrow, who would be there for you? And who would you be there for if they needed you? Take the time today and build a strong network, so you have your safety-net-work when you need it.

As my coaching business slowly began to take off, so did my relationship with Anne. Over the summer we had been growing closer, and thanks to my sessions with Maria I had also realised 'what was wrong with me' in regard to why my relationships in the past had not been working out.

To some extent, all my life I had been searching for what Maria called "high-heeled rejections." Anne cannot wear high heels. She would have loved to wear them, but due to her car accident and a nerve damage in her right leg she struggles to walk to this day. I learnt that high heels did not matter too much, and Maria even called them "shallow."

In hindsight I smile and shake my head at how I behaved in some of my previous relationships. One of my most spectacular surprises came when I got together with someone who had told me that she was my age when we met. Several months later, during a weekend trip, I discovered her real age by peeping into her passport at the border checkpoint. What I saw was shocking and I am sure you will laugh out loud now: she was ten years older than me. But what was even more extraordinary was my reaction. I was clearly struggling with the fact that she had lied to me, but I did not have the guts to end the relationship, likely very much out of fear of being alone.

With Anne things were very different. Not only did I check the passport early (joke), but from day one she was a very straightforward person. Someone who had no time for nonsense, as life had thrown a fair share of challenges at her. I felt her genuine interest in building our relationship together and so it was only a logical progression when she moved in, together with that cat named Sebastian. Over the summer I had had the opportunity to spend time with Sebastian at Anne's place and although I was told that I had a cat allergy, I truly started to enjoy his calm and peaceful way of being. There was something I felt I could learn from him. So, I had absolutely no objections to Sebastian moving into Kim Tian Road together with Anne.

Having been single and living alone for the past three years I would be lying if I said there were no teething problems moving in together. I guess all three of us had to find our place and our way of sharing our home. But it did not take too long, and soon I was smiling when I thought of coming home from a business trip or a client meeting, as I knew Anne and Sebastian would be there waiting for me.

As the year 2014 came to an end, everything had truly changed. I had started the year working at P&G being single and ended it by following my passion as a self-employed coach, in a lovely new relationship with Anne and living together with her and Sebastian the cat. What a transformation. But things did not stop there.

As Anne was 39 and I was 44 then, we had not much time to waste if we wanted to bring children into our family. We both felt ready and wanted to have children together and so we started trying for them.

Under Every Roof a Sorrow

It was in late January 2015 when Anne came to me in the morning, and I could feel something was different about her. She looked at me, smiled mischievously, and then showed me her pregnancy test. The markers were clearly visible. She was pregnant. Wow, wow, wow! I could feel tears coming to my eyes, as I gave her a kiss and a big big hug. We would have a child and I would become a father.

For more than 40 years, the thought of becoming a dad would have rather scared me, but in that moment, I felt full of joy, confidence, and happiness. We both were so excited, but this was only a home pregnancy test and we had to validate it.

Over the coming weeks we made several visits to the doctor. Things were going well. When I looked at Anne I could not stop smiling, and she smiled back at me beautifully, in her quiet, serene way. We would have a child. But our pregnancy apart, life was not so easy, as I was still trying to find customers whilst at the same time learning more about how to coach and support my few existing clients.

I was working 'full-on' and also travelling a fair bit, mainly to Hong Kong where I began to establish a coaching collaboration with 'Airplane Roland' and his team. The trips to Hong Kong were usually tough. I took the first flight from Singapore, leaving home before 4 am and then coming back the next day, normally way past midnight.

In early March 2015, I was on one of those trips. At 6:30 am my plane to Hong Kong was about to take off when I received a message from Anne. She was ten weeks pregnant at that time. "I am bleeding ... going to the hospital now." The plane took off, and, for the next three and a half hours, the only thing I could do was worry.

As if it were an omen for what would unfold that day, the descent into Hong Kong was completely terrifying with strong gusts of wind and severe turbulence. It got so bad, the pilot had to abort the landing procedure just a few metres off the ground. We were diverted and landed in Shenzhen after another hour of circling in the air. Still on the runway, I immediately rang Anne. The news was terrible. "There is no heartbeat. We lost it," she told me quietly.

After waiting for hours on the plane in Shenzhen, I made my way to Hong Kong and then finally back to Singapore that evening. The next day we went to the hospital for the heart-wrenching removal procedure. We struggled, having lost Wolfina, which is what we had called the little one in anticipation. The days and weeks afterwards went by in a sad blur. For both of us, the feeling of becoming a father and mother had been absolutely terrific and a long-held dream. We did not want the dream to end there and then. With the biological clock ticking for both of us, we decided to try further for children with IVF. This was very tough and at some junctions even brought our young relationship close to the brink.

The complicated hormonal treatment with daily injections, regular visits to hospitals, the constant hope, and unfortunate disappointments took a massive toll on us. It was very hard, especially for Anne. In hindsight I now think that IVF requires strong counselling support for the couple. We did not have this but were trying to work it out by ourselves.

After six rounds of IVF, a lot of emotional turmoil, as well as physical health and financial struggles, we very sadly decided to bury the dream of having children. It was a difficult decision, also as adoption was a path we were not fully prepared to go down. I am sharing the situation here to illustrate the truth behind a German saying my sister used to remind me of: *"Unter jedem Dach ein Ach."* – "Under every roof (there is) a sorrow." The German *'Ach'* is an expression for sorrow, adversity, problems, or difficult situations we have to deal with. Connecting the *'Ach'* with 'every roof' means that there is basically no household that doesn't face any problems or challenges. I am sure you have some sorrows of your own that immediately spring to mind.

Here are some of the 'sorrows' I have come across when talking with others and working as a coach:

– An alcoholic family member, whom everyone tries to help, passes away.
– A brother keeps overeating, damaging his health.
– A cheating spouse leaves the family and the young kids behind.
– A brother struggles with a gambling addiction, which brings financial and emotional turmoil to the whole family.
– A daughter is diagnosed with autism.
– A wife suffers with regular and deep bouts of depression.
– A beloved husband and caring father commits suicide.

Nobody's life is perfect. We all struggle with something at some point. Even if someone's life looks picture-perfect on the surface, there is very likely something underneath that 'roof' which is causing grief, sorrow, or disturbance.

On the other hand, that very struggle with our problems is also part of what makes us human and what can connect us more closely with each other – if we let it. By sharing our adversities, we often come to realise our burden is not that heavy and, more importantly, that we are not alone in our concerns and worries. But this kind of personal sharing is not always easy. To share what is really going on requires the ability to be vulnerable. It also requires compassion from the listener. But it is in exactly this kind of exchange that a strong bond is created. And therein lies the magic of human kindness as a wonderful source of positive energy and connection.

As you go through your day, I would like to invite you to reach out to someone you know and trust and share one of your sorrows and ask about one of the other person's challenges. From my point of view, this ability to share both our joys and our sorrows is a big part of what makes our lives so precious and meaningful. You may just feel a wonderful rush of encouragement and camaraderie; as the saying goes: Be kind, for everyone you meet is fighting a hard battle!

Having made the difficult decision to put our wish for children aside, we had to make a Plan B. This was not an easy undertaking: setting up a family with children is something that cannot easily be replaced by other things. The following short story helped me personally at that time not to give up and to keep looking for alternative options together with Anne.

There Is Always Another Option!

Once upon a time, there was a small business owner who had a huge debt to a loan shark. Every month, the interest rates would increase, and the burden of instalments threatened the good man with losing everything he had worked so hard for.

In an attempt to negotiate some relief, he went to the loan shark, who was an old, nasty, and remarkably ugly man. The loan shark listened, deceitfully nodding his head to the pleading of the business owner. And it transpired the loan shark had a goal in mind: marrying the delightful, intelligent, and beautiful young daughter of the business owner.

After the business owner had stopped talking, the loan shark said, "I am happy to release your burden of the loan if you give me your daughter's hand in marriage." The business owner was devastated and begged the loan shark to consider any other solution to the situation.

"Well," said the loan shark, "we could make it a fair gamble and see whether luck is on your side. Come to my house with your daughter tomorrow afternoon." The business owner did not know how to tell his daughter, but eventually summoned all his courage and spoke to her. Her response was telling. "We will find a solution, Father."

The next day, the loan shark met the two in his garden. He said he would place two pebbles into a bag, one white and one black. The daughter would then have to reach into the bag and pick out a pebble. If she picked black, the debt would be wiped out, but the loan shark would then marry her. If she picked white, the debt would also be wiped out, but the daughter wouldn't have to marry him.

Standing on a pebble-strewn path, the loan shark bent down and picked up two pebbles. As he was doing so, the daughter noticed that he picked up two black pebbles and placed them both into the bag. The loan shark then asked the daughter to reach into the bag and pick one.

The daughter was perplexed and nervous. The situation seemed hopeless, as she quickly contemplated her choices:

1. I could refuse to pick a pebble from the bag, but this would not resolve my father's loan situation.
2. I could take both pebbles out of the bag and expose the loan shark for cheating, but this might make things even worse.
3. Or ... I could just go along, pick a pebble from the bag, knowing it was black, and sacrifice myself for my father's freedom.

Have you, dear reader, ever been in a dilemma like that, where every possible option seemed unacceptable, where there was no way out 'alive', almost as if someone was holding a gun to your head? How do you react in such situations? Do you panic? Do you try to run? Do you freeze? Do you give up?

Here is what the daughter did: "Please give me a moment to gather my nerves as this will be the most important choice I may ever have to make." With that, she took a stroll through the garden. Her mind was racing, but she managed to take some deep breaths and regain her composure. There must be another solution, she thought. She refused to give up. And looking down at the pebble-strewn path, she had a flash of genius.

She went back to the loan shark and drew a pebble from the bag. But before looking at it, she dropped it 'accidentally' into the midst of all the other pebbles on the ground. "Oh, how clumsy of me!" she exclaimed. "But," turning to the loan shark, "never mind, if you look into the bag for the one that is left, you will be able to tell which pebble I picked."

The loan shark had been outsmarted. The pebble left in the bag was black. He didn't want to be exposed for cheating, so he was forced to play along, pretend that the pebble the daughter had dropped was the white one, and clear her father's debt without making any claim on her.

Just Married

For us the search for an alternative approach to having children was not as easy as pulling a pebble out of a bag. But it was possible. There were other options to explore. What it would take as a first step was to apply Phra Chaibodin's "accept, accept, accept." This was very tough. It took both of us quite some time and, honestly speaking, even today these 'what might have been' thoughts come up occasionally. But life moved on and we both had to move on with it. And move on we did, getting married in a wonderful setting at Singapore's Mount Faber.

Our wedding was our special day. I still remember the feeling of pure joy and happiness when we put our rings on each other's fingers and exchanged our wedding vows: "I, Joerg Kuehn, take you, Anne Nim-Sie Chan, to be my wife and my love from this day forward. I promise that by the end of our long lives we will look back and smile at the wonderful times we shared, the tough moments we managed, and the most amazing family we built.

In times of crisis, I promise to share my thoughts, fears, and hopes respectfully so that we overcome them together and grow stronger as a team. You are my base camp,

Marrying beautiful Anne

my friend, my coach, and my lover, with the cutest smile on earth. I promise that my love and care for you as well as my stunning jokes will make you smile every day.

You have experienced difficult losses in your life. I promise that I will not walk away but keep walking beside you. Together we will show the world that growing old in style, in love, and in happiness is the ultimate pinnacle of success."

"I, Anne Nim-Sie Chan, take you, Joerg Kuehn, to be my husband, to have and to hold from this day forward, for better, for worse, for richer, for poorer, in sickness and in health, to love and to cherish, till death do us part.

I am honoured and privileged to be given the opportunity to love you and to be your lifetime partner. I promise to exercise my leg every day, so that I can continue to hold your hand and walk with you on our exciting new journey together.

I promise to encourage and inspire you, to indulge you whenever I can, and to laugh at your jokes, even when they are not funny. I promise to remind myself, every day, to cherish and adore you, and to choose my words carefully, especially when we are having tough conversations. I promise to build a family with you – filled with love, joy, and compassion. And together, we will make our dreams come true."

We still keep these vows in our kitchen today, and sometimes taking a look at them is a wonderful reminder of the journey we are on together. Clearly, there are those difficult days, and during the time of the IVF, life was really hard. But we always found a way to move on together, and I am convinced that our vows have helped us to do that, particularly because we have been able to talk about things and find the 'always another option' together.

And whilst our wish for children was not meant to be, there was something else which came into our family, and which in hindsight feels such a blessing to have stumbled upon.

Stumbling on Happiness

The year 2015 ended on a very sad note. Anne's cat Sebastian had been quite ill for a while and needed daily injections to cope with his diabetes. He also required a special diet of broccoli, carrots, and other vegetables to help with his digestion. By the end of 2015 things took a turn for the worse, as he struggled to eat any food at all, and so eventually Anne had to make the incredibly difficult decision to let him go.

Some might say that letting go of a pet should be something we can deal with. But Sebastian had been a constant part of Anne's life for twelve long years. He'd been handed over to her outside a tube station in London, when he was only six weeks old. The size of a child's fist, Anne had held him close to her chest and brought him home.

From then on, they had to find their way through life together. Anne to this day says that it was Sebastian who kept her going when things at work and in general were nearly unbearable. Both moved to Hong Kong and eventually to Singapore together. Seeing Sebastian go was sad and difficult also for me who had experienced the beauty of life with a cat for just a year. But eventually he was gone, and we had to move on again.

After three months of 'cat-less living', we considered getting a new one and decided to go on a search without hurry. Entering Mrs Wong's cat shelter at Bukit Timah Road, we were greeted by more than a hundred cats. Our 'target cat specification' was very clear: male, black, and with a long tail, like Sebastian.

As we started looking around for that 'perfect fit', one cat seemed highly interested in us and even jumped on us. This cat was the total opposite of our 'ideal': a female cat with a three-colour pattern and only half a tail.

We were not sure what to do with it, and meanwhile the only black, male, long-tailed cat we saw at Mrs Wong's was hiding under a cupboard. The next day, I asked Anne: "Do you think there was any meaning behind this cat jumping on us, almost choosing us? Should we go and get her?"

Anne said yes, and soon the cat, which was called JW2, came home with us. (JW stood for Jurong West, the district of Singapore where she was found.) We decided

Rosie jumping into our life

Rosie without fur

to give her a proper name and called her Rosie. She clearly was not the prettiest cat on earth, especially after she had moulted nearly all her fur in the first few weeks.

She had come with a massive cat flu, sneezing all over our apartment, and during her first night she was so scared that she stood still under the table and did not move until early morning. Things got worse, and eventually we even brought in a cat whisperer who told us that it was us who made Rosie insecure. At that time we were going through another round of IVF together, and deep down Anne was still grieving Sebastian and not able to let Rosie fully into her heart yet.

It was not until we went on a trip to Europe and our good friend Heiko, a cat whisperer in his own way, took care of Rosie for two weeks. It was as if she had needed this space, the time alone in the flat, interspersed with the regular visits by Heiko. When we came back, we found a transformed cat. Her fur had grown back, and she was now the confident feline who accepted the central leadership role of the household, with her two human servants returned to start a proper cat-life family.

Apparently, Sigmund Freud once said, "Time spent with cats is never wasted." And Rosie proved that there had been a meaning behind her jumping on us. With her friendly temperament she was there to support us and our relationship, as she gave us something to love and care for. At the same time, she enjoyed the attention, the cuddles, the play, the naps, and of course the food schedule, which was totally under her control. Gradually she promoted herself to a proper CEO – Chief Enjoyment Officer – whilst making our flat a real home.

Even though she may never make it to a boarding school or an Ivy League university, we truly love coming home and being together with her. Rosie has helped us a lot to deal with the 'sorrow under our roof' of not having children. Initially she had been totally 'out-of-spec', but I am convinced we 'stumbled on happiness' when she chose us and we made her part of our family.

So, what lesson is Rosie's story telling us? I think it shows us how adaptability works, which is beautifully described by Harvard psychology professor Daniel Gilbert in his ground-breaking book *Stumbling on Happiness*. For me, Gilbert's two key lessons are:

– When we imagine our likely level of happiness, sadness, or other feelings based on hypothetical future events, our mind adds or leaves out key details without us realising it.

– When events actually happen and the hypothetical future becomes today's reality, our psychological 'immune system' distorts our perception of events to shield us from undesirable effects like pain or depression.

What this means is that we might have a clear perception of how we wish things to turn out and life to evolve. We might for example have this picture of a perfect

Stumbling on Rosie-Happiness

family with children around us when we grow old, but actually, as in our case, life may have different plans.

Still, it is our natural desire to become happy within the circumstance we live in, even if at the same time those 'target circumstances' have not turned out exactly the way we had wished them to be.

When you look at your life and the things you desire, is there perhaps something you could accept and open your heart and mind to? Is there an opportunity trying to find you, which might eventually provide you the happiness you needed to 'stumble on'?

Take a breather, be still, open your eyes, smile, and perhaps just let it 'jump' on you: you never know what's round the corner ...

X Years No Beers

Ever since my time in the Thai monastery in 2013 I had wanted to make a change in one area of my life: alcohol. But it was not until more than five years later that I truly began to do something about it.

By that time, multiple things had happened which made me question my relationship with alcohol. I had been a social weekend drinker since I was probably

15 years old. And you can bet I did not miss many weekends of partying or at least enjoying some beers or glasses of wine during the 32 years since then.

I would never have called myself an alcoholic, as I was fully functioning, but I did nearly burn down my parents' kitchen once and got myself into some other minor troubles. Drinking will do that, but I always enjoyed the feeling of immediate relaxation, joy, and relief when that first drink was running through my veins.

But the number of drinks I consumed gradually appeared to increase, and when I did an actual count for one of the months in late 2017, I estimated I'd had about 70 drinks. Probably still manageable, but given I was drinking only every 3–4 days, you can work out that the number of drinks per session came to maybe 7–9. That's almost 'Olympic level'. And with those 'peak performances' came the blackouts, which seemed to increase during those weeks and months.

Nothing much to worry about I thought, but some mornings I found myself waking up and wondering whether I had done something stupid last night, embarrassed myself, or said something highly controversial. It started to dig into my soul. As I was also trying to lose weight, I thought, why not give alcohol a break for a while? They say, "When the student is ready, the teacher arrives." In my case, several teachers showed up in quick succession.

First was Peter, who took me through a life-changing eight-week meditation course. Peter's German-style 'tough love' pushed me hard at times, but really helped me a lot. Peter had not had a drink for eight years. He asked me, "Why don't you try to quit at least for the duration of the course?"

At the same time, someone very close to my heart was going through a severe health crisis, awaiting a significant surgery. This person had struggled greatly with alcohol, and a return to their old drinking habits after the operation would mean a high risk of premature death. A rehab or therapy programme was not an option for my loved one, and so I spontaneously proposed we both go off alcohol so I could provide support and be a real companion along the way. Little did I know how tough it would be.

But then another positive thing happened. My good friend Mark introduced me to the wonderful institution of *OYNB – One Year No Beer*[18] which helps people re-assess and change their relationship with alcohol. I signed up first for the 90-day challenge and later extended it to 365 days.

At the start, going alcohol-free was tough. When the weekends came around and I saw Anne ordering her pint of Guinness, I felt a sense of envy and a deep-rooted urge to have one myself. Yes, it was tricky. Going alcohol-free also meant that the good old drinking sessions with my football mates were not appropriate for a while. I missed these opportunities for socialising, the interactions, and the camaraderie a lot. But I kept on the path and tried to focus on a few close friendships with people who would be there despite my 'staying on the wagon'.

They say alcohol is the only drug you "must apologise for not consuming," and in some social settings it certainly felt that way. But to be honest, it was probably more my own perception that the pressure to drink existed, rather than people really forcing me to drink.

You would assume that giving up drinking would have to be good for both body and soul. But a few months down the road, I started to question everything. If someone had told me that I would not have a drink – or a hangover – for six months, I would have imagined me skipping down the road every morning full of energy, joy, and happiness. But that was not the case.

In fact, the very opposite was true. Life at times felt even more problematic than when I was drinking. Only later would I learn that this is the natural flow of things. Life has its ups and downs. In the past, I had numbed the downs and revelled in the artificially induced highs, blackouts notwithstanding.

Now, there was no more numbing, and it took me probably a year and a half to realise that coping with feeling down, tired, or frustrated is also possible without that immediate relief of a drink. After that time, I began to appreciate that it's not only possible, but actually quite liberating not to have to have that drink.

When now soberly observing other people drink, I also noticed that for many drinking is not a problem, as they can sit for hours, sipping delicately on one or two drinks. It dawned on me that I can't do that. My speed was different, and on many occasions, there was no limit, which made me push the needle too far at times.

Looking back, going alcohol-free has made me live my life in a more honest way, and I surprisingly feel freer. I also sense that it has made me a better coach, as I am showing up more congruent and present, and based on this my coaching income has almost doubled over the first two years since I stopped drinking. Beside this, I believe quitting alcohol has also provided me with more calmness, focus, and a growing level of self-confidence.

It hasn't been a one-way street. Stopping drinking has taken some things out of my life that I honestly truly miss, but it has also put in so many more new and wonderful things that I'm extremely grateful for. And so, the bottom line is this: I feel I get more out of my life now, which is something I'm genuinely happy about and quite proud of.

Oh, and here's the rest of the story: the person close to my heart came through surgery extremely well and since then is in much better control of alcohol! I tell you this story not because I think *you* should change your life, but because I wanted to share my personal experiences and learnings. But if you sense there is something in your life that's having a significant negative impact on your happiness and contentment, why not consider taking a break from it? There are lots of helpful resources out there, and the benefits are just too great to not give it a try.

How to Leave Paradise?

Christmas 2017 was different to previous years. Anne and I stayed in Singapore as we had completed the sixth cycle of IVF and were hoping desperately that this time it would work out. To minimise the risk, we decided not to travel to Germany, but stay in Singapore instead. After nearly 17 years in Asia, this was my first time celebrating Christmas in 30-degree heat. It was nice but felt very strange indeed.

Between Christmas and New Year's Eve we then got the sad message that Anne was not pregnant and with that the year ended on a very low note, as we came to the conclusion that the physiological and emotional turmoil these rounds of IVFs were having, especially on Anne, had to stop. But "when one door shuts, another door opens." For us this clearly took some time, but it became obvious that we wanted to make the most of life and of our Plan B.

With this, one key question arose for both of us: "Where do we want to live in the long term?" Our life in Singapore was very well established, very comfortable, and to a certain extend we were cruising. My coaching business was going well, I had built a good network of clients, was lucky enough to make a stable income which allowed me to even save some money, and I was also closely connected with other coaches as part of the Singapore chapter of the International Coaching Federation (ICF). I had a strong network of good friends around me, and we were living in a beautiful place, with swimming pool and sauna just a few floors down by lift.

But a deeper concern seemed to come up for me in 2018. I had been 'home far away from home' for nearly two decades by then. And somehow this tied into the question, where do I really belong? Sometimes I felt anxious seeing myself being stranded in Asia like 'circling in an orbit'. Stuck in a beautiful place, for certain, but a place where I somehow did not really belong, and without the possibility of coming back into the 'orbit' that is home.

At the same time though my life was wonderful, and Singapore provided such a convenient place to be. It almost felt like paradise. What do you do, when you consider paradise is probably 'not for ever' and there might be something else which is more important than this great *dolce vita*?

I once again went back to my mechanical engineering roots and started to write it all down. Anne and I had long conversations and began to look at where we could and wanted to live. With no children but a 'Zen' and very composed cat Rosie in our 'backpack', we were quite flexible as to what to do and where to go next.

We looked at various options where life could take us, and it quickly became clear that for Anne London was where her heart was. Every time she spoke about it her face lit up. I personally had not really spent time in London and had literally zero network or connections in the UK. But moving there would also bring me closer to my family and my home in Eastern Germany.

Entering a period of meticulous decision-making preparation with long pros-and-cons lists, as well as many very insightful conversations with my friends, things started to become clearer. Whilst it would be a massive step to leave Asia, it was also a step that could offer excellent learning opportunities for us both individually and as a couple. We also realised that a major life change of this kind requires a lot of energy and focus to build up a new existence from scratch. We felt at an age where this would still be possible and that perhaps we should do it sooner rather than later.

The conversations and email exchanges with my friend Juergen especially helped me to look at what such a move would entail, not only in the short term but more importantly how it would fit into the longer term and bigger life picture. Juergen reminded me that my life had begun to move into its second half already, and he asked me what a happy and fulfilled life would be for me?

Pondering this made it clear that I wanted to "live a healthy life, in a functioning and fulfilled marriage, with good friends around me, financially secure at a home that I was looking forward to coming back to every day, working in a job that is meaningful, enjoying life by continuously learning more about myself, people, and life in general." Especially the last part about 'learning' was what began to tip the balance towards starting a new chapter and journey in London.

In contrast to my previous adventures, this time I would make a big life change together with someone else – Anne. This made many of the next steps easier and clearer, as we could talk them through together and then move forward. We used the rest of 2018 to look at our financials, to map out a move and business plan, as well as do a 'reconnaissance' or 'scouting' in London together.

On that trip I also paid a visit to the National College for Hypnosis and Psychotherapy as I wanted to go back to school and learn more about psychology. All boxes were ticked in a positive way and with this, Anne began to manage our actual move plan in a stunning Excel spreadsheet with meticulous perfection.

On the 15th of April 2019, after many weeks of sorting, packing, and preparing, we were ready. Five hours before our departure, the agency collected Rosie in her large 'business class suite', and soon after that Anne and I made our way to the airport together.

I can't really describe what I felt, as there were still so many organisational details on our minds. And perhaps it is very difficult to grasp what it meant, as two decades in Asia came to an end together with a new beginning back 'home' in Europe and London. But London and Europe were about to drift somewhat apart, as we made our move when the whole world was talking about Brexit. Opposing the tide, on April 16th we made our 'Brentry', moving into a small flat near Earl's Court in West London. Rosie arrived alive and well a few hours after us and with this, we slowly began to build a new life. Little did we know at the time that only a few months later, the whole world would come to a complete standstill.

The following funny little story which happened after being here for some time nicely summarises how we felt and how things would work out. Its title and very British sense of humour would soon become essential for most of us from March 2020 onward.

Every Crisis Presents an Opportunity

It was a lovely Saturday evening in 2019, when at 10 pm our only toilet got blocked, triggering the 'collateral beauty of a plumbing crisis'. Let's go through our little drama blow by blow.

We started our adventure by searching the net for a London based plumbing company that could help us on Sunday morning. Oh, and we required a plumber with knowledge of macerators, which is a pump-like device connected to the toilet. Having started to make calls early on Sunday morning, it took only three hours until Plumber Number One arrived, but unfortunately, he had no macerator knowledge.

He called his colleague, Plumber Number Two, who arrived at 2 pm. Plumber Number Two quickly established that we needed a new macerator, which he promised to install early Monday morning. He was a nice guy, and since we had to pay him for a minimum of one hour and it had taken all but a few minutes to give us the news about the macerator, he kindly took on some other work we needed done and installed a new radiator thermostat. That was helpful, but we still had no toilet. We had to look for creative toilet solutions, which were found in local cafés, shops, and pubs. Thank you!

On Monday at noon, a vegetable blender arrived by courier. A quick call to Plumber Number Two confirmed that this was not the macerator we needed. Still, we learnt that he would be on his way to install the real macerator soon. Two hours later, he was here and did so. But – oh shit! – it turned out the pipe was blocked. Enter Plumber Number Three, recommended by Plumber Number Two, as he was a 'blockage expert'. He tried his best with a massive industrial hoover, to no avail. And, wouldn't you know it, he could not use his high-resolution pipe camera because our pipes had 'elbow joints'. He reckoned it would be best to lift all the floorboards and tiles, to see where the main stack was. Also, could we get access to the downstairs neighbour?

Now, our downstairs neighbour had not been our best friend since a recent Friday evening when I was hammering together an IKEA cupboard. Still, we asked him if we could have a look, and he kindly let us in. Plumber Number Three got no new insight from the visit downstairs, but my wife wondered why one of the walls downstairs featured water stains. Our neighbour seemed surprised himself. It turned out that Plumber Number Two had installed the thermostat incorrectly and created a leak into our downstairs neighbour's flat. Blimey!

On the positive side: the downstairs neighbour turned out to be quite friendly and even offered the use of one of his three toilets. Back at the flat, we called Plumber Number Two, who in the late evening turned up to disconnect the radiator. It was now Monday near midnight. We had spent over £1,000 for a toilet that was still blocked, a disconnected radiator, and a neighbour's damaged wall. And we were still bathroom beggars.

On Tuesday morning, we made an executive decision to change plumbing companies. Plumbers Number Four and Five arrived in the afternoon. They were unsuccessful in unblocking the pipe but came up with a medium-impact solution to resolve the situation, which still entailed breaking tiles and somehow laying a new pipe through the kitchen by Wednesday.

At long last, and thanks to our managing agent, we got a call from the 'real' blockage experts, Plumbers Number Six and Seven, who promised to charge us only if they could indeed unblock the pipe. On Wednesday morning – with street wisdom and some pretty smart efforts – they unblocked the pipe within half an hour. Yippee!

And why am I telling this story? You might think, well, shit happens. And, yes, it certainly does (once the facilities are unblocked), but that's not the point. I tell it for two reasons. Stuff like this doesn't just happen to you, even though it may seem like it sometimes. We all endure our share of trials and tribulations, be they of a plumbing nature or otherwise.

And I tell it because I strongly believe this plumbing crisis taught us an important lesson: each crisis presents us with opportunities. Here's the good that came out of this episode:

1. My relationship with Anne, which had always been good, improved further as we managed the crisis as a team, enjoying our lovely early breakfasts and/or late dinners in the establishments of our temporary bathroom sponsors.
2. The relationship with our neighbour improved.
3. We found some really good plumbers, tipped them a bit, and have had super service for other plumbing issues since then.

It's seldom the case that our tales of woe don't contain some silver linings. We sometimes just have to open ourselves to recognising them. So, my challenge to you today is this. Whatever crisis you are currently going through or are about to encounter, ask yourself: what are the golden opportunities in it? Where are the silver linings? How can you use this crisis to your advantage and manage to see it as a blessing in some way?

Just as thunderstorms bring rainbows, crises beget opportunities. Maybe, just maybe, there will be a bit of collateral beauty – or even a pot of gold – that appears in the wake of our next crisis.

And how much we all needed this frame of mind when only a few months later the world ground to a shuddering halt: Covid-19.

The World on Hold

Our first few months in London were full of things we had to organise. Buying furniture, opening a bank account, applying for National Insurance, getting a tax number, arranging for pre-settled status (important with Brexit), completing the company set-up, the list went on … Fortunately, things worked out well, mainly because Anne had done a fantastic job in meticulously mapping out all the steps that needed completion with her Excel spreadsheet magic.

Arriving in London, we moved into a smaller space compared to Singapore, which was something we had to learn to arrange ourselves with quickly. But the one thing that stood out during our first weeks and months for me were the birds. I usually get up very early and when the city is still quiet, it is wonderful to hear familiar birds greeting the new day together at sunrise. Strangely enough the birdsong made me feel at home, back in Europe, after nearly two decades in Asia.

But 2019 was also a tough year, as my mum went through a challenging health situation which required a significant surgery. But now being based only a short flight away, I was able to visit her more frequently than I would have been able to from Singapore, and fortunately the surgery and subsequent treatments went well, so that she was able to recover fully. During that year, I still commuted to Hong Kong for work once a month. This was nice on the one hand, as it kept me closely connected to Asia, but also challenging on the other, as the jetlag was a big struggle, making these trips usually very exhausting. Overall, though, we managed well through 2019 in our new little home in West London, and we were looking forward to 2020, for which we had already made many nice plans.

In January of 2020, I went on my monthly trip to Hong Kong. Little did I know then that this would be my last trip for a long, long time to come. Right after I had landed in Hong Kong, the first Covid cases were reported in Wuhan, and very soon after the world came to an unforeseen and complete standstill.

I still remember when the first travellers infected with Covid-19 had landed here in the UK and were escorted to a segregated clinic on special buses with drivers in full protective gear. We knew little to nothing about the virus at that time; nobody had any idea what change and challenges we all would have to deal with in the coming two years.

The following story is a very personal account of how Covid-19 began to hit home, and the trauma it could inflict on sufferers as well as friends and families.

Even if You Think You Can Manage – Reach Out!

The principal of the National College for Hypnosis and Psychotherapy, Shaun Brookhouse wasn't feeling his best in March 2020. He "didn't think it was anything in particular," he "just felt a bit unwell."

Shaun took a week off work, but things soon got worse, and people around him started to worry when his breathing became more laboured. One friend eventually insisted on calling an ambulance, and Shaun reluctantly agreed.

From then on in, he does not remember anything – until five long weeks later, when he was revived from an induced coma, as the doctors tried to bring his respiratory tract back online. It turned out Shaun was one of the first Covid-19 patients in the UK. When he arrived in hospital, the pandemic had only just begun, and the attending physicians had very little knowledge of the illness and its treatments.

Shaun's chances of surviving were not very high, given his age and his weight. But thanks to the heroic efforts by doctors and nurses – as well as what he calls "the lucky fact" that he was at an NHS teaching hospital, where, in addition to normal patient care, research is carried out on new and better treatment methods – Shaun made it. He survived.

Shaun Brookhouse

This should be where the story ends and where the Hollywood movie does the equivalent of a 'happily ever after', but in Shaun's case, what came next can teach us an important lesson. When he came around, he did not know where he was, as the coma drugs had quite a strong psychotropic effect on the brain. He did not know the people around him and, even more concerning, they did not seem to have clear faces, instead, all of them seemed to have beards!

What was that about? Of course, it turned out that the hospital staff were wearing masks, shields, and full protective gear. Seeing the funny side of this, Shaun later noted that "In one respect, it was kind of galling, because the women's beards, especially, seemed to be so much better than mine, much fuller and lusher."

Waking up also brought a big concern for Shaun. "Where are my friends? Did I offend people? Is that why no one is coming to visit me?" Again, looking back, it all made sense: the world had descended into lockdown, with no-one allowed to visit patients in hospitals.

After one more week on an ordinary ward, Shaun wanted to get out as quickly as possible. Back home, he slept badly. "I had regular night terrors with all sorts of hallucinations," triggered mainly by the coma drugs.

He had good friends around him who made sure that he was looked after, but Shaun being Shaun, he soon told his friends that he "was fine and able to manage" by himself now. He didn't want to impose or get on their nerves, so he "was okay now." But deep inside, he was not okay. Like many trauma survivors, he went through a difficult post-crisis period and wanted to dissociate and just be by himself.

For several months, Shaun now began to isolate, sitting at home proud and unwilling to ask for help. He struggled with physical weakness, sleep deprivation, old unresolved psychological issues, difficulties differentiating between what was real and what were hallucinations. And there were those haunting feelings of survivor's guilt – a typical phenomenon in trauma patients.

As a practising psychotherapist for nearly three decades, Shaun knew exactly what was going on and thought if anyone could manage his mental health, it was him. But it turned out he was not able to manage it. It got so bad that at one point he saw no way out and contemplated suicide.

Fortunately, he realised he needed to ask for help before it was too late: he reached out to people around him, found a therapist he trusted, and eventually came out the other side. Sharing Shaun's story is close to my heart.

The Covid pandemic has impacted most of us in many ways. Many of us have had difficult experiences. We've gone through a variety of health, professional, and personal challenges, dealing with the mental health impacts of lockdowns together with the constant uncertainties and changes to the way we live.

Whilst we usually adjust and somehow learn to live with such changes, under severe strain our mental struggles can become overwhelming. Yet, as in Shaun's case, the world, and indeed we ourselves, may still expect us to 'get on with it'.

And further crises – both personal, such as financial, health, or employment related, or global, such as climate – and all kinds of other struggles still lie ahead. We are going to need a lot of resilience to find our way in this ever-changing world. At times, this can feel like a lonely, uphill, and hopeless battle.

It doesn't have to be. Even if you think you can somehow manage and don't need any help when things get bad, please do reach out to a family member, a colleague, a friend, a coach, or a therapist. In Shaun's words, "Having good people around you, people who care for you is essential. If you don't have them, you've got to reach out. You've got to ask for help. It does not help to think you know better. There's no shame and no weakness in saying, 'I'm struggling, I need some help'." And here is the thing. People want to help. Let them.

Companies on the Brink

By March 2020, Covid-19 had begun to spread quickly. The early indications that it could potentially become a global pandemic had turned into reality. Panic began to take hold. Not only were the first deaths recorded, but the new illness was so contagious that it began to run havoc, spreading across populations around the world. Health services and governments were working frantically to try and contain the outbreak.

We still didn't know about the full scale of the crisis. Limited testing and surveillance meant that during the early weeks of the pandemic, case numbers were completely underestimated, obscuring the extent of its outbreak. I still recall the British Prime Minister Boris Johnson in the early days pushing for "a strategy to get to herd immunity as soon as possible." To do so not only ran the risk of millions of people dying, but also held the threat of completely overwhelming the health system. And at various stages during the pandemic, images of people waiting and dying in hospital corridors or even outside hospitals proved how acute the situation was.

Recognising the danger, the UK government soon changed its strategy and on the 23rd of March 2020 Boris Johnson announced the first official lockdown, as Parliament introduced the Coronavirus Act 2020, granting the governments of the home nations emergency powers and authorising the police to enforce public health measures. From one day to the next, life came to a standstill, as only frontline and essential workers were allowed out. The rest of us had to strictly stay at home with only one outing a day for exercise and the essential grocery run allowed. Life switched to a curious state of hibernation. But there was still a whole world of businesses out there, desperately trying to come to grips with these unprecedented circumstances.

For me as an executive coach it was really hard. I saw first-hand how businesses which had been successfully grown over a substantial period of time were suddenly on the edge of extinction. I still remember talking to a client who struggled to hold back his tears. "Joerg, in the last four days I have lost all the business that I had gradually built up over the seven years. My clients just cancelled all contractually agreed commitments due a lack of business and utter uncertainty."

It was heart-wrenching and devastating to witness. But I had to help and support my clients as much as possible, whilst at the same time trying to cope with this new situation myself. Very quickly it became obvious that at least for the foreseeable future, we all would need a new way of doing things. Each of us had to adjust. And so, by the end of March 2020, we all desperately needed some life hacks to deal with this adverse situation.

Three Magic Life Hacks to Prepare for Adversity

In his novel *Siddhartha,* Hermann Hesse tells the story of a young monk's quest for enlightenment – the Buddha narrative. After living an ascetic life in the forest, Siddhartha continues his journey, to live among 'real' people. Along his path, he enters a large town where he gets invited for a 'job interview' with the successful businessman Kamswami. As the interview begins, Kamswami asks Siddhartha: "What is it that you've learnt? What are you able to do?"

"I can think. I can wait. I can fast," Siddhartha replies. "That's everything?" Kamswami asks, to which Siddhartha responds: "I believe that's everything!" This triggers Kamswami's next question: "And what's the use of that? For example, the fasting – what is it good for?"

"It is very good, sir. When a person has nothing to eat, fasting is the smartest thing he could do. When, for example, Siddhartha hadn't learnt to fast, he would have to accept any kind of service before the day was up, because hunger would force him to do so. But like this, Siddhartha can wait calmly, he knows no impatience, he knows no emergency, for a long time he can allow hunger to besiege him, and he can laugh about it. This, sir, is what fasting is good for."

Kamswami was impressed and, after a short test in reading and writing, the businessman made Siddhartha an offer to stay and work with him. Goal achieved!

Walking into a job interview today with only these three skills might not necessarily land us the position, but I think there are some great insights to learn from Siddhartha's story, not only when it comes to interviewing, but in relation to how we adjust to change and how we react to a global crisis like Covid-19.

I can think!

Operating with a calm and clear mind is a key enabler of success. And when thinking translates into developing a set of daily activities that move us closer to where we want to be, there is a high likelihood we will eventually reach our goals.

I can wait!

Being able to plan and play the 'long game' helps us not getting carried away by short-term detours, obstacles, and setbacks. Patience is a virtue. When we're able to wait, it allows us to achieve what is truly meaningful and important.

I can fast!

Siddhartha's third skill gave him resilience to withstand hunger, with 'hunger' in the story serving as a metaphor for difficulties and disasters of all kinds. Siddhartha did not need to take 'any' job, but instead could search and wait for the right fit. That not only provided him a substantial degree of freedom, but also gave him the confidence to meet the businessman eye-to-eye.

For me, these three skills are exceptionally valuable in our times of constant change and adversity. Especially skills two and three can help us to not lose sight of what is truly important in such a situation. Without these skills, we can become lost, impatient, and we may overlook signs that tell us something is wrong. This, in turn, can make us stressed and tense. We lose focus, which can lead to muddled thinking, subpar decisions, and even 'becoming poisonous', as we saw in the tragic Ignaz Semmelweiss story.

Hermann Hesse summarises the concept beautifully: "When you throw a stone into the water, it falls quickly by the fastest route to the bottom of the pond. This is the way it is when Siddhartha has an aim, an intention. This is what fools call magic, thinking that it is brought about by demons. Nothing is brought about by demons; demons do not exist. Anyone can do magic, anyone can reach his goals if he can think, wait, and fast."

At the beginning of Covid-19 we all started to develop a Plan B, on the go. For me it meant that all my coaching switched to video calls over night. The first few weeks were utter chaos and I worked crazy hours, especially trying to support my key client in Hong Kong, whose business had grown from 20 million US dollars revenue to a stunning 100 million in the five years I had worked with him. But as most of his clients were airlines, in 2020 the USD 130 million which had been in the books for that year were suddenly at risk and so was the survival of this healthy company. From one day to the next it was on the edge of extinction.

We frantically worked on stabilising the cash flow, reducing commitments to suppliers, and cutting costs. This sadly also meant letting go of 50% of the workforce, whilst all other team members graciously accepted voluntary salary cuts. But during this second quarter of 2020 it was by no means clear whether these measures would allow the business to survive.

On a personal front, the lockdowns meant I was now spending much more time with our Chief Enjoyment Officer, cat Rosie, at home. She loved it and we clearly needed her services as we were desperately learning to cope with our new reality. But surprisingly soon it felt as if we were adjusting. For me it was remarkable to see how the whole world was somehow able to continue its existence despite being locked in at home. Nobody would have thought this possible.

To me, this tells us a lot about how adaptable we can be when needed, how much resilience there is inside each and every one of us. And it also shows that we are powered by a 'supercomputer' which, if used well, can help us through even the biggest crisis.

You Possess a 'Supercomputer'. Use it!

One of my New Year's resolutions for 2020 had been to regularly pick up the guitar and improve my playing. I had specifically set out a goal: 'Plug and slap technique in full swing by the end of the year'. But during the first two months, I must shamefully admit, I picked up the guitar far too little to really make any progress.

I guess if we take stock of our New Year's resolutions, a similar pattern often emerges. We are highly motivated in January, but as the year progresses, we do not really find the time and brain space to accomplish much of what we intend. Our busy lives with seemingly millions of priorities take over.

As part of a mindfulness programme, I learnt some intriguing facts around why we struggle so much to consistently take the actions we know are beneficial and important to us. It has to do with how our brain works and how we process information.

In his book *Flow,* Mihaly Csikszentmihalyi[19] describes how we receive environmental input through any of our five senses. The amount of these external inputs can be very large and this means that every second we are bombarded with millions of bits from the environment. Yet Csikszentmihalyi's astonishing finding is that the conscious mind can process only about 120 bits per second.

To give some context of what these numbers mean, when someone is speaking to us, we need about 40 bits of information per second to listen and process what is being said. I believe this fact explains why we struggle to listen to more than one person at the same time and, in general, have a problem with multitasking. Our conscious mind is constantly busy focusing on the important bits of information.

Is it any wonder, given the mental overload, that we easily forget we were planning to go for regular jogs, eat better food, or play the guitar? Hand in hand with the limited conscious bandwidth problem, some 47% of the time our mind is wandering. It makes you appreciate a little better the difficulty involved in 'consciously' shaping our own destinies and why most of our New Year's resolutions go down the drain by the end of the first month.

But here's the good news: recent research [20] also revealed that we have a very powerful subconscious mind, which can process up to about 11 million bits per second (see next image). This enables us to drive a car and talk to someone, all while listening to the radio in the background.

The subconscious mind is what really rules us. Research shows that 95–99% of our daily lives are not controlled by our conscious efforts, but by our subconscious mind. What this clearly tells us is that we have very little chance to really make sustainable changes in our lives unless we adjust the necessary 'programming' deeply rooted in our subconscious 'super-processor'.

There are the two primary ways to take more control and effect change at a faster and more reliable pace, which was essential for all of us during the time when Covid-19 started:

1. Increase awareness:

Effective tools here are meditation, breathing exercises, and mindful breaks in general, which can help us to become more aware of the present moment. By simply observing what is going on within and around us, we can stop 're-acting' and take back control of the steering wheel of our lives by starting to 'act'. Covid-19 definitely gave us the chance to take a break and revisit how we were living our lives. But acting in line with your intentions once or twice isn't enough, which brings us to number two.

2. Create positive & healthy habits:

If we want to sustain changes in our behaviours, we need to make the action in question a daily habit, like brushing our teeth. James Clear, an expert in creating new habits, summarises the keys to building successful habits as follows:

- Make it obvious – create the right environment and commitment.
- Make it attractive – do something you enjoy kicking off the ritual.
- Make it easy – reduce obstacles and do the activity for two minutes only, but consistently, each day.
- Make it satisfying – reward yourself after the habit and never miss twice!

If you struggle to establish a certain routine, perhaps apply one or all of James Clear's four powerful tips. With a little diligence, especially in the early stages, you will develop compelling new habits and you may surprise yourself by getting things done you feared were totally impossible. And all because you have turned things over to your magical 'supercomputer': your subconscious mind.

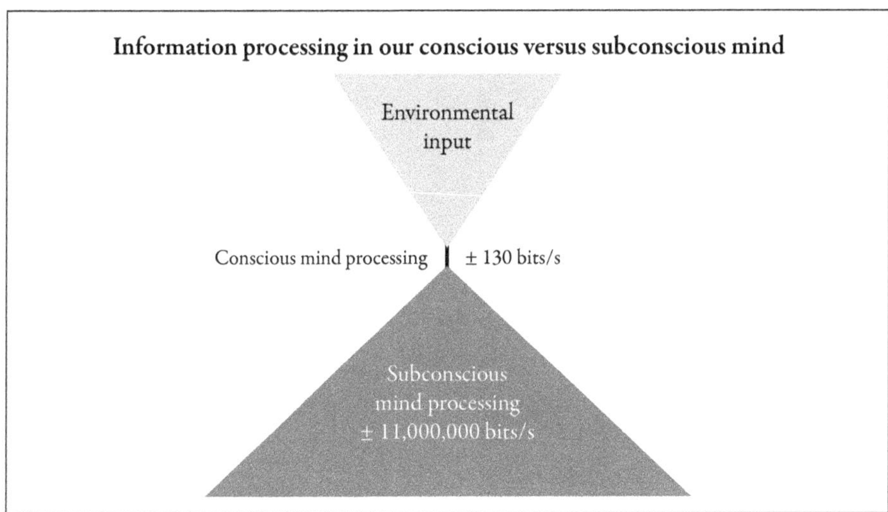

Processing power of our subconscious mind

With the onset of Covid-19, suddenly a lot of our daily habits were up for questioning, as almost every daily routine was impacted in one way or another. There was no more commute to work. There was no more office. Work had to be done online. Children had to be home-schooled. With non-essential shops closed, we had to shop online. Workouts had to get done at home. And on and on the list went. In this respect, it was a good opportunity to develop new routines, because there was time for something new.

An amazing tranquillity settled over London as everyone started to find their own ways to deal with the crisis. It was a remarkable reboot of our daily habits, and I probably should not say this, but I personally felt the first lockdown was quite an interesting experiment to put our 'normal life' on pause, checking whether we wanted to change anything, and if so what.

For me, the guitar together with a new friendship not only helped me through lockdown, but also supported me to make progress with my New Year's resolution. I must confess that deep down, I had always held the dream of being a 'rock star'. I love music and I love to sing even though my failed ukulele-busking audition in Singapore in 2012 brought home to me that I am probably not as talented as I thought I was. But for many years, and especially when out partying, I found myself in a 'dreamy' state standing in front of stages, admiring the musicians playing their instruments and singing their songs.

Despite multiple attempts at trying to learn the guitar, including going for regular lessons, plus even giving a little home concert with my good friend Mattias

My guitar

Hulting in Singapore, I never made any real progress towards my dream. Most importantly, I did not come to a point where I had established a regular routine playing and hence improving my guitar skills. But Covid-19 changed that, based on a new and incredibly fruitful 'friendship symbiosis' that came paired with new habits.

In 2019 my brother-in-law had turned 60 and in the run-up to his birthday party, I had had the idea to sing him a little song accompanied on the guitar. But doing this on my own was hopeless, and people would most likely have laughed, or reacted in a similar way to Sebastian the cat in Singapore, who occasionally would run to the door screaming "Get me out of here!" when I was strumming my guitar and singing away.

But on this occasion, I decided to reach out to a good friend of mine in Germany: Torsten. I knew his father Ralf is a musician who knows my brother-in-law Juergen quite well, and I thought he might be up to do a little surprise gig together. After Torsten had connected us, I asked Ralf whether he would be up for us to practise one or two songs together which we could play for Juergen's birthday in October 2019.

Rock stars Ralf & Joerg

Ralf was more than up for it and had even rewritten a song for the birthday 'boy'. Living 1,000 km apart, we practised mainly by ourselves and then gave ourselves a few days before the actual party in East Germany to fine tune. Our performance went very well, and I truly enjoyed the collaboration with Ralf, based on whose guidance I was able to play and somewhat sing along. He had made me a 'rock star' in my own little way.

When Covid then locked us all in at home, I saw my guitar on its stand and Ralf came to my mind immediately, and whilst it is somewhat impractical to connect via video call and make music together, we found a surprising way to make it happen, which was in no small measure due to Ralf's innovative approach to continuous experimenting and learning.

We set up our first call at the end of March, and I am glad to say we have not stopped since. Every two weeks we connect. Ralf will show me new songs, and we then just play along together. I love the German 'melancholy rock' band Element of Crime, and Ralf totally took this new genre onboard, even purchasing a book with Element music and learning the harmonica accompaniment.

I am not a rock star, but I now can play a few songs, and doing this regularly with Ralf brings a smile to my face. We were even practising for a little gig together in June 2022 in front of probably 100 guests, but more about this later.

So, Covid has enabled an amazing guitar friendship and our regular bi-weekly connects were keeping us both sane in times when the world sank further into uncertainty and continued peril. Thanks, Ralf, for all your help, support, and the wonderful times together!

The first lockdown came to an end in the UK at the beginning of May 2020. By then, more than 30,000 people had sadly lost their lives, making the UK one of the worst affected countries in the world. Boris Johnson announced his conditional plan for lifting lockdown, and from June 2020 there was a phased opening of schools and non-essential shops. But the pandemic was far from over: guidance to keep working from home remained in place, with all non-essential travel either banned or reduced to a minimum.

Then, during the summer of 2020 infections were levelling off and it felt as if everyone was taking a breather, with the weather improving and the economy gradually at least partly reopening. Overseas travel was still impossible and while sighing this brief sigh of relief, everyone was also already bracing themselves for autumn and winter, when things would very likely take a turn for the worse again.

But the summer of 2020 gave us all a short break from the pandemic, its rising death toll, and the constant risk of overwhelming health services. It gave us a temporary 'somewhat normal life' which was fuelled in the UK by the government's 'eat out to help out' initiative. Many of us indulged in a nice meal and a drink or two (mostly socially distanced and outdoors), partly sponsored by the government.

Anne and I used the summer well and went on a wonderful short trip to Cornwall, desperate for some sunshine and outdoor time. Gosh, was it lovely to sit by the sea watching the sun set, enjoying life as if we had never lived or had only a short time to go.

We also still sneaked away on a brief break to Norfolk before the difficult autumn and grim winter of 2020 began. After restrictions had been eased over the summer, and with case rates starting to rise again in September, a rule of six was introduced which meant that only six people were allowed to meet indoors. At the same time, it was recommended that all non-essential workers move strictly back to working from home, and a 10 pm curfew was imposed on the hospitality sector.

By the beginning of October, more than 42,000 people had died of Covid-19 in the UK, and the UK government now introduced a set of three tiers within which the restrictions would be tightened, depending on the number of new cases as well

Sunset in Tintagel with Anne in August 2020

as the capacity situation in hospitals. But by the end of October 2020, a full lock-down was announced to 'prevent medical and morale disaster for the NHS'.

Five weeks later the lockdown ended officially, and the country returned to the three tiers. But soon after that, and with case rates now increasing dramatically especially in the South, Prime Minister Johnson introduced a fourth tier and announced stay-home alerts for London and the South of England. During the month of December and over Christmas more and more areas were now added to tier four. Eventually, on the 6th of January 2021, the whole country entered the third complete lockdown.

By that time, we had all been living nearly a full year under the grim influence of the pandemic. Going into another lockdown, it felt as if this crisis would somehow never end. It felt as if we were caught with no way out. Stuck in an ever-repeating cycle of lockdowns, gradual release of restrictions, and lockdowns again. It felt like Groundhog Day …

Three Wonderful Tips for Our 'Groundhog Days'

On February 1st weatherman Phil Connors, together with his producer Rita and cameraman Larry, makes his way from Pittsburgh to Punxsutawney, where, on February 2nd, a groundhog named Phil predicts whether spring will come early, or winter will continue its icy grip for another six weeks. German-speaking immigrants initiated the tradition of Groundhog Day back in 1887.

Connors makes no secret about his dislike for the trip, as he finds the small town with its narrow-minded people "so uninspiring." His plan is to get done with the Groundhog Day report quickly to be back in Pittsburgh for the 5 pm news.

But life has other plans for the obnoxious weatherman as he enters an endless loop of waking up day after day at 6 am to Sonny & Cher's *I Got You Babe,* with the same day that he'd lived through the day before repeating itself, and the same people doing the exact same things.

That's how the movie *Groundhog Day,* starring Bill Murray and Andie MacDowell, starts out. The film has prompted Oxford Dictionaries to define the 'Groundhog Day' phenomenon Connors experiences as, "A situation in which a series of unwelcome, monotonous, unpleasant or tedious events appear to be recurring in exactly the same way."

Looking at where we stood with the Covid-19 pandemic during the winter of 2020–21, it often felt as if we were all stuck in our own Groundhog Days. And we all really started to have had enough of it! I was wondering at that time whether there was anything we could learn from the movie that would help us through this hopeless daily pandemic grind?

And yes, I believe there were some interesting lessons! As the story unfolds, Connors does everything he can to escape the ever-repeating cycle. He descends into binge-eating, getting drunk, robbing a bank, stealing the groundhog Phil, and even trying to kill himself multiple times.

Nothing works. That's when he learns three important lessons, which I think we can all apply whenever we are at risk of descending into the *tristesse royale* of Groundhog Days, whatever they might look like:

Accept – In a conversation with his producer Rita, she encourages Connors to accept the situation and even look at it as a blessing, rather than a curse. This becomes a game changer for the weatherman, as he begins to add new meaning to his days, exploring the endless possibilities presented by a day you get to 'redo' over and over until you get it right (greetings also to Phra Chaibodin ;-)).

Play – In his attempt to win over Rita, he embarks on a journey of learning new skills in a very light-hearted and playful way. He becomes an expert in ice-sculpting and learns to play piano like a virtuoso. He also learns to speak French, so he can recite romantic poetry to her. This touches Rita's heart, not to mention the hearts of competing TV crews.

Care – Having accepted his fate and now enjoying Groundhog Day as a daily experiment in living, Connors begins to genuinely care for the people around him, performing a long list of good deeds, such as catching a boy falling off a tree, changing a flat tire for three old ladies, rescuing the mayor from choking on a steak, and simply buying coffee for his crew.

Accepting his fate, enjoying play, and genuinely caring for the people around him is what eventually breaks the cycle. At the end of the movie, he wakes up in Rita's arms: the spell is broken. It's the 3rd of February, and a new life begins. One analysis of the film comes to the remarkable conclusion that Phil Connors lived his Groundhog Day an amazing 12,395 times or nearly 34 years.

Fortunately, the Covid-19 pandemic would not persist for quite such a long time, and at the start of spring 2021, children began to go back to school, and life gradually and slowly returned to more or less 'normal'.

The philosophical weatherman Phil Connors nicely put it thus: "When Chekhov saw the long winter, he saw a winter bleak and dark and bereft of hope. Yet we know that winter is just another step in the cycle of life."

With this, I suggest keeping these learnings of our 2020–21 'Groundhog Winter' alive. For whenever life grinds us down with an endless loop of 'unwelcome, monotonous, unpleasant, or tedious recurring events', let us accept, play, and care. If we take on these lessons, I am convinced we will be able to make it through our next Groundhog Days, however they may present themselves, with much more to show for the time spent.

The second Covid-19 wave, sweeping over us during the difficult winter 2020–21, peaked in mid-January 2021, and was deadlier than the first. During the four months from November until February alone, more than 76,000 people in the UK lost their lives. The NHS and its brave nurses and doctors were at breaking point. But there was a new ray of hope: On 8th December 2020, after a heroic research and development effort by multiple institutions around the world, Margaret Keenan, a 90-year-old grandmother, was the first person to get vaccinated in the UK. Soon the vaccine rollout began on a grand scale, which would help to provide high levels of protection and eventually bring Covid-19 under control.

I personally had been very busy during the winter, trying to help my clients (and myself) to cope with the economical and emotional burdens the pandemic had put on us. It was not easy. Happily, I had my own support structure in the form of regular video chats with friends, long walks with my friend Sebastian, the presence of cat Rosie, as well as conversations and new activities I embarked on together with Anne.

One such new and a little crazy activity was winter swimming. During the first lockdown in March 2020, out of boredom, I had signed up for an eight-week on-

Anne & a swan: ice-swimming in December 2020

line course with the 'iceman' Wim Hof. His self-help approach is based on breathing exercises, meditation, and most importantly exposure to the cold. He had developed it after tragically losing his wife to suicide. Trying to come to grips with his own desperation, he found remedy in the cold. The course was interesting, and by the end I felt the daily five minutes of ice-cold showers he 'prescribed' were indeed invigorating and helping me to stay more focused and in the present moment.

But it was not until October 2020 that Anne happened upon an opportunity to make this crazy cold exposure a regular hobby and 'team-building event'. Doing some research, she learnt about the Serpentine Swimming Club in Hyde Park, which offered swimming 'all year round'. Unfortunately, they had put a stop on taking on new members. Still, the old rule applied: "If you really want something, the universe conspires." Anne had put herself on the waiting list and when the window for new members briefly opened in October 2020, we jumped on it.

We had our first dip at temperatures of around fifteen degrees, which felt cold, but still manageable. Soon we would start to experience what cold really means.

As autumn moved towards winter, the days and especially nights became colder. But the 'Serpies' had told us to swim at least twice a week in order to acclimatise to the gradual descent of the water temperatures. It was tough, but each time we overcame that scary moment of getting into the water, it was as if every other sorrow and worry just disappeared. It was simply too cold to be worried about anything other than breathing and swimming and surviving.

We usually left the house around 6:30 am in pitch-black darkness. Sometimes it would rain or even snow, and this together with the wind made me shake my head each time we walked towards Hyde Park and the cold water. "How on earth can I go for a swim outdoors now?" It was insane. But strangely enough, it was something that helped a lot to keep us both sane during the pandemic. Because after coming back home and gradually getting warmed up, there was this feeling of inner 'cosiness', pride, and joy. Very difficult to explain, but simply wonderful.

I am to this day puzzled how Anne of all people could come up with the idea of doing winter swimming. She grew up in hot Singapore and owing to her accident still struggles with a nerve injury in her right leg. But I am amazed how each time we arrive at the Serpentine in what looks like a scene from the movie *Frozen,* she bravely puts on her swimming cap and walks in. I cannot stop smiling and shaking my head in disbelief and admiration at her bravery! Well done you!

With cold swimming helping us through the difficult pandemic winter, another and different angle to Shackleton's adventure began to intrigue me, based upon which I wrote the following short story.

What Are You Most Looking Forward to?

As we recall: Ernest Shackleton, together with twenty-seven brave men, left South Georgia in the southern Atlantic Ocean in December 1914 on a ship with the incredibly apt name *Endurance.* They experienced terrible weather conditions, got stuck in an icy lockdown for nine months, lost their ship, floated on ice floes for another seven months, sailed in their lifeboats through a hurricane which even sank a 500-ton steamer, and then, after all that, a large part of the crew waited another five long months for the return of the men who had gone looking for help. But finally, they were rescued.

While they endured unbelievable hardship together, I have often wondered what it was that kept them going and not giving up. According to several journey reports one of the key things – besides the strong camaraderie, daily routines, and Shackleton and Wilde's tremendous leadership – was the crew members sharing with each other what they were looking forward to when the expedition would be over.

During the long evenings they sat down and talked about what kept them going. Some were looking forward to "fantastic steaks," some to "a pint in the pub," and some longed "to stroll down High Street with their wives." Whatever it was, nearly every evening they exchanged their stories and wishes for

Wednesday Night Football (WNF) in London

the future, for a time when they would have made it back home. This is how they kept their hope alive, like a North Star shining brightly even in the darkest, coldest, most hopeless hours.

In the difficult winter of 2020–21, we were all stuck in a dark and cold place. We had to endure the ongoing lockdowns, with no clear picture as to how and when we would move back into a somewhat normal life. It was tough. But similar to Shackleton's men, I believe we all had something that we were looking forward to doing, when the world would open up at some point.

I personally was looking forward to playing seven-a-side football on Wednesday nights again. I missed the banter with the teammates, which actually starts several days ahead of the game when the line-up is being discussed on the WhatsApp chat.

I missed walking to the sports field with a good podcast in my ears, and I especially missed the hour of rigorous exercise where everything seemed to fall off my shoulders and there was nothing on my mind besides playing the game with the pure enjoyment of a kid.

I missed coming home, taking a hot shower, being totally exhausted and yet feeling so happy. I even missed the next two to three days when my whole body ached, and I wondered whether I'd be able to play again the following week. But come Monday, I usually had a smile on my face, looking forward

Anne as captain of a narrow boat

to doing it all over again. So, seven-a-side football on a cold Wednesday night was what I was looking forward to the most.

We are now past Covid-19, but there are other challenges that await. You may encounter times when things are really tough and perhaps even bleak or hopeless. In such moments I would like to invite you to ask yourself, like Shackleton's men, "What am I looking forward to, when this is over?"

Paint an image, together with the sounds, feelings, and smells in your head and heart in as much detail as possible. Just as with Shackleton's men, a compelling vision of the future, along with actual plans for what you're going to do when your challenge is over, can get you through even the toughest of times. It keeps reminding you that 'This too shall pass'. No challenge lasts forever. While it does, keep calm, carry on, and look forward to whatever it is that makes it worthwhile to keep going.

In April 2021, both case and death rates of Covid-19 started to decline, and gradually restrictions were lifted. Children went back to school, non-essential shops began to open, and to my own personal delight, Wednesday football resumed: the long and difficult winter was behind us.

The pandemic was not over yet, but the NHS vaccination campaign proved a resounding success. Anne and I had been included in some of the earlier batches, and by May 2021 we were both completely vaccinated. With summer around the corner, restrictions were eased further, and it was now even possible to book some holidays within the UK.

Like most people in London, Anne and I were desperate for some time outdoors and away from home, and so we booked a short trip to the south coast of England near the New Forest, spending time in nature, by the sea and even on a narrow boat. It felt like a wonderful reawakening of life after such a long spell of darkness.

With Covid restrictions eased, the football 2020 Euro Championship was partly played in the UK. For me this presented a wonderful opportunity to watch some games at the legendary Wembley Stadium. On the 29th of June 2021, I went to see the highly anticipated knock-out game England versus Germany with my English friend and football mate John. We knew only one of us would be really happy after the game …

It was one of the first matches where up to 40,000 fans were allowed into the stadium. I will never forget the atmosphere. Before kick-off, German and English fans sang *Sweet Caroline* together, and it was as if the result would not matter too much, but that we all enjoyed being alive and singing together after such a long time of lockdowns and restrictions. Simply wonderful!

Sadly for me, and joyfully for John, England beat Germany and advanced further in the tournament. The upside of this for me was that I then even had a chance to watch the semi-final England versus Denmark, this time together with Anne. And this game would teach us an amazing life lesson.

How to Be Resilient When Life Puts You 1-0 Down

Wembley, 7th July 2021: 60,000 mainly English fans were hoping their team could make history by reaching the final of a major tournament for the first time in 55 long years. My friend Roland had bought tickets for this game more than two and a half years ago, but due to travel restrictions he could not make it. He graciously invited me and Anne to go and watch the game, which would be an absolute treat for us.

In the 30th minute, the Danish player Mikkel Damsgaard put the ball down for a free kick 25 yards from the English goal. After a moment of preparation, he took one final look at the goal and smashed the ball into the back of the net. Denmark 1 – England 0.

We observed English hearts sink and the whole stadium fall into a silent shock. Memories of the many failed attempts during the last six decades haunted people's minds. Would this be another failure? The tension, panic, and agony became tangible.

At this point of growing despair, I could see the England manager Gareth Southgate standing on the touchline gesticulating. He was urging his players to keep calm and stay focused. In the press conference afterwards, he explained that he had discussed with his players the possibility of going one goal down. He mentioned that when bringing up the thought of trailing the game during the pre-match discussions, "several players looked on in horror." But Southgate had prepared his team, and he had a plan.

The plan was not to react to the nerves of the occasion and stay focused on executing the original game plan. And indeed, only nine minutes later, the English team was able to equalise with a nicely executed attacking play, and in extra time England took the 2-1 lead. The final whistle sent the nation into 'dreamland', as they had reached their first final in nearly six decades.

Why am I telling this story? I believe there is one key lesson from Southgate's and the team's reaction to the setback of going 1-0 down: resilience! Southgate describes resilience as "something that cannot be easily taught but must be experienced by working through challenging life situations."

He himself is something of a resilience expert: At the age of only thirteen, he was released from Southampton, because he was perceived as not good enough. Later, at Crystal Palace, he was struck off the youth team and was told by his coach, Allan Smith, that he might want to "become a travel agent" rather than pursue a career as a professional football player.

But Southgate stayed calm and focused on his dream, which was to play for England one day. His resilient attitude allowed him to reach this goal at the age of twenty-five. It then helped him again to get through the dark moment when he missed the deciding penalty kick in the 1996 Euro semi-final, and when he got sacked as Middlesbrough manager in 2009. (And after the Euro 2020s heart-breaking penalty loss to Italy, he probably needed that personal resilience more than ever!)

Working through all these low points and treating them as precious learning opportunities not only helped Southgate bounce back, but it also made him a humble and authentic leader who truly inspired the English nation, especially after the long and difficult Covid-19 months.

I believe Southgate's lessons can be applied way beyond football and Covid-19. I want to invite you to use some of his ideas as you work to become more resilient. Appreciate the opportunity for demonstrating calm and resolve when life throws you curveballs or showers you with challenges – even if they feel unbearable. Embrace them. And when you are close to throwing in the towel and giving up: stay calm and focus on your goal by asking yourself:

1. What similarly difficult life situations have I faced and mastered before (evidence begets confidence)?
2. Who of my friends, coaches, mentors can I talk to (a problem shared is a problem halved)?
3. What is the worst case / best case that can happen, and how can this help me to break the 'catastrophising cycle'?
4. What valuable life lesson am I learning here, and which skills can I build?
5. What first small step can I take today/now? Don't procrastinate!

Answering some of these questions will help you to stay focused on your goals in the face of adversity. And *that* will give you the ability – even when you're 1-0 down – to not give up, but to 'keep calm and carry on'!

Keeping calm and carrying on is what we all had to do since the pandemic brought the world to a standstill. During the summer of 2021, the world carefully opened up further, but a third wave, fuelled by the new Delta variant, emerged in July 2021. Fortunately, the rates of deaths and hospitalisations were much lower than with the first two waves, in no small measure due to the successful rollout of the vaccination programme.

By now international travel was slowly becoming an option again. Although a lot of paperwork needed to be filled in, it was the window for me to go back to Germany for the first time in nearly two years. My parents had both turned 80 in March and June that year, but there had been no chance for me to be with them due to the quarantine requirements.

But at the beginning of August, I was on my way. I still remember sitting on the train home to Saxony from Frankfurt and blasting *Fields of Gold* by Sting in my headphones. Gosh, was it nice to see my family and friends again. I absolutely enjoyed this trip and the time spent together after such a long time of restrictions. We were back to life and how wonderful that was!

But we still weren't out of the woods: towards the end of 2021, Covid-19 sent another warning when the Omicron variant arrived, causing record levels of new infections. The good news though was that the symptoms were much milder and so hospitalisations and deaths remained low. Christmas 2021 was still a bit nervy, watching daily case rates hitting several hundred thousand, but the vaccines held and so restrictions stayed at bay, to be lifted completely by the beginning of 2022 in most countries.

It felt like Covid-19 was over, and Anne and I went on several trips, to the New Forest, the Lake District, Pembrokeshire, Cornwall, and Snowdonia. One would have thought that now, more than two years after the first Covid-19 cases were detected, the world would erupt in a never-ending celebration, that finally the danger was behind us, and we could go back to our normal lives. But strangely enough it did not feel that way.

Yes, we all began to travel and enjoy our time again together with loved ones and doing the things we had missed during the past two years. But the world had been shaken to the core and was struggling to fall back into a balance. Supply chains were disrupted, the cost of living increased dramatically due to higher energy prices, and at end of February 2022 Vladimir Putin decided to invade Ukraine. This sent a shockwave of further grave implications through Europe and the whole world.

Covid-19 was behind us, but new volatility, uncertainty, complexity, and ambiguity was awaiting us. Living in our VUCA world is likely to be a challenge that is here to stay. It feels as if we are never really able to close our days, as this restless world seems to continuously drag us into its conflicts, worries, and ongoing changes. Therefore, it is essential that we are able every day to set our very own boundaries and to really differentiate between work and our personal lives. To enjoy *Feierabend* even if the work for the day is not yet finished!

What Is Done Is Finished – *Feierabend*

My favourite Buddhist monk and comedian, Ajahn Brahm, once told the story of a fellow monk, who was overseeing the building of a new hall in his monastery in southern Thailand. The work progressed very well until the beginning of June. That's when the rainy season sets in, usually lasting until October. During this time, the monks stop doing their regular work and spend more time in contemplative study and meditation. It's often referred to as 'Buddhist Lent' or 'rain retreat'.

As the daily monsoon downpours began, the abbot ordered work to cease on the construction site and sent all the workers home. Now, it so happened that during that rainy season some visitors came to the monastery and saw the unfinished building, with the abbot sitting quietly in reflection.

With no builders in sight, a visitor asked the monk when the construction of the hall would be finished. The abbot, without hesitation, answered, "The hall is finished!" The visitor was a bit confused and asked: "But I cannot see the roof. There are no windows. The floor is not properly done yet, and there are cement bags lying around everywhere. It surely is not finished." The abbot smiled back at him and gently replied, "The hall is finished. What's done is finished!" and he went away.

Beautiful. What's done is finished. In other words, what you've accomplished to date is complete. What you've done is what you've done. Is this any cause for concern? Is it a reason to be dissatisfied? Be happy in what you've done. Don't look at it as simply a stepping stone to something more and then something more, and something more beyond that. And don't obsess about what you haven't done yet. That's a recipe for unhappiness, as you'll never feel really fulfilled.

Ajahn Brahm's little story reminded me of the German concept of *Feierabend*. Literally translated, it's a combination of the words 'celebration' and 'evening'. And no, it doesn't mean 'happy hour'. Its original meaning is not a time to party, but a time to make a clean break when work ends, and to really disconnect, allowing us to have fun, to relax, rest and recharge.

It might seem surprising that Germans, who are often stereotyped as efficient and hard workers, cherish their leisure time and will stand up to protect it, but work and leisure can be seen as complementary, not conflicting. Using quality time after *Feierabend* can help us effectively decompress from the stress of the day and approach the next day of work with a fresh pair of eyes, rested hands, and a new perspective. And doesn't that make us more productive?

Encouraging employees to make a clean break and leave work behind when the day is done certainly can help improve productivity, but what happens when there are no clear boundaries between work and home, because you're working at home?

Observing my own work habits during the pandemic, it felt as if the boundaries between work and leisure time had been blurred to say the least, if not in fact completely obliterated. With no clear commute home after working hours, I caught myself sneaking into my office after *Feierabend* to check on new emails or messages from a long day of work. It doesn't help that my office is part of the living room and accessible 24/7.

Studies show that we have been working longer hours during the pandemic. In the US and UK, our average daily working hours increased from 8 and 9 respectively to 11 hours. The effects are higher levels of anxiety, stress, incidents of burnout, and depression – and very possibly lower productivity, despite the increased time spent working.

As working from home is something that will likely stay with us far beyond the pandemic together with uncertainty and volatility, I would like to encourage you to try and establish a clear break from work every day.

In the morning, set a specific time by which you will finish your work. Call this time of the day *Feierabend*. Go ahead and actually put it in your calendar. As you approach the end of your workday, outline what still needs doing tomorrow and put it on your to-do list. Then, shut down your computer, switch off from work-related communication and tell yourself loudly: "What's done is finished!"

Once you've made this clean break, do something that nurtures and recharges you to 'celebrate' your 'evening'. Enjoy this precious time off with activities that are totally yours and see if you don't just surprise yourself with how much more gets done the next day, as you approach challenges with a fresh and recharged mind.

All You Need Is Love

But the Covid period was about to end for me with something very special. Something that not only the Beatles had been singing about. It was a party which had been in the making since just before the first Coronavirus patients were identified. A party, which formally ended Covid for me and many of my friends.

On 16th November 2019 I had sent an email to family and friends inviting them to celebrate the 'half-time of my life' by the end of May in 2020. I could have also called it the '31st anniversary of my 19th birthday', or simply let them know I would be crossing the half-century mark. Many signed up, and by February 2020, the organisation of the event was done.

But sadly, we all know what happened after that. The world came to a standstill for two years due to Covid. It was impossible to even think about having a party and celebrating with friends. By the end of 2021, I started another attempt at organising the event, and with the world opening up again, it became more and more likely it could happen in June 2022.

As the big day drew closer, I was quite anxious about how it would go. I had big hopes for it, as it would be a day when many people who mean a lot to me and who have witnessed and helped me in all kinds of situations in my life would come together. I wanted to say "Thank you." Many of them knew each other, but a lot also would meet for the first time. When preparing for the party, I had an image in mind: a large group photo of happy smiling faces against a beautiful sunset.

Historic football game with friends from all over the world in June 2022

But before that was possible, there was a lot to prepare, such as organising an eleven-a-side football game, which entailed a whole lot of details including pitch booking, jerseys, referee, water... Beyond the football, there were other logistics to be handled: booking a venue, hotel accommodation, a DJ, and arranging for the dinner menu, table allocation, speech, dress code, taxi logistics, guitar songs ...

The list looked completely overwhelming at first, but I learnt a very important lesson when executing it. I learnt to lean on people! My father brokered the connection to the football club and venue. My good friend Juergen organised the taxi transfers, 'volunteering' his son Joerg as a driver. Anne supported me with all the communications. Rock-Opa Ralf helped me with the guitar songs. My sister, Heidi, prepared toys for the little ones. Martin volunteered as referee. Thomas and Marcus agreed to be captains for the football game. Linda volunteered as photographer. The other Linda organised a photo-box, and the list went on. It felt as if everyone was chipping in, and just like that, the burden on my shoulders dwindled and I started to smile, relax, and so was able to enjoy the beautiful day.

The football game ended in a dramatic, but well-fought, draw due to last-minute VAR (Video Assistant Referee) intervention, something which the highly competent referee, Martin, had strangely enough predicted before the game. The penalty shoot-out was an absolute nail-biter with Lucky Strike FC beating Happy Feet United 10-9 owing to a magnificent performance by Zafer – the black cat from the Bosporus.

178

Party animals

The party had wonderful costumes and an atmosphere of friends and family coming together, celebrating life after two years of Covid madness. My speech went well. Our guitar songs with Rock-Opa Ralf had everyone singing along and legendary DJ Dirk Duske smashed the dance floor. It was just wonderful!

I could not stop smiling. I relished reuniting after such a long time with people dancing, talking, drinking, laughing, and enjoying themselves. Even now, many months later, I still feel deeply touched. The youngest participant, little Leni, was not even one. The oldest were my mum and dad, at 81. Everyone connected with each other. Everyone was positive and happy. And then there was this image of the large group picture of happy smiling faces against a beautiful sunset. See for yourself on the next page!

Now, you may wonder why am I talking so much about this event? In hindsight, what I felt during that evening, in the time since, and what I took away from this wonderful day was LOVE – the deep caring love and feeling of being supported. That sense of not being alone, of belonging. That feeling of lightness. The sense that others have your back. The uplift in someone giving us a smile or making us laugh. The gift of simply being together in joy and supportiveness.

I not only wanted to bring a little of the spirit I felt at the party to you, but also to remind ourselves of what it is that is really important to us. I strongly believe, when all is said and done in our lives, we will look back and ask ourselves, "How much did we love?" Can we not love a little more every day? Of course we can. And that will make all the difference.

Rock stars in action

This wonderful party brought not only the Covid pandemic to a fantastic personal closure for me, but it also functions as a highlight to celebrate one decade of change – my own personal walk of change. I had embarked on the Camino de Santiago in May 2012. Ten years later, in May 2022, nearly everything in my life had changed. The various stages and steps have been described in the second part of the book.

Part three will now focus on what to do with these changes. How to put them into action. How to walk the talk and with this to make a difference for others and how to make a difference for you.

The big team picture

Part Three
Walk the Talk

It was in August 2011 when I discovered that fateful message on my then girl-friend's mobile phone. Looking back, I think it is fair to say that at the age of 41 that message triggered a proper midlife crisis in me. After yet another failed relationship, I was single once again, with a substantial mortgage to pay on a house I moved into alone, with my health not the best, and working in a job I did not like. I was grinding through life.

But then I started to follow my inner voice and with some luck as well as the support of my boss Jeffrey, I was able to begin my journey on the Camino de Santiago. After a good start, the walk step by step broke me apart, but it then also rebuilt me by teaching me that I was okay! I did not have to prove myself to meet other people's expectations. It taught me that it was time to go my own way, doing the things in my life I was truly passionate about.

Thus, that message in August 2011 had turned into an initial spark which generated great personal upheaval, but most importantly also extensive learning, growth, and change. But my life would likely not have changed for the better with the walk alone.

It was the many other little steps that I took after the Camino, like spending reflective time in the Indonesian mountains, getting fired as a part-time monk, establishing a regular meditation practice, starting my coach certification, having regular philosophical conversations with my friends, and, most importantly, going through the eye-opening process of Maria's therapy, which eventually helped me to change my life.

One decade on, I can say that nearly everything is different. I am happily married to Anne, I have moved from Singapore to London, I have stopped drinking alcohol, I play the guitar regularly with my friend Ralf, I live together with a delightful cat named Rosie, I have written a book, I have made new friends, and, most importantly perhaps, I have quit my well-paid corporate job to follow my passion as a full-time coach. This also meant being a student again, undertaking further studies towards becoming a psychotherapist.

I also have a stronger support network. My clinical supervision with Steve, my own therapy, an extended network of good friends, and of course my beautiful 'lieutenant' Anne are there for me when the going gets tough. With all these changes implemented, I believe I can say that the midlife crisis is behind me: I now feel settled, calm, and fulfilled in going my own way. There is clarity where my life is going and where I want to go.

If I tried to articulate this 'life destination', or perhaps better 'life direction' today, I would phrase it as: becoming the best coach possible, to touch and improve lives. You may ask: but what happens to all the other important parts in your life outside of coaching? My answer is that I see them as entwined with my life mission of becoming the best possible coach. As an effective, knowledgeable, and authentic coach, I believe it is important that 'I live what I preach'; in other words, that 'I walk the talk'. For me this means I do not only coach through my sessions, but I coach through the way I live my life.

When I am working with clients on their personal development and improvement, I also need to ensure that I take care of my own personal development. This includes maintaining a good mental and physical health, living in a loving and fulfilling relationship with my wife, and retaining a strong network of support around me. It also requires that I make quality time for myself, to reflect and continue to grow, so that I juggle the different priorities successfully.

This is clearly not easy and demands continuous dedicated effort and focus. But in doing so and in living my life towards becoming the best possible coach, I believe I not only 'walk the talk', but I also 'walk in my clients' shoes'. Having to manage my life with its ups and downs and its conflicting demands, I am also reminded of the challenging situations my clients go through.

Fortunately, I have 'borrowed' a little tool, which I will share with you soon, that helps me and many of my clients to stay the course during the sometimes challenging ebb and flow of our daily journey.

With Part One describing my 800 km walk on the Camino de Santiago and Part Two exploring my 'walk of change' in the decade since, Part Three of this book now shifts gear. Through the eyes of some of my coaching clients, we will look at how they have implemented lasting changes and improvements. Changes which enable them to 'walk' their 'talk', and which also show how this required me to engage with continuous learning and development.

For me, coaching and getting coached is an essential part of modern life. When I started my studies to become a psychotherapist in May 2019, Shaun Brookhouse, at the time Principal of the National College for Hypnosis and Psychotherapy, asked us new students two questions.

Firstly, he wanted to know which of us still went to church regularly. Out of the twelve participants, two hands went up. Secondly, he asked, who of us still talks regularly to our neighbours. Only three hands went up. He smiled and said, "This is the reason why you are here!"

What he meant was that in the past people had means to deal with their emotional or mental challenges by talking them through with good friends and neighbours, besides being integrated in a church or other religious community. Now this is not the case any longer, and so psychologists, psychiatrists, psychotherapists, counsellors, and coaches are needed to help fill this gap.

Some of you perhaps already have had experience working with a coach or a therapist, but for many it may also still be a bit suspect, or at any rate you may feel unsure whether and how individual coaching works and what difference it could really make. And so here in Part Three, I would also like to lift that veil of myth around coaching and therapeutic work a little.

In the words of my good friend Pfeffi (aka Detlef), I invite you to "look over my shoulder" when I work with clients through coaching programmes. My hope is that through my sharing how clients have changed their lives, you may see some parallels to your own life situation, identify one or another new idea or tool, or perhaps simply gain a changed perspective which could be valuable for you on your own personal journey.

There are of course obvious – and also some not so immediately apparent – parallels between our walk of life and an 800-km pilgrimage. And there are also parallels between walking the Camino and a coaching programme. All of these challenge us constantly: we want to reach certain goals, and to do so we have to put in effort, make decisions, adjust our route and our pace according to what we can achieve, and, most important of all, we somehow must keep going, every day.

In doing so, we may experience times when we are at risk of losing faith in our powers. Times when we struggle to get up in the morning. Times when we must deal with injury, illness, or simply exhaustion, and their implications. Times when we meet good people who help us along our journey, but also times when we walk with people whose company we would rather not have to endure.

The German football manager Jürgen Klopp once said: "Life is not a 'request concert', we must work with what we've got!" I believe this is just as valid for a tough pilgrimage on the Camino de Santiago, and it also applies to a coaching programme: we encounter adversities, walk through storms, get drenched by pouring rain. Occasionally we get lost, tired, and deflated, and at times we just feel lonely and forlorn. But we also have the good times, when we are progressing well, when we enjoy every step, when the weather is beautiful and the landscape just glorious. We celebrate our successes with magnificent people who support us, and together we create wonderful memories.

In life, in a coaching programme, and on the Camino, we are all on our own personal journey; on paths that present us with ups and downs, difficulties, daily routines, surprises, and joys. As I was putting these stories together, an interesting pattern emerged. A pattern that more or less mirrors the stages, steps, and lessons of my own walk on the Camino. And so, bearing these similarities in mind, I invite you to come on a journey through some real-life transformations.

Why Walk Through a Coaching Journey?

When I embarked on the Camino de Santiago, I had a lot of questions on my mind, together with some unresolved issues. You may remember my Wheel of Life, which looked far from round at that time. My career, my health, personal growth, fun, leisure, and recreation had all scored rather low. But the area with the most disappointing score related to my repeated failure to retain longer-term relationships. In 2012 I could feel deep down that something was not right in my life and the Wheel of Life exercise made this abundantly clear and visible in front of my eyes.

As we go through our lives, we all may have certain areas where we are challenged or where we feel we could do with some more clarity, growth, or support. I believe that a basic, essential, and necessary element to embark on a coaching journey – beside the personal desire to change, improve, and develop as an individual, be it at home or at work – is a clear reason *why* we want to change: something that we want or need to amend, resolve, or transform, and that we are willing to address consciously and constructively.

Mikhail Gorbachev's answer to the journalists, which was translated as "change before you have to," pointed to a clear reason why the East German government had to change: the status quo had become untenable. Circumstances had developed to a stage where the old approaches, behaviours, and leadership style simply did not work any longer, and if the government did not change, then change would be visited upon it by the people, with potentially disastrous consequences.

Sometimes, for us, this 'why' may not be so clear, but register as the subtle feeling that something needs addressing. That is still good enough, as it provides fuel to go through the challenging process of self-discovery and change. A 'why' – be it loud and clear and signposted by external conditions, or subliminal and sensed more than reasoned – together with an open mind, as well as the willingness to change are the key ingredients for a successful outcome.

The following story describes such a 'why' at the start – and at the heart – of a coaching engagement, and how this was translated into remarkable personal growth and transformation.

For confidentiality reasons, names and backgrounds in all case studies have been changed.

Dream of Changing Your Life? The Trick Is to Believe You Can Do it!

It was a February morning when Marie emailed me, asking whether I would consider coaching her husband Peter, a successful civil engineer, who had been thriving in his career across eight different countries over the last eighteen years. By that time, he was working with a well-known multinational company, and he was greatly appreciated both, by his team and his clients for his expertise, solution-orientated approach, and management style.

One might have thought the story of Peter's life was the very definition of success: he had money, he travelled worldwide, and he had earnt his professional respect. But during our complimentary session, Peter, a man in his forties, confessed:

"I admit, I am very good at my profession. However, what I do is not my chosen path, and I'm frustrated because I don't like what I am doing. It doesn't give me satisfaction. But I don't know how to move forward or change. My biggest fear is that I will still be doing the same thing in ten to fifteen years."

So, Peter's 'why' was strong and very clear. He wanted to change something in his work, because by just continuing the professional path he was currently on, he felt he was wasting his life.

Peter's story touched me, as I recognised in him a similar frustration and resignation as the one that drove me to change my life. Before we started our coaching programme, I asked Peter to draw a picture of his situation and bring it to our first session.

The picture he drew was gloomy and its meaning was quickly apparent. It symbolised Peter's dilemma of wanting a career change but feeling paralysed by procrastination and fear of not earning enough money, hitting a brick wall again and again, with the clock ticking all the time.

Peter described himself as "being trapped in a box at the bank of a wild and fast-flowing river. I can see the good life calling on the other side of the river, but there is no hope to get across alive."

We started working closely together, beginning to identify Peter's passions and talents. As it turned out, he had a massive drive for developing and selling sustainable products in areas where they were unavailable at that time. He yearned to work autonomously and make use of his creativity. He was fed up with the, to me painfully familiar, 'Sunday blues' he felt before each looming Monday.

It was obvious that by staying put as an engineer, Peter was squandering his life, wasting his talents, and, above all, he was losing the satisfaction, hap-

Peter's drawing of his situation at the start

piness, and immense sense of purpose that a fulfilling career can bring. Looking at the root causes for why Peter was stuck, we found answers in his past, which had established his personal belief system.

Growing up in a tough working-class area in Leeds, he had learnt from his father, an industrial steel welder, that "A job is something you have to hate." When Peter was twelve, his mother left, and he had to take care of his two younger siblings. This challenging situation ingrained in him a deep conviction that he had to take care of his siblings' wellbeing first, above his own. This, together with the fact that money had always been short, helped to explain why Peter was so afraid to take a leap of faith towards a more fulfilling career.

During one of our sessions, as we were digging deeper, Peter drew a bubble chart of his current set of beliefs (see next image on the left side). As homework I asked him to try and replace the old negative beliefs with new, more empowering ones. What he shared in our next session totally blew me away. Please have a look for yourself at the right-hand side of the next image.

In Peter's new 'belief flower', 'Leeds' became 'New Yorkshire'. The depressing slogan 'Work = No Life' was replaced with 'Love Work Life'. 'Responsibility' was replaced with 'Remember Dubai', in reference to Peter's and his wife's first successful experience abroad. Instead of putting the 'Kids First' he wrote 'Go For It Dad', which he was convinced his children would say to him about his yearning. Peter's plan was a soft transition, so 'Take care of family'

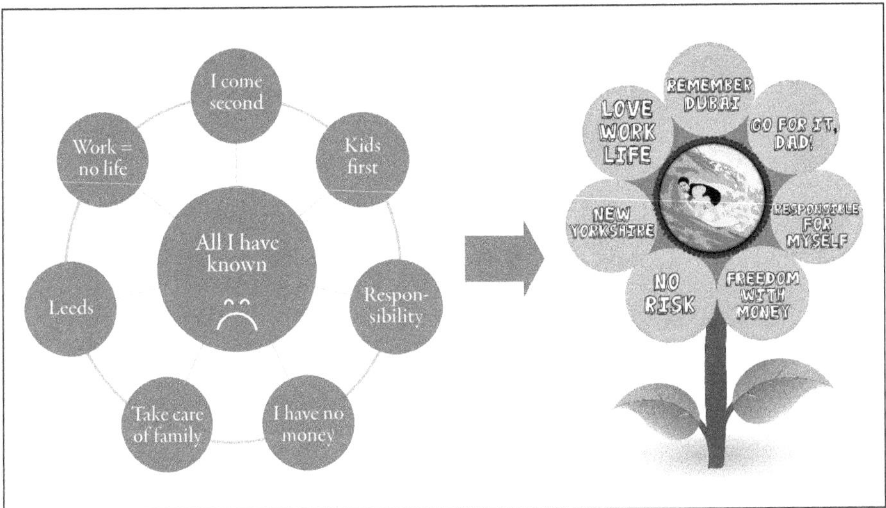

Peter's old and new belief flower!

was replaced with 'No Risk', as he decided that he would not leave his well-paid job until there was a clear and safe alternative in place.

With the petals of the belief flower now displaying new beliefs, Peter had only one thing left to draw: the heart of the flower, the essence of his change. In the middle of the flower, Peter put a surfer. This symbolised the balance and focus required to cross the river full of insecurities, worries, and uncertainties. What an inspired idea!

The rest is Peter's history: during the following year, he learnt the nuts and bolts of how to run an internet business from scratch. During the first seven months of selling self-designed sustainable products through his own website and company, he generated the same revenue as he earnt working as a civil engineer in a full year. And so even though he continues in his old job for now, there is a bright future ahead of him, and every day he is getting a little closer to the other side of the river.

None of this would have been possible if he had not taken the plunge, if he had not changed his negative beliefs into new, more empowering ones. Go for it, Peter! Keep pursuing your dreams and make your new belief flower grow further and further!

As Peter's drawing very vividly showed, he was stuck. On the one hand there was this deep lack of fulfilment in his job, even though he was very good at it, on the other hand, there was his concern about taking care of the family and being financially secure, which led to a continued internal cycle of start/stop, or as Peter had painted it, 'hitting a brick wall'.

And while it was not clear to Peter what and how he could change his situation, he knew that he simply had to change. The clock was ticking, he was not getting any younger, and he was watching his life running through his fingers.

His 'why' was absolutely clear: continuing on the current path would have been possible, but one day he would have reached the end of his life, wondering what on earth he had been doing with it, and he would have had to conclude that it had all been wasted. That was no longer an option worth pondering. Still, it required a lot of courage to take the first steps and then follow through on his personal transformation, which Peter did so beautifully and successfully.

What Do We Really Need?

Once the 'why' for change and improvement has been established, the question then is how to action it. In my own case and before even thinking about going on a pilgrimage, I participated in a mindfulness workshop, where my inner voice kept shouting at me "Go for the walk!"

Once I was given the green light to really go and walk the Camino, I had to sort out my backpack. This, you may recall, was when I learnt my first invaluable lesson. My backpack had started out weighing 26 kg, which would certainly have killed me. So, I had to cut down, throwing out anything that was not essential, which brought up the all-important question: what do I really need?

When embarking on a personal development or coaching journey, the question of what we really need is a crucial one as well, since there is always the risk of 'putting too much in the backpack'. As for a long hike, and as in real life, during a personal development journey we must take care to strip down to the essentials needed for success.

Much as every additional gramme on the Camino could contribute to further exhaustion or even injury, on a personal development programme we need to have a clear and structured focus on the things we want to change, improve, or achieve, and take those with us, leaving the rest behind for the time-being. Or, to put it differently: hunting too many targets poses the risk of us losing sight of what we are chasing and ending up not achieving what we set out to.

The story of Peggy impressively and also dramatically highlights how important it is to be clear about what we really need, and then follow that through.

From Handcuffs to a Dream Job – The Power of Setting Boundaries

It was a Thursday evening and only a few days after her second daughter was born when the police knocked on Peggy's door at her apartment in Singapore. She was informed that her abusive husband had jumped bail, that the police were searching for him, and that they had an arrest warrant for Peggy. In front of her daughters, she was put in handcuffs and taken to the police station.

Three hours later, she was released on condition of her turning up on Monday for a court hearing, where she had to either provide information on her husband's whereabouts, which she did not know, or pay SGD 20,000 bail as she was his next of kin. Peggy was devastated.

Her only way out was to ask her mother for help, despite not having a good relationship with her. To Peggy's surprise, her mother agreed to pay the 20k bail that Monday. After this incident, Peggy filed for divorce, but she now had to move back in with her mother. This was far from easy. Her mum was a tough and headstrong person: everything had to be done her way.

On the positive side, her mother pushed Peggy to further her education, and so Peggy did a bachelor's degree with an Australian university, whilst working full-time in a customer service job and raising her two children as a single mum.

Shortly after she had completed her degree, Peggy received the awful news that her mother was in the final stages of terminal lung cancer. Peggy decided to quit her job and move to a new role, now working twelve-hour night shifts in the health sector. This way she was able take care of her mother and children during the day whilst working at night. I have no idea how Peggy did it ...

Being ill, Peggy's mother was now sometimes even more difficult to deal with than before, but again she pushed Peggy to take up a master's programme and offered to pay for it. This is when I met Peggy as part of the well-regarded women mentorship programme Protégé, which is run by my good friend and former mentor coach Louise Tagliante.

After Peggy had shared her life story in our initial session, we both cried. In our second coaching session, I asked Peggy about her biggest wish and what specifically she needed the most in her situation. "I just want to have a day off with my kids," was her immediate response. Asking her what she would need to do to get a day off, there was a long silence. Peggy then hesitantly responded: "I need to ask my two brothers to step up, to care for our mother and help me free up my time."

Peggy appeared scared of having that conversation with her brothers, but soon realised it was necessary not only for her, but for her children. And so, in our session she promised to ask for support.

The next day, Peggy gathered all her strength and told her brothers that she could not keep going and needed their urgent help. To her immense relief and surprise, her brothers agreed. On the following Saturday, Peggy enjoyed a full day off together with her children, relaxing and strolling through the malls, relishing some delicious ice cream.

Peggy had started to set boundaries, and it worked. A few months later, she successfully completed her master's course and flew to Australia to receive the degree. Her mum had always told her that she would wait for Peggy to complete her studies, and only two weeks after Peggy was back in Singapore, her mum passed away. It was a difficult time for the family, but still, life had to go on.

Over the course of the previous five years, Peggy had saved every cent, and so she was able to take over the flat from her mum without taking on additional loans. This was a remarkable feat considering her circumstances, and for the first time she could offer her two daughters their very own family home.

But after years of caring for her mum, raising her children and furthering her education, Peggy began to feel burnt out, mainly from the long night-time working hours. She knew she needed to set further boundaries and find work in a daytime job.

Peggy's dream was to provide training, as she loves to share knowledge and see others grow. When an internal regional trainer position became available, Peggy applied for it and got the role. Her dream came true. She started designing and delivering regional training programmes, working directly with the global Learning & Development teams in Europe and the US.

When I asked her what the biggest lesson of her personal development journey was, Peggy modestly smiled and said: "I learnt to put my foot down and create me-time. This was and still is what I really need! Once or twice a week I get up early, walk to the beach, close my eyes, and let the wind speak to me. That brings a smile to my face because I am no longer afraid to set boundaries. In doing so, I have created my very own space to breathe and live freely."

The one thing that Peggy needed the most was to take care of herself. She needed to put herself first, for a change, so that she could have the necessary energy, time, and focus to support the people around her. To do that, she impressively developed her ability to set boundaries as a key enabler to stay more balanced and healthier, whilst still being there for others.

Like Peggy, we all have certain things that we really, really need. Some might be obvious, and some might be hidden. But to find out what it is that we truly need is essential for our personal growth and to live healthy and fulfilled lives.

If I were to ask you right now, what is the one thing that you really, *really* need in your life, what would it be? Perhaps make a quick note of it. This will help you later to create your own Life Compass, towards the end of this part of the book.

Know Your Direction and Your Destination!

In Part One of the book, we learnt how Alfred Nobel's life direction changed when he read about the 'merchant of death' having supposedly died. We also heard about the old Egyptian belief that we might be asked at the end of our hopefully long lives whether we had joy and whether we brought joy to others. And Bronnie Ware shared with us the five biggest regrets of the dying, which she discovered when working in a hospice.

These stories can give us some inspiration and encourage us to reflect where our own lives might be heading. Sometimes this can be a challenge. Life planning is no easy, straightforward, or short-term process, even though we must make decisions every day that determine the direction we are taking in our lives.

You may also remember my third evening on the Camino, when I painfully realised that it was still more than 700 km to go. But that night I also visualised sitting in the cathedral in Santiago. This powerful image enabled me to continue walking the next day: I was very clear where I was going and even a small step would lead me in the right direction. If I were to ask you about your life's destination or direction, how would you answer the question? What is your direction?

Alice's story struck me in this regard. She was at a point in her life where she knew she had to change direction but was not so clear how to do that. In working through a coaching programme, she clearly defined and implemented a new direction for her life.

From 'Having Had Enough' to 'Being Enough' – Three Tools for a Successful Mid-Career Change

I met Alice also as part of the Protégé mentorship programme. She had just quit her well-paid but unfulfilling job in the financial services sector. Before then, she had thrived in a highly successful twelve-year career across several excellent employers and high-profile leadership roles in Europe and Asia: "I was successful but bored at work, whilst failing at being a good mother and daughter at home. I had had enough!"

In our initial conversation I met an impressive, driven, outspoken, and highly intelligent executive who seemed stuck. Over the next five months, we used three simple but powerful tools which supported Alice in finding more clarity about her future direction, and helped her transition into a job that provided her with what she was looking for.

Tool 1: Harrison Career & Personal Development Assessment

We started with the Harrison assessment,[21] which is a psychometric tool that I use with most of my clients. It helps to create very valuable personality insights and awareness by completing a brief 20–30-minute online assessment.

Developed by the American mathematician and psychologist Dr Dan Harrison, the assessment is based on the 'enjoyment performance theory': things we love, we become better at quickly, so we get good feedback, and hence enjoy doing them even more. In the personal development section, the assessment offers what is called a 'paradox report', comparing two usually opposing traits. The theory behind this is that every strength has the potential to become a weakness, if it is not balanced through other traits or becomes too dominating.

Looking at Alice's Harrison Paradox report, it became clear that she seemed to have a tendency to put others first. With this she risked self-sacrificing, which can be seen in the darker circle in the lower right quadrant in the next image. Whilst this was not so prominent at work, she was surprised to realise, and confirmed, that it was certainly a feature at home and in her personal life.

When we ran the career options report of the Harrison assessment, which lists the jobs with the highest likelihood of being enjoyed by Alice, we were astounded. To our surprise, we saw many creative roles as well as counselling/psychology jobs featuring in the top ten of Alice's enjoyment potential. This was in stark contrast to the rational work in a bank that she had been doing for the last twelve years.

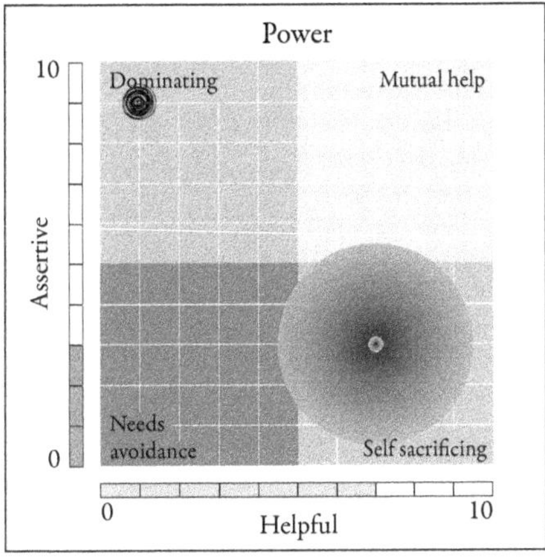

Alice's Power-Paradox of the Harrison Assessment

Careers With High Enjoyment Potential	Estimated Career Satisfaction
Packaging Design Specialist	91.7%
Marriage and Family Counsellor	91.6%
Music Director	91.5%
University Art Teacher	91.1%
Secondary School Arts Teacher	90.6%
Film/Television Director	89.6%
Graphics Design Specialist	88.5%
Fashion Designer	88.3%
University Psychology Teacher	87.2%
Educational Psychologist	86.7%

Alice's career options report

Tool 2: Morning Pages – The Artist's Way

Alice related that she had always been a very creative person who loved to draw and write when she was young. But sadly, she had long since buried those passions. With the luxury of a career break now, I introduced Alice to Morning Pages, which is part of Julia Cameron's *The Artist's Way*[22] approach and which Maria had applied so successfully with myself. The goal of Morning Pages is to reconnect us with our intuition and inner voice by handwriting three pages every morning with whatever comes to our mind.

Alice had a very strong inner voice, and it turned out that all the answers she needed to fix her professional life were found in her personal life. The Morning Pages frequently featured her parents and how they played an important part in her situation. It mattered more to Alice how they felt than how she felt herself. Alice had picked a degree that would guarantee a well-paid job and that thus enabled her to financially support her parents as well as her sister for the last twelve years.

Alice had not asked for consent from her family when she handed in her resignation because she just simply had "had enough." For closure, she now needed to know that her family was happy for her to depart from her previous roles and to spend some time without an income.

As they truly loved her, the answer was clear, and moving ahead, Alice was able to relieve herself of a massive burden by getting 'permission' to seek out a meaningful job, rather than just a job that paid well.

Tool 3: Career Wheel

After we had the personal side sorted, it was now time to define what could be the right next job for Alice. Here we employed the Career Wheel, a powerful tool that I was introduced to by my former mentor coach, Jennifer Anderson who had published it in her book *Plant Yourself Where You Will Bloom*.[23]

The Career Wheel, similar to the Wheel of Life, captures several key criteria which can be important for career development, like for example personal talents, interests, income expectations, or the working environment. It can be used both to define the perfect role, by setting out specific requirements for each of the criteria, and to compare different job opportunities by rating the fulfilment of the various criteria.

Alice did an amazing job at laying out the most important requirements for her perfect role, which enabled her to identify and valuate future job opportunities within the Career Wheel. In her own words, she realised that "people and values mattered more over environment as well as lifestyle." She loved "making complex things simple" and "helping people grow."

The challenge now was to find a job that would fit with Alice's documented requirements and newly created insights about her personal and professional life direction. When searching for available opportunities, it turned out that a former manager of Alice's was establishing an Asia-wide Learning & Development team in her company. And even though Alice did not have much experience in the HR/L&D area, her sponsor leaned forward and offered her the role, which she successfully started at the end of her sabbatical.

In her own words, Alice's transformation reads like this: "They say happiness is priceless. That is true and I will also say 'there is a high price to pay for unhappiness. The longer you wait to address it, the higher the price'. For me, unhappiness amounted to ninety percent of my monthly credit card bills. I removed luxurious holidays, fancy meals, lunchtime shopping triggered by pre-lunch meetings and all the late cab fares. My parents, my son, and husband are visibly happy that I am happy to be making the most of the time I have with my family as well as at work. For once in my life, I have moved from 'I've had enough' to 'I am enough'."

Alice's story highlights that her life's direction needed a change. Through the work with her subconscious mind in the Morning Pages, together with the Harrison assessment, as well as the Career Wheel, she realised where her life was going: she was not happy in what she was doing at work as she mainly did the role for the money and to support her parents.

By talking to her parents, she received 'permission' to earn a little less but work in a job that was more fulfilling. Once it was clear where she wanted to go, it became easier for her to identify what steps would be required to move towards that new revised direction.

Alice's story, and to some degree also the stories of Peter and Peggy, affirms that there always is another option. Similar to the legend told earlier in the book about the young woman who picked the black pebble out of the bag and with this helped her father to release his debt with a threatening loan shark, these three coaching stories describe how individuals have found their very own 'pebbles' which changed their future direction in life. They didn't take these steps alone but worked with me as part of a coaching programme. This in no way speaks against them, but rather for their understanding that support in a crisis can be very helpful until the challenging situation has been overcome.

My question to you then is this: what is the right 'pebble' for you? What is your direction? No worries if you cannot answer this question right away, as we will be covering it in more detail soon.

Who Is Walking 'Coaching Caminos'?

After that difficult third evening on the Camino in 2012, from Day Four onward, I started to settle into a better walking rhythm and was able to look around with open eyes at who else was walking with me.

Perhaps you remember Mr Lionheart, who, aged 75, fell in love again, or the magic duo of Kyrill and his dog Kira who only had a budget of €6 per day but exuded so much peacefulness and harmony? Or you may recall Marie getting to grips with the situation of her ailing father. Every pilgrim I met on the walk was carrying something in their 'backpack'. Something they wanted to resolve, look at, digest, learn about, release, or heal.

Having 'met' some of the people I encountered on my walk, you may be wondering: but who goes on a coaching journey? Who are the people who embark on such a personal development programme? The answer is very simple: it's people like those I met on the Camino, people like you and me.

Currently my youngest client is in his early twenties and my oldest client is approaching the graceful age of seventy. I work with people who lead thousands of employees and who have very comfortable incomes, but I also have clients who struggle to afford coaching and with whom I find a dedicated financial arrangement.

As a coach, I am grateful that every day I am exposed to a wide range of interesting people from different continents, cultures, educational backgrounds, industries, religions, as well as personal interests and passions. Of course, with this diversity there also comes a wide range of coaching topics we are working on. That's why, as a coach, I'm constantly updating and expanding my toolbox, always thinking about the right tools to be applied. That is often not easy, because every customer situation is very specific. I therefore would not do justice to the complexity and individuality of the various client situations if I attempted to list all the coaching topics here. But some examples of individual coaching challenges which clients try to work through may include:

- Feeling stuck or finding yourself at a personal or career crossroads
- Manage stress and create more personal energy
- Overcome self-doubts and constant worrying
- Rekindle motivation as well as passion and establish more meaning in life
- Manage conflicts and difficult conversations
- Deal with highly charged emotional situations and feeling overwhelmed
- Learn to delegate and create a high performing team
- Establish effective time management and focus
- Enhance decision-making skills
- Understand personal values and develop life goals
- Build trusting and collaborative relationships
- Enhance leadership presence and communication
- Acquire new skills and develop an alternative career path

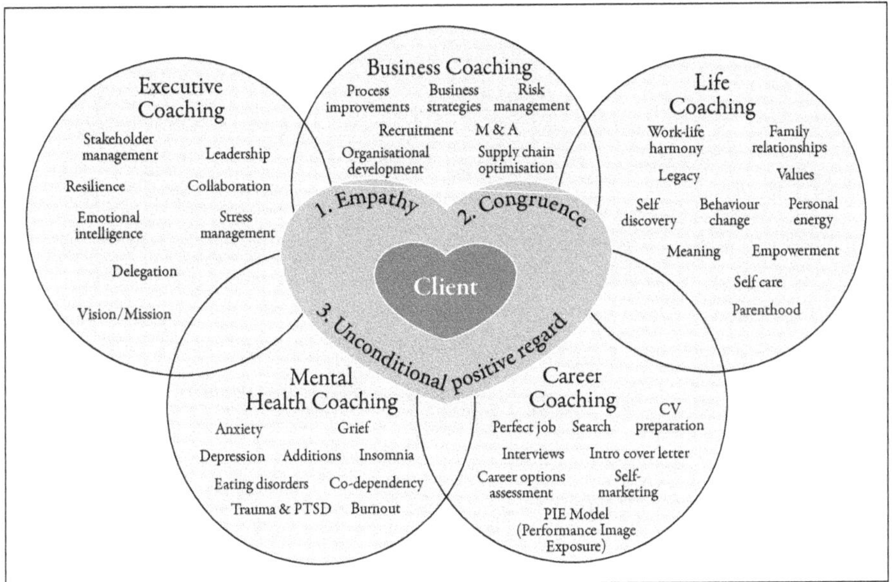

My coaching services

Even though this is only a small excerpt, these examples certainly show how varied the specific customer topics can be, which in turn underlines the uniqueness of each individual situation. Because of this, there is in the coaching industry a large variety of specialisations through which coaches help their clients across various topics and coaching fields.

But I strongly believe that whatever it is that we discuss in our coaching programmes, it usually links back to a very individual core inside. A core that, with its personal values, dreams, and expectations, has been shaped to a good part by the experiences and people in our past. In the snapshot picture above, I have summarised the five coaching services which I am offering to my clients together with examples of potential topics in each of them.

These different types of coaching do not exist disconnected from each other, because at the heart of it all is the client, and when looking at my clients, I always see them as whole human beings who have a professional as well as a private life, and these are intrinsically linked to each other throughout the person. And so, when initially we might be working mainly on executive coaching or business-related topics, we may soon discover areas in the client's personal life that influence the performance and effectiveness at work and vice versa.

Jeff Bezos, founder of Amazon, talked about 'work-life harmony' as an alternative approach to the well-known concept of 'work-life balance'. Bezos declared:

"The reality is, if I am happy at home, I have 'tremendous energy' when I go into the office. And if I am happy at work, I come home with the same energy." [24]

I believe it would be difficult to deliver sustainable and long-term peak performance at work without setting a harmonious foundation in one's personal life, and so I support my clients in a holistic fashion, putting the client relationship at the core of each coaching engagement.

In therapy, this relationship is also called 'therapeutic alliance' and numerous studies have proven that the quality of the coach-client relationship is a vital factor for clients to reach their objectives.[25] Such relationships are never static, they evolve over time in a dynamic fashion. Earlier in the book we talked about 'rupture and repair' as a core concept of building strong relationships, which is also very much valid for the coach-client relationship.

The American psychologist Carl Rogers, one of the founding fathers of the humanistic and client-centred approach in psychology, has identified three key attributes for therapists and coaches to build strong and effective client relationships:[26]

1. Empathy: Understanding the client's subjective experience and feelings in a compassionate way enables the therapist to view things from the client's perspective and encourages the client to become more reflective and understanding of themselves.

2. Congruence: Inner experience and outward expression matching makes the coach genuine, real, authentic, and trustworthy, serving as a model to encourage the client to be their true selves, without wearing a mask.

3. Unconditional positive regard: The coach genuinely cares for the client without evaluating, rejecting, or judging the client's thoughts, feelings, or behaviours and with this accepts/values the client for who they really are, without any provision.

Utilising these three ingredients is important for the coach to build a strong alliance and to set the stage for a successful development of the client, as it provides them with a safe and confidential space to explore and share even uncomfortable or sensitive information.

Looking at my own coaching work, it is fair to say that my main target group are executive clients. This stems mainly from the fact that I have been working in leadership roles for two decades myself and therefore can very much relate to these clients' challenges.

I also feel that I can make a great difference in this field of coaching, as being able to successfully support an executive, who now or in the future may be responsible for hundreds or even thousands of employees, I can touch and improve a large number of lives.

You may ask, why then is it necessary to study psychotherapy, and how does this come into the picture if my main target are business owners and executives? Up until 2018 I practised executive, life, and career coaching. For several of my clients I felt that I could have done a better job in supporting them, but I lacked the psychological knowledge about areas such as trauma, anxiety, addictive behaviours, or depression.

At the same time, I think coaches look more at the present and into the future, as opposed to diving deeply into previous experiences that might have shaped the client's current behaviours. I felt that in my ability to support clients, there was a gap which I had to close.

I therefore looked for additional qualifications in the psychotherapeutic arena, because I believe it can make me a better, more effective, and holistic executive coach. With this additional knowledge, I can work with my clients on practically any topic and access the client's past experience as a 'treasure trove' to enhance self-awareness as the foundation and prerequisite for personal development.

Taking this holistic approach, a coaching engagement usually flows across multiple pillars of the coaching services I am offering. The following story demonstrates how these pillars can work together well, so that the client can achieve the targeted improvements and transformations.

The Shiny Eyes Index

Hugo was in his late thirties and working for a medium-sized company in Austria when we connected for a 'chemistry call'. I usually do not enjoy these calls very much, as they feel like a job interview, at the end of which the client decides whether they want to work with me as coach or not.

Hugo had been referred by his line manager, whom I had coached several years ago as part of an executive coaching programme. In the Zoom call, I met a quiet, focused, and very observant man, whose eyes and questions felt almost a bit intimidating. Later on, I realised that this had more to do with my own insecurity about meeting Hugo for the first time and my trying to impress him, than with anything he did or said. I wanted to 'win' this coaching engagement, because I felt it could be a very interesting journey together, since Hugo was an operations director, a field I had spent a lot of time in myself.

Fortunately, Hugo's impression and feedback from our first conversation was positive and so our coaching programme started with a three-way meeting together with his line manager. I find this is a particularly professional way to kick off an executive coaching programme, with the line manager involved, as it helps to lay out the expectations clearly.

From our three-way meeting I could tell that Hugo and his boss had a collaborative relationship, and so there was a lot of overlap between Hugo's objectives and those of the line manager. We basically had two key goal categories to focus on:

Goal Category	Line Manager's Objectives	Hugo's Objectives
Improvement in current leadership style and skills	Develop more resilience to take things less personally and to heart	Resolve inner conflict between emotion and logic to reduce time/energy losses and create more inner harmony
	Hone leadership style by delegating more effectively and bringing people along on the journey	Enable versus execute – learn to delegate more
Strategic direction: future career	More clarity as to whether Hugo continues his career as a generalist or specialist	In the future I want to set up something which is scalable with a self-organised team, less dependent on me: "Stop cooking myself and start making the recipes and cooks better"

Along the journey we added one more goal, which I will describe below, but the above table gave us an excellent indication of what we had to do. As usual at the start of a coaching programme, I asked Hugo to complete the Harrison assessment together with a reflective questionnaire.

I like my clients to focus on their strengths and so limit their number of improvement areas, which is in line with the philosophy of Gallup's well-regarded CliftonStrengths approach.[27] The idea of Don Clifton, an American psychologist, author, and entrepreneur, is to look at "what's right with people rather than what's wrong with them."

Debriefing the Harrison assessment, we identified a lot of strengths. Hugo was a self-motivated, persistent, open, and reflective, analytical leader with strong decision-making skills, who loved to innovate whilst maintaining a very organised and optimistic approach.

As development areas we decided to focus on self-acceptance (the tendency to like oneself) and assertiveness (tendency to put forward one's personal wants and needs).

Getting started, a key goal for me is helping my clients generate self-awareness in the areas we want to improve. This includes identifying anything that might trigger them, as there are quite often underlying lessons to be learnt.

With this we used the Thoughts Feelings Behaviour (TFB) worksheet, developed by Aaron Beck[28] as part of Cognitive Behaviour Therapy (CBT). Hugo's homework was to observe any situation or interaction over the coming two weeks which might trigger him emotionally.

The task sounds simple but can be challenging as Hugo had to record on a printed worksheet any trigger situation, together with the respective thoughts, feelings, and actions. He did a meticulous job by creating a trigger journal and in our next session we debriefed some key trigger situations including:

- Impatience when Hugo wanted to get things done immediately
- Emotional defensiveness when someone questioned his or his team's performance
- Struggle to communicate bad news

The related thoughts and feelings led us to investigate Hugo's past a bit more, to understand where some of those triggers could have originated from. To do that we used the Harvard Business Review (HBR) article about *Family Ghosts in the Executive Suite.*[29]

The article talks about the fact that early in our lives, family dynamics can shape many of our 'key behaviours and attitudes toward authority, mastery as well as identity'. In simple terms this means that executives might revert to childhood behaviour patterns when certain interpersonal dynamics are at play in the workplace which may remind them of previous family dynamics.

The article is guided by the principles of family systems theory developed by Murray Bowen,[30] psychiatry professor at Georgetown University, and describes how individuals cannot be understood in isolation from one another, but rather as systems of interconnected and interdependent individuals.

Hugo completely blew me away with how thoroughly he analysed his 'ghosts from the past'. Literally writing a small personal essay, he focused especially on values, roles, and expectations which he felt had shaped him and his behaviour. His meticulous homework became a game-changer for Hugo, enabling him to understand and begin amending his behaviour in trigger situations which in turn would substantially enhance his effectiveness as a leader:

"My parents divorced when I was eight and I was then living with my mum. She was a very busy executive working long hours. Therefore, I was responsible for running the household. Every day Mum gave me yellow Post-

Its, with tasks I had to complete. In the evenings she would check what was completed. I hated and dreaded these evening 'appraisals'. Whenever some Post-Its were not completed, I needed to defend what had happened. The 'appraisals' made me anxious and emotional, as I might not have met Mum's expectations or was at risk of being scolded."

Talking through this in our session, Hugo paused and then, shaking his head, he said: "It does not feel right to have such a responsibility at that age. I would never expect this from my own kids!" That was a very important realisation and helped Hugo enormously to better understand his past as well as in becoming more tolerant with himself and others in pressure situations. He now knew where his (over)reactions came from. The awareness of his old core beliefs or 'ghosts from the past' was visibly challenging for him to digest. Other old core beliefs of his included:

- I must resolve the issues by myself.
- I have to function.
- I must meet expectations.
- My own needs don't count and so I put them second.

With this we had more clarity as to why Hugo struggled to delegate and why he sometimes took things so much to heart. Under pressure he was reverting to the behaviour of the 'evening appraisals' as an eight-year-old.

With these new insights in place, Hugo began to work on the triggers and gradually became more comfortable with them. This was possible because on the one hand he had understood what was happening, on the other hand we employed the concept of Transactional Analysis (TA), a psychoanalytic theory and therapy method wherein social interactions (or 'transactions') are being analysed. Developed by Eric Berne,[31] TA says that we tend to interact with each other from one of the following three ego states:

- Parent (critical/controlling or nurturing/structured)
- Adult (resourceful and in the here & now)
- Child (adapted/destructive or free/cooperative)

In trigger situations at work, when for example Hugo became defensive, it was obvious that there was a communication between a controlling parent ('a person questioning Hugo or his team') and an adaptive child ('Hugo at eight years old').

A key lesson of transactional analysis is that communication between adult and child can be stopped if one party moves into the ego state of an 'adult', thus creating communication channels across, as shown in the following diagram.

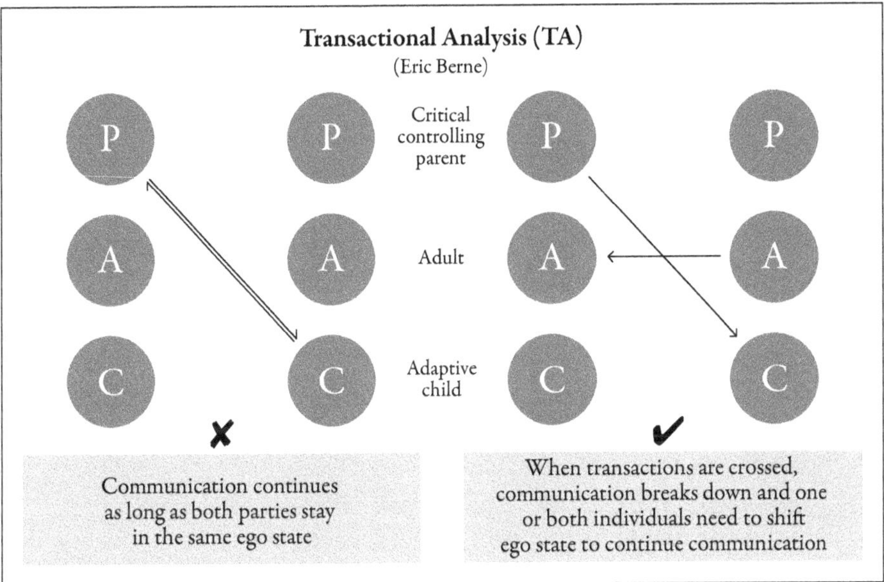

'Breaking communications' in transaction analysis

Reminding himself that he was not the powerless eight-year-old any longer in such situations, Hugo began to switch more and more into the adult ego state, staying more present, resourceful, and with the facts. With this, he could work on solutions without getting carried away emotionally by falling back into previous behaviour patterns. As a result, his triggers reduced, and he began taking criticism less personally. Interestingly, this also enabled him to identify tasks which he could delegate, as opposed to doing them himself.

Now, please understand, this was not as fast and easy as it may sound here. It was a process we worked on for several months in our sessions. It was also accompanied by setbacks when certain situations made Hugo react emotionally.

But that is normal. Every behavioural change is usually accompanied by taking steps forward and occasionally tripping up. But in such situations, it is crucial to firmly hold onto the steering wheel and to keep going in the right direction: gradually the new behaviour becomes more of a routine, and those emotional triggers reduce further and further.

Learning about and acting on his triggers at work also seemed to make Hugo a better father and husband at home. Applying the TFB worksheet, he began to understand situations when the interaction with his wife and children triggered him emotionally.

As in the office, he now refused to get carried away, stayed calmer, and communicated his wants and needs more clearly. Again, this was no easy or straightforward process, but step by step he began to resolve difficult situations at home more effectively as well.

Earlier in the book we talked about Michael Singer's teachings, which propose that our answers are inside ourselves and not outside, and you also perhaps remember Ajahn Brahm's monk showing us that thinking about pulling teeth with pliers alone does 'not hurt'.

Hugo seemed to demonstrate all these lessons very well, and he gradually became more comfortable with being uncomfortable. This made him more composed, focused, resilient, and less distracted by parallel thoughts and priorities. He began to create more inner harmony for himself, which also included self-care through regular running sessions and time out just for himself to recharge.

He delegated more to his team, took things less personally, and created free space for strategic considerations, including participating in external conferences and knowledge-sharing events. We began to talk about how he could optimise and restructure his organisation. And interestingly enough, this exploration would also give us an answer to the second category of our coaching objectives: the direction of his own future career.

Exploring whether he was more of a generalist or specialist, it was critical for Hugo to maintain a high level of passion for his work. I asked him to describe what a perfect week would look like, but in our next session he came back with an even better discovery. Over the weekend he had spoken to his wife, who had mentioned something very wise.

During their conversation his wife asked Hugo: "Do you remember when you worked in business consulting? You went to Germany and pitched your creative solution for how this car company could reduce their waste? I still recall when you went out that morning you had shiny eyes. And when you came back that evening you had shiny eyes. I felt this was a time you were at your peak. Completely passionate."

Wow! Hugo of course remembered that client, as during that time he "had woken up at night, writing down a revolutionary approach, pitched it the next day and then oversaw the successful implementation." With this we knew what we had to do to find the perfect future career development for Hugo. Whatever it was, it had to create 'shiny eyes'.

Defining it more precisely, Hugo described it as "developing revolutionary ideas and putting them into action!" Having established this, we could practically test any future career opportunity and rate how it would score on Hugo's 'shiny eyes index'.

The answer for Hugo's second category of coaching objectives was therefore to pull him out of the daily operations as much as possible and create free space for him to "think outside the box and implement ground-breaking new approaches."

Together we also developed an idea for how Hugo could do that: he needed to give more decision-making power and responsibility of the daily execution to his team. He had to create a self-organised team, which would identify the work it needed to do, manage prioritisation, and then execute independently.

With that in place, Hugo would have more free capacity to 'flow to work', create new ideas, and implement them. This would not only give him shiny eyes, but also make his boss happy, as Hugo could drive important strategic initiatives prioritising the biggest commercial benefits.

And that's why we are currently working on an organisation development programme as an additional coaching programme objective. To do that, we review the team's roles and responsibilities and help Hugo to access and transform his team step by step towards a more self-organised approach.

This not only seems to create more shiny eyes for Hugo and his boss, but also for the people working for him, as one team member recently said: "When you tell us about a new project, you put down the 'lighthouse' for us, the goal where we want to go. You motivate us and then we all pull together to get there!"

During the one year we have been working together now, Hugo has gone through a substantial personal and professional transformation. He is getting less emotionally triggered, and so his head and gut are more synchronised. He stays calmer and communicates his wants and needs clearly. This not only makes him a more effective leader who delegates well, but also an even better dad and husband at home. Thus, Hugo keeps creating shiny eyes for himself, the people around him, and of course definitely for me as his coach :-)!

Working Holistically as a Coach

Central to Hugo's story is an approach and a philosophy that recognises that while a client may be a busy and successful executive, they are first and foremost a human being who has been shaped by their past experiences and who has a personal life with all the complexities and priorities this by definition entails. Incorporating all

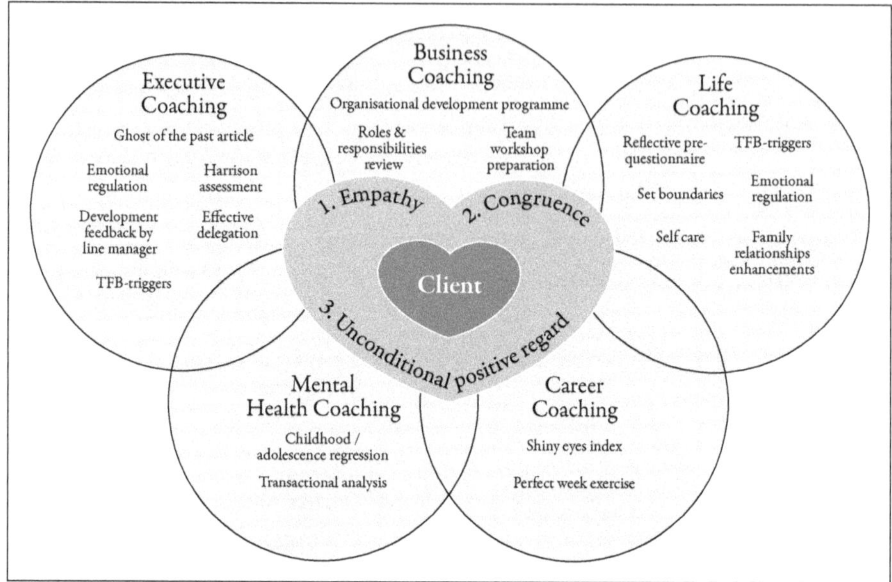

Coaching services and topics in Hugo's case study

these aspects in an executive coaching programme, working holistically and being flexible in flowing across various coaching services can therefore be instrumental to achieving positive outcomes.

Hugo's story shows that we worked well across all five coaching pillars, with the tools and areas covered as in the personalised diagram above. At the heart of our work together was a robust coaching alliance since we created a very trusting environment where Hugo was able 'think out loud'.

For me as his coach, working with Hugo honestly does not feel like work at all, it feels more like a creative and close collaboration, where we are producing a little magic in each session. All of this of course happens with Carl Rogers' three key attributes at heart from my side as the coach: empathy, congruence, and unconditional positive regard.

Hugo's is a 'good news' story. But life as a coach and therapist is not always as rosy as his case might suggest. It can get tough, as challenging as the patch I was hitting on the Camino de Santiago nearly two weeks in, when I started to fall apart.

As a Coach the Going Can Get Tough

I had worked very closely together with Gavin in an executive coaching programme for about three months. He was in his late thirties, based in the US, and worked in a global sales role he had just taken over. Our work was mainly focused on supporting him in settling into his new responsibilities. The business and Gavin were under substantial pressure, mainly because of new regional and local competitors.

Working together, I was impressed by Gavin's drive and eagerness to learn and improve. But it was not easy. There were a lot of trips, conferences, as well as conflicting priorities in Gavin's challenging business schedule, which made it difficult for him to free up time and space to concentrate on the coaching.

We had focused our efforts on helping Gavin develop a better balance between being hands-on in specific sales projects and maintaining the strategic oversight needed to be successful in the role. Beside this we also talked about his personal life, where together with his wife he was trying his best to support their daughter through a difficult period at school. This also caused some financial concerns for Gavin, which occasionally made him feel worried and low.

By the end of our coaching programme, Gavin was in a better place overall. He had established a more balanced routine at work and made some progress on the personal side. After the programme had finished, we loosely stayed in touch.

About eight months later, he suddenly sent me a text message. He was struggling to get into work. I was on a business trip myself at that time, and after a brief phone call, I felt it was best to refer him to someone professionally qualified whom he could talk to face-to-face.

Together with his wife he went to see a local psychotherapist and after a few sessions was referred to a psychiatrist at the regional hospital. There, he was prescribed medication to support him with symptoms of anxiety and depression.

Sometime later I reached out to him, and we had a brief video call. Seeing him after nearly eight months I was concerned. He had lost a lot of weight and I got the sense that he was a bit nervous and restless. But Gavin reassured me that he was okay: he was training for a marathon and looking forward to an upcoming trip up-country.

I then did not hear from him for about three weeks and so I dropped him a message to find out how he was doing. With no reply for several days, I contacted his wife and received the following message: "Dear Joerg, I am sad to inform you that Gavin has sadly taken his life!"

I cannot describe how much this message hit me. I still remember that I had to sit down in our living room in London, trying to grasp what was written on my phone's display. I felt shell-shocked, helpless, and overwhelmed. It was an early morning, so I woke up Anne and told her what had happened. I needed to speak to someone.

I then contacted Gavin's wife to share my condolences and offered my help to support her in any way possible. Understandably, she was utterly devastated and trying the best to keep her head up in such unbelievably difficult circumstances.

I also got in touch with my own coach to talk about the situation. What had happened was sad enough, but I felt that there was perhaps more that I should have done from my side. Could I have seen certain signs in Gavin? Should I have called him more frequently after our coaching had ended? Should I have contacted his wife sooner? Question upon question, together with a heavy feeling of guilt.

I hoped I had done the right thing by referring Gavin to a local therapist and felt he was in the best possible hands there, as he was then further referred to a psychiatrist and receiving medication. Still, and even though there was perhaps not much I could have done differently, to this day it startles and deeply saddens me when I think of Gavin: a friendly, good-hearted, honest, hardworking, and down-to-earth manager, father, and husband.

Many months later I spoke to his wife. She was still struggling. But thankfully, she and her daughter had found support in a strong network of friends and family. Life went on. Somehow. But the sadness and grief will probably never leave them.

Gavin's case is certainly extreme, but it shows that we as coaches and therapists are taking on a great responsibility. Our work is not just about having 'a good chat' with a client and charging money for it. And that is why our training and continued personal development is so important.

Through my studies and the supervision towards qualifying as a registered psychotherapist with the United Kingdom's Council for Psychotherapy (UKCP), I began to become more equipped to deal with difficult client cases as well as with challenging personal situations for myself.

Ultimately, my goal is not to practise as a full-time psychotherapist, but as mentioned earlier, to become the best possible coach for my coaching clients. For me this entails being able to support them with any possible psychotherapeutic challenges they might face, including, for example, insomnia, depression, or trauma.

The UKCP registration process is comprehensive to say the least. Nearly four years in, there is still quite some work to do before completion. I still have to write a thesis as well as a large-scale paper about 'my fitness to practise as a psychotherapist', complete three more essays, and eventually pass a final panel interview to establish my 'psychological maturity' to receive my UKCP registration.

Part of this process is also to collect 450 client therapy hours, which I started after receiving my intermediate certificate in hypnotherapy and psychotherapy in

November 2020. Since then, I have been allowed to work with psychotherapeutic cases, and this has come with a completely new dimension: beginning to work on client cases with psychotherapeutic challenges, as compared to my usual coaching clients, was tough. I am glad that I have the weekly support of my clinical supervision sessions with Steve.

I enjoy Steve's approach, as he is not giving me the solutions, but usually asks me what I think would be the best course of action. This forces me to think things through and identify ideas on how to move forward, gradually building confidence.

But at the beginning it was really difficult, and I would like to share an example here which brought me to the edge and made me question whether I would ever be able to become a psychotherapist.

Am I a Failure as a Therapist?

Miriam contacted me through the Hypnotherapy Directory, which is a UK portal for hypnotherapists. In her introductory email she mentioned that she was struggling with severe feelings of sadness, tremendous stress, and very low energy. She was hoping to find a way back, to begin enjoying her life again.

During our complimentary video call, I met a soft-spoken woman in her late thirties. She was a divorced mother with a fifteen-year-old son, living together with her new partner and her son in the North of England.

Miriam worked as a data analyst in a tech company, but I could tell the job was draining her. She felt underwhelmed by the scope, unsupported by her boss ("to say the least"), and she struggled with feelings of guilt, questioning herself as she had been working "in much higher profile roles in the past."

At the same time, she was wrestling to support her son who was at risk of not doing well in his upcoming General Certificate of Secondary Education (GSCE) pre-assessments. She also struggled to support her partner who had recently started a small business which took him away from home for most of the week. Miriam had a lot on her plate. This made her feel exhausted and overwhelmed.

She had tried various therapeutic and coaching approaches to find a way out of her difficult situation, and having experimented with life coaching, counselling, Eye Movement Desensitisation and Reprocessing (EMDR), a type of rapid eye movement therapy, as well as Cognitive Behaviour Therapy (CBT), she now wanted to try out hypnosis.

When she shared the various approaches she'd tried before, I felt a knot tighten in my stomach. I suddenly feared she was looking at me now for *the* solution. To this day I can feel the pressure and anxiety rising inside myself when I look back. I had to find a way, ideally via hypnosis, to 'fix' Miriam's complex situation. A massive task.

With these considerations we embarked on a hypnotherapy programme together. In her reflective questionnaire she was very detailed and talked about growing up as a "gifted" child who was excellent at mathematics but struggled very much to build friendships. Most of the time in her past she had been by herself. "I felt I was different."

Asking her about social support in her current life, it turned out she had a very close girlfriend, who had unfortunately recently moved across the Atlantic to the US. I realised that she was pretty much alone as she also did not have close bonds to her family.

Starting our work, Miriam told me that she felt very unfocused and distracted, and nearly all the time had a feeling of "multiple videos playing in front of my mind's eye." She had severe difficulties in focusing and staying on task. This also showed when, during our second video call, we were trying some basic hypnotic inductions. Miriam struggled to let go and begin to relax. Her mind was in a constant frenzy.

As homework, we agreed for her to try out a relaxation technique with a ten-minute Progressive Muscle Relaxation (PMR) recording. In our next session she came back disappointed as it had "absolutely not worked." She asked whether I had other ideas? I struggled to find solutions and felt after other professionals had not been able to help Miriam, the pressure was now on me to find that 'magic bullet'.

As the classic hypnotherapeutic approaches seemed not to work for Miriam, we tried out the psychotherapeutic technique of focusing. Developed by the philosopher and psychologist Eugene Gendlin, it can be used in any kind of therapeutic situation. It helps clients to connect with the 'felt sense', which is something we experience, but usually struggle to put it in words.[32]

Using this technique, clients may for example describe "a dark, heavy and slowly rotating cloud in the chest." Exploring the 'felt sense' further can enable clients to gain more clarity about what they feel or want, and with this create new insights and awareness about their situation. This can stimulate change and healing.

In our work, Miriam discovered through focusing that a significant shift in her overall happiness had occurred when she was seven years old. It turned out she had experienced a traumatic event. Initially she did not want to talk about it.

During one of our next sessions, she broke into tears, sharing that it was a tragic road accident, which had taken the life of her aunt, someone she was very close to. Speaking softly, Miriam described that it was a big loss for her. Aunty Claudia had been her main emotional support with whom she had spent a lot of time during her childhood, also because her own parents were rather distant. Her father was a lorry driver, away most of the week, and her mum worked in a local hospital without much time for Miriam due to her shift work. Miriam was left to her own devices, also because she was seen as "very self-sufficient and highly intelligent."

But after her aunt's sudden passing, Miriam felt very much alone and forlorn. Things turned worse when she approached puberty. She desperately wanted to belong and build friendships, but instead was ridiculed as the "nerd."

I could sense that her childhood and early adolescence had hurt Miriam a lot. At the same time, I felt under pressure to help her and 'make her better'. In our fifth session, Miriam's speech was suddenly a bit slurred. Even though we had not talked about alcohol or drugs, I felt that she was perhaps intoxicated. I was not sure how best to bring this up. On the one hand, I wanted to preserve our steadily developing therapeutic alliance. But at the same time, I felt I could not just move on, and so I gently shared my observation about her slurred speech. Miriam went silent. She shook her head and then shared that she was occasionally drinking white wine. She drank to "get through the difficult lunch time," when working from home. She usually had a few glasses and at times a whole bottle, but had to finish this routine before noon, so that her son would not notice it when he came home from school. Miriam went on to tell me that occasionally in the afternoons, after drinking alcohol, she would feel so bad and guilty that she would injure herself with a small knife on her forearm.

On one hand I was glad that Miriam trusted me to talk about her challenges. But I was, in all honesty, overwhelmed by how problematic this must be for her. I felt anxious and I worried about being able to support her and finding a solution.

I believe Miriam sensed my insecurity. She was opening up in our sessions, but I could also feel – or at least thought I could feel – that she was getting impatient. She wanted a breakthrough: she wanted to come out of her difficult situation quickly.

Talking about the case in supervision was helpful for me. I received a lot of good insights from Steve. He focused on the positives: Miriam seemed to trust me. Sharing a personal situation which neither her son nor her partner knew about must have been a big step for her.

At the same time, she was a very smart person. She tried to understand and change her situation through a cognitive approach. In Steve's words, this caused the risk of me "to collude with Miriam." He meant that I was trying together with Miriam to find that silver bullet, which could make all her problems quickly go away.

Steve was right, I had spent hours and hours trying to research how best I could help her, based on the symptoms she described. But the more I was reading, the less confident I felt as to whether I was able to make a difference. Steve then told me the following story:

The Wind and the Sun were talking one day as they observed a man sitting on a bench. It was rather cold, so the man was dressed in a scarf and a coat. Out of the blue, the Wind suggested a little challenge to the Sun. The Wind said, "I'll bet I can blow that man's coat off."

The Sun scoffed. "I'll take that bet and I'll raise it. You can't do it ... but I can," said the Sun. "You?" answered the Wind. "What power do you have? No way." And so, the contest was on.

The Wind began to blow in chilly gusts from the north. The man tugged his coat tighter around his neck. So, the Wind kicked up the intensity of his speed a few notches. As the Wind blew stronger and stronger, the man struggled to sit upright on the bench. The more powerfully the Wind blew, the tighter the man wrapped his scarf and coat around himself. Now, the Wind was blowing at full force, and it was freezing cold. The man, gripping the bench with both hands, pulled up his knees and huddled in a kind of ball in a desperate attempt to keep from freezing. No way to take of his coat! The Wind had failed.

Now it was the Sun's turn. The Sun began to smile. With a kind and friendly look, it simply glowed without exerting even the tiniest fraction of the effort the Wind had put in. In the warm sunrays, the man started to feel comfortable. He straightened up on the bench, stretching his legs and loosening his scarf. As the Sun continued to casually beam its rays, the man began to feel quite warm. Then, he started to sweat. He mumbled to himself, "Crazy weather. Never seen anything like it. But I'd better take my coat off before I roast." The Sun had won.

I asked Steve why he'd told me this story. Steve, being Steve, played the question back to me. "Well," I said, "perhaps I am trying too hard to impress

Miriam and find the magic solution for her problems. Maybe I should just be with her, like the sun, and let her decide herself how to work through the discomfort she was experiencing."

Steve smiled. "Yes, support Miriam with warm rays and stop trying with brute force to find that magic bullet to fix her problem!" The best I could do for Miriam was to be there. Sit with her. Be the sun. Support her with warm rays. Yes, it sounded logical. But man, it was hard.

The more Miriam shared with me about her helplessness and hopelessness, the more I struggled to hold my own in our sessions, still sensing a constant inner need to help. It was tough and I could feel nervousness setting in every time during the build-up to our next session.

Looking back, I believe there was a point when Miriam came to the conclusion that I could not help her. Yes, she had trusted me, but I had 'failed' her as a therapist. I was not able to provide her with the tools to come out of her situation.

In our tenth session she told me that she had quit her job and would soon begin to hand over her responsibilities. After that she planned to take a break and then focus on a new job search. This was the point she stopped coming to our sessions.

I struggled, because very similar to my most difficult day on the Camino on the 18th of May 2012, I felt I had failed. My basic instinct was to call up Miriam and offer my help and new ideas.

Fortunately, Steve was there to help me keep my head above water. In his typical style he asked me what it would do if I now reached out to Miriam. I realised that it could perhaps even have negative consequences, as she might feel obliged to come back to our therapy sessions, even though deep down she did not feel I could really help her.

It was tough, but I stayed put. The weeks ticked by. Talking it through in supervision, Steve invited me to watch a short two-minute video about empathy by Brené Brown, an American professor and author, well known for her research on vulnerability, shame, and leadership. The video, which we had watched already during our studies, really opened my eyes. I've probably watched it once a week since. Please check it out for yourself.[33] Brené Brown talks about four key qualities of empathy:

- Being able to take the perspective of an individual in a difficult situation
- Staying out of judgement
- Recognising the emotions in the other person
- Communicating to them the emotional impact you've seen and heard

"Empathy is feeling with people," she says. It requires that "we connect with something inside ourselves, which knows that feeling." And this is what makes it so difficult! It can be hard, connecting with a painful and perhaps dark place inside us. And so, we're habitually tempted to 'make things better' or dish out advice. Sitting with our own pain, as we relate to the difficult situation of the other person, can cause us agony and discomfort.

But if someone shares something really difficult and challenging with us, the person is probably not looking for proposals on how to immediately resolve the situation. They are looking for an empathic response, so they don't feel alone. Brown suggests when someone is in a difficult spot, a more appropriate response could be, "I honestly don't know what to say now. But I am so glad you told me!" She believes that rarely can a response make something better. "But what makes something better is connection!"

With the wisdom of hindsight, I believe this is what could have helped Miriam, and I now realise that I was not yet ready then to support a client with the complexity of her situation. The problem was not that I had to learn many more and new techniques. No, I strongly felt that the gap was inside myself. I had to learn to connect with these dark and difficult feelings inside myself to really be able to *be* with clients and build that connection of empathy, whatever the situation might be. I needed to learn to 'be the Sun', instead of blowing like the Wind.

During those weeks, it was helpful to remind myself of the story of Joe Simpson, the young mountaineer who broke his leg in a hopeless situation and then found a way back by "thinking straight and making decisions." I had to think straight and make decisions to move forward. I also had to see the situation as a challenge, not a threat, because as we have seen earlier in the book, not doing so could even have a negative impact on my health. I had to move on and find a way to support clients with more complex situations than my coaching clients.

Sometimes, when the student is ready, the teacher arrives. In my case it was two teachers who showed up, nearly at the same time.

The Power of How We Store Our Emotions

The first teacher came in the form of a Continued Professional Development (CPD) course about trauma and Post Traumatic Stress Disorder (PTSD) as part of my studies. The course was taught by Geoff Ibbotson, who had worked for twenty-two years as a GP and fourteen years as a therapist in a Clinical Psychology Department. He was also an expert witness in PTSD for more than twenty years.[34]

Up until then, I had learnt new knowledge, tools, and therapeutic approaches in my studies, but as was clear from Miriam's case, I did not have the conviction and confidence to work with hypno-psychotherapy clients who were dealing with complex challenges like hers. Attending the course changed this.

It not only gave me the knowledge I needed to help clients create lasting changes in the way they feel and manage their emotions, but it also gave me new insights into why so many of us, including myself, at times struggle with overwhelming worries, fears, and doubts. A key lesson from the course was that this may have to do with how we process stressful past events, as we create explicit and implicit memories.

Explicit memories are detailed, fact-based, verbally describable events, which we can choose to recall or not. Such memories have, as I would put it, a 'content, time, and location stamp' and are properly filed away in the 'this is what happened there and then' part of our memory.

Implicit memories, on the other hand, represent sensations and emotions generated by stressful events, which aren't stored in our brains. They are stored in our bodies, so we can respond faster the next time we are exposed to the same or similar – potentially dangerous – situations.

In contrast to explicit memories, implicit memories are not properly filed away and cannot, therefore, be recalled at will. They get triggered by associated stimuli such as sounds, smells, flashback thoughts, or certain words. As they have no 'timestamp', we experience them in our body as 'real' in the 'here and now', and we quite literally start 'sweating' with no conscious thought involved: in an instant, our feelings can become disturbing to the point of being completely overwhelming. This is how soldiers with PTSD may react in utter panic when a door slams, as to them it may sound like an explosion.

When we are in that state of being, we can't think rationally. We are slaves to our emotional responses, and those are usually either panic responses or avoidance behaviours. There is no freedom in that emotional prison and no chance to expand our level of accomplishment and confidence in our abilities. Gosh!

But here's the good news. The tools I learnt in the workshop can help clients to consciously process these emotions and start to file them away more effectively. Fortunately, many of us do not have to deal with the emotional fallout from seriously traumatic experiences like those on a battlefield or resulting from terrible accidents. But we still must occasionally reckon with overwhelming worries, anxieties, and fears, especially at times of great uncertainty and change.

The new approaches I learnt are based on a technique which is called personalised imagery and I will soon share a captivating example of how they can be put in action. In the workshop we also practised with each other, and I could feel right away through my own experience how powerful they were. They touched me and changed me in a way that I cannot really explain.

I noticed after the workshop that I began to feel calmer and more composed in sessions when clients shared uncomfortable or distressing information. I began to feel more capable and equipped, and so started to be more comfortable with being uncomfortable. With this I 'sat more with the clients'. This sounds straightforward, if not indeed obvious, but the reality is that before the workshop I was mostly on the lookout for what I could do next. With what technique, clever solution, or idea could I 'step in' and help the client?

Now, I felt calmer. There was no need to perform, no need to fix. I could be like the Sun. And as the Sun, I was more prepared to connect with the darker parts inside myself when clients were sharing difficult situations. Through this, I became more empathetic and hence started to make a deeper connection with my clients. I had processed some of my own challenging past experiences through the workshop and with this was ready to work with others more from my heart and gut rather than my brain. And then the second teacher, Steve, would impart another important lesson on top of the fundamental shift inside myself through the trauma and PTSD course.

Do We Carry Somebody Else's Burden?

Right after Miriam's case, I worked with other clients whose circumstances deeply touched me. One case I struggled with particularly, because it involved childhood abuse. Again, I was very much sucked in and became entangled. Day and night, I was thinking about ways how I could help my client deal with her complex issues.

As time went on, I noticed I was beginning to go beyond the scope of my role as a therapist. I researched various options around how the situation could be resolved and even drafted some communication for my client. At one point, I found myself waking up at night, trying to work things out for her. That was when I realised, I needed to discuss the case in more detail with Steve, and I'm glad I did, as it taught me a very profound lesson.

Sharing the case, I was hoping for some good advice on how to alleviate or resolve it. But considering my extensive experience of working with Steve, I should have known better. Instead of giving me a ready made solution, he started asking me specific questions which forced me to think about the challenge from a different perspective.

220

As a result, I had a not-so-surprising insight: "Perhaps, again, I was going too far in trying to help this client!" I was beginning to "do the actual work for the client" instead of "supporting her to develop and own a way forward." It sounds strange but saying this out loud made things suddenly clear.

Talking further with Steve, I was reminded of a deep paradox for coaches, therapists, and other service providers who work in helping and caring professions. On the one hand, our job is to help our clients feel better, supporting them in achieving the things they want to achieve. On the other hand, we cannot do the work for them. This would be a recipe for burnout for us and disempowerment for the client. But at the same time, we depend on successful outcomes for our clients to pay our bills. So, the temptation is always there to do at least some of the work for the client.

My favourite monk, Ajahn Brahm, described this situation in the compelling story of a young medical doctor who came to see him, deeply in distress and about to quit his profession. The young doctor had cared for a patient over several months, trying to save his life. But it was not meant to be, and the young doctor felt hopeless.

Ajahn Brahm told him something very profound: "My young friend, you are a wonderful doctor, and you will help a lot of other patients. Please keep in mind: your job is not to cure. Your job is to care. If you do that well, that is good enough. You cannot expect to cure everyone." [35]

My supervision session with Steve ended with a bang when he asked me casually whether I knew the film *Life of Brian*. At the end of this darkly satirical comedy, there is a scene where people are carrying crosses towards their crucifixions, when a spectator offers one of the cross-carriers a little relief. With a smile, the cross-carrier agrees and immediately disappears. Suddenly, the helpful spectator is carrying somebody else's cross towards his own execution, as trying to explain to the guards what had happened obviously falls on deaf ears.

While this is classic Monty Python humour, it brought the lesson home to me. I was beginning to carry the burden for my client. And she wasn't the only one. I did it for several others too.

Not only as coaches and therapists, but sometimes also as friends we are tempted to be nice and help others as much as we can. We spend a lot of time supporting, pleasing and caring for others, be it at home or at work. This can easily get to a point where it's too much, a point where we carry too many other people's crosses, which puts us at risk of collapsing ourselves.

Sometimes, we need to restrain our natural urge to help, and set some boundaries. In doing so, we may feel guilty at times or selfish about 'abandoning' others, but it's important to *care,* not to try to cure.

In this supervision session, which happened soon after the trauma workshop, I realised what Nivida Chandra, a psychologist and research scholar, put very well in the following quote: "Health is the ability to let others take responsibility for themselves. It is the ability to say no when your own energy reserves feel empty." [36]

With the new insights from the trauma workshop, Steve's teachings on not carrying other people's crosses and 'being more like the Sun', I began to approach my therapy and coaching sessions differently.

I started to 'be more' with the clients in their situations. I did less problem-solving inside my own head. I began to feel more with the client. At times this can be challenging, but it is part of the process to connect with the client and hence also with the occasional dark place inside myself.

Yes, sometimes I still fall back into problem-solving and need to remind myself to allow the client to do the work, rather than me putting ideas forward. Some client cases also trigger my 'own process' which means that they can point to areas which I personally need to resolve, further develop, or in which I need to grow. This, I am sure, will be a continuing learning journey.

But with the strong support I receive through my clinical supervision sessions, as well as my own therapeutic path, I feel more equipped, confident, and ready to work with hypnotherapeutic clients. Clients such as Jackie, with whom I started to work after the trauma workshop and Steve's pivotal teachings.

Stepping Out of Abusive Relationships

I got the email from an associated psychotherapy clinic in West London, which occasionally refers clients to me. The email included a request from a potential client, who was "looking to get back into therapy, exploring perhaps a different approach."

A few days later I was in a complimentary video call with Jackie. I met a friendly, open, and well-spoken office manager of a medium sized marketing company. She seemed very resourceful, having singlehandedly supported the CEO and his leadership team with organising conferences, handling correspondence, designing marketing campaigns, and managing recruitment drives.

Prior to her current employer, Jackie had worked for seven years in a smaller agency. Her boss there was on the one hand a brilliant marketeer, but on the other hand an impulsive, aggressive, and at times even abusive bully. When she spoke about this assignment, her voice softened, and her gaze lowered. She still seemed to struggle with it.

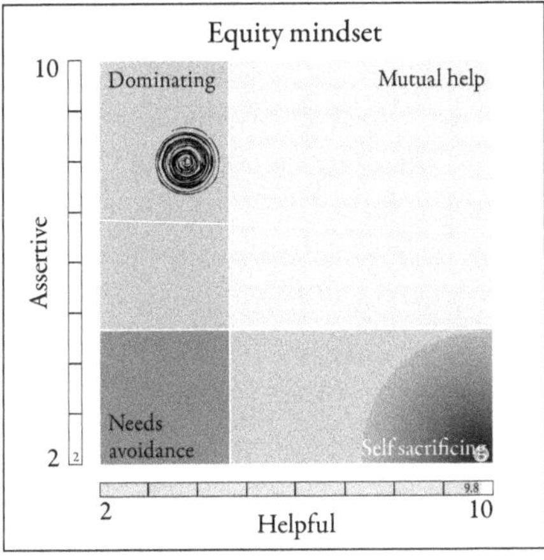

Jackie's Harrison Paradox report

Asking her what would be helpful to achieve in therapy, she shared that she wanted to stop being a people-pleaser, become more focused, and decide what she wanted to do next in her career. After a long pause she added: "I want to have my own voice and heal my trauma."

I listened. Like the Sun, sensing the pain in Jackie's words. I sat with the discomfort inside myself together with Jackie and her need. By the end of the call she said, "Let's work together!"

In her reflective pre-questionnaire Jackie shared more details about the abusive seven-year-long working relationship. She also talked about an abusive boyfriend with a "short fuse, who was verbally and physically aggressive as well as dishonest" to her.

There seemed to be a pattern, which we needed to understand better. The questionnaire also asks for five accomplishments which Jackie answered with: "This is a hard question. I know it sounds silly but I'm really not sure. Perhaps in the top five is actually speaking to you."

I had once read the saying: "The heaviest weight at the gym is the front door."[37] As with regular exercise, which requires us to overcome the inner hurdle and get going, it is that very first step which can be the most difficult for people struggling with emotional challenges. The step to ask for help. I admire Jackie for taking that courageous step.

In our first session we debriefed the Harrison assessment. It showed a lot of strengths, which I believe had made her so effective and successful in her job. She was very open and reflective, with strong analytical skills, as well as a warm, empathic, and diplomatic communicator. She enjoyed innovating, was very helpful to others, and had an excellent balance between being organised and flexible.

The one key improvement area that stood out was assertiveness, defined in the Harrison assessment as the ability to communicate our own wants and needs. Jackie's score was close to zero, which could likely be related to the abusive relationships she'd experienced at work and in her personal life.

In the Harrison Paradox graph, assertiveness is linked to helpfulness, one of Jackie's key strengths. But given the low score in assertiveness, Jackie's normal behaviour range tended to reside in the self-sacrificing quadrant (the darker circle on the lower right side in the previous image).

You might wonder what the red 'typhoon' in the upper-left quadrant is about. This represents the so-called 'shadow behaviour' into which Jackie could flip under great stress or pressure. According to Carl Jung, the Swiss psychiatrist and psychoanalyst, our inner psychological shadows are usually stored in the unconscious mind and can be composed of repressed ideas, instincts, desires, as well as shortcomings.[38]

My therapist Maria used to teach me the HALT formula, which suggests we are especially prone to flip into our shadow behaviours when we are Hungry, Angry, Lonely and/or Tired.

As Jackie and I got to work, a very sad episode in her life emerged. When she was sixteen, her mum was diagnosed with a rare form of cancer, and after an initial recovery she passed away, when Jackie was eighteen. Her mother had been a key source of strength for Jackie, and I could sense that losing her at the time was still hard for Jackie today.

On the professional side, Jackie shared details about her current workload that led to draining fourteen-hour days. She seemed to have no personal life, as there was also work to be done on weekends. Jackie was contemplating a career change and switching into marketing, given her passion and talent for creative storytelling. But at the same time, she was very scared of such a change. We had work ahead of us.

As had been mentioned in the initial referral email, Jackie wanted to try out a different type of therapy, specifically hypnosis as she had read a lot of positive things about it. Many people who hear the word 'hypnosis' may immediately have a stage hypnotist in mind, doing all kind of nonsense with his subjects for entertainment. This is absolutely not what therapeutic hypnosis is about. It is also not about the therapist putting the client to sleep.

So, what is hypnosis? Hypnosis in the therapeutic realm can be seen as an "altered state of consciousness, in which a person's attention is detached from his or her immediate environment and is absorbed by inner experiences such as feelings, cognition and imagery."[39]

It is important to note that clients under hypnosis are not asleep. They are, rather, in a calm state, which helps them to connect with their subconsciousness. As we have seen in the story about the supercomputer earlier in the book, the subconscious mind has huge power. Accessing that subconscious part of our brain can therefore be extremely powerful, to which end hypnosis can be a very effective tool. In this regard it is also important to note that clients under hypnosis in most cases still communicate with the therapist.

When working with Jackie, we tried out a hypnotherapeutic approach, which resembles a walk in nature. After some deep and calming breaths, the client is asked to close their eyes and, in their imagination, enter a natural scene, such as for example a forest or some other peaceful, natural scene. This is usually done by helping the client with phrases like:

"Now that you are calm and relaxed, I want to invite you to a peaceful natural scene. It could be a quiet scene that you are familiar with or a beautiful natural scene in your imagination. With your eyes closed, observe all the wonderful different colours and shadows. What are the various smells that you may notice? What are the interesting sounds that you can hear? Take your time and immerse yourself fully into your own safe natural space. Perhaps now you can see a stream of water or another connection to water with a small bridge over it."

I usually ask the client to give me a gentle nod once they have settled well into the calming natural scene and found the bridge. In most cases this works well and so I invite the client to find leaves on the ground and gradually begin dropping them from the bridge into the stream of water, each leaf representing something the client wants to let go.

To support the experience, I may say things like: "And as you gently drop these leaves into the water you can see them landing on the surface and being tenderly carried away. With each leaf, you let go a little more of the things you want to let go. Yes, with each leaf the weight on your shoulders gets a little less. And you let go more and more."

I allow the client as much time as they need and ask them to give me a nod when they are ready to move on. From there the guided visualised walk leads the client to a peaceful and quiet place in the natural scene, where they can find valuable personal resources to help with their situation and ask questions they might want to ask. This phase concludes the hypnotherapy session, with the client strengthening their confidence and resourcefulness.

It is magnificent what this little exercise can do. For Jackie it brought up resilience as an additional resource, together with a great release of sadness into the stream, making her "feel lighter and taking a step in the right direction."

In our next session Jackie shared about conflict situations where she interacts with dominant men like her previous boss or boyfriend. She seemed frightened to talk about these situations and was quite fearful of those men. All the pain and the emotional scars had made her sceptical of human nature, a position which she described as "a lonely place."

The seven years working with her previous boss seemed to have been especially traumatic. And so, in one of our sessions we worked through the trauma-release hypnosis, which I had learnt in the trauma and PTSD workshop.

After a brief induction, the client is guided to zoom out of their situation and then, on a timeline, to float backwards, until they hover safely and in a secure distance above a potential past traumatic event. It is important that the client does not go back into the actual traumatic situation, but floats in the safe space above it.

From that safe and secure position, the client can observe what has happened in a dissociated manner and thus gain important observations and lessons. It is also possible for the client to bring out the younger version of themselves into the safe space above.

I know this must sound like science fiction to you, but in a close therapeutic alliance this hypnotherapeutic exercise – and here especially the interaction with the younger self – can be a profoundly healing and cathartic process. Sometimes a hug can bring tremendous relief. The client also has a choice to bring up any other persons who were involved in the situation. They may request an apology or even do some 'payback' with that person to begin resolving the event.

I have witnessed this exercise provide a lot of help, support, and healing, especially where the process of taking traumatic 'implicit memories' through a cognitive process proves challenging. But this work is never easy or straightforward and should only be applied by qualified and trained therapists. It also involves various continuing exercises, combined with supportive conversations in the safe space of the therapeutic alliance. Through these, step by step the client can begin working through and releasing traumatic experiences.

After our first trauma release session, I asked Jackie what she had advised the younger version of herself in the difficult situation: "Get the fuck out!" she said right away and truly meant it, with anger and a fierce energy in her voice.

The question now was: how could we translate this cathartic hypnotic emotional experience into an actionable way forward? Jackie surprised me with how she approached this in one of our next sessions, when she suggested for us to "take a step back, break it down, and put a plan together!"

As a 'plan', Jackie was referring to sources of strength which had supported her over the years when things were really dark. What she came up with almost reminded me of my own How To Love Myself (HTLM) programme. Her key action items to stay more in control included:

- Move my body daily through yoga & running
- Make a to-do list for the week
- Eat nourishing and good food at fixed times
- Phone my grandmother
- Talk to friends
- Be proactive & reach out
- Be honest with myself

After we had worked together for several sessions, Jackie began to feel "somehow, weirdly a bit more in control." Yes, she was still struggling with the fact that her current job was something she did not enjoy. And yes, she was still working far too many hours, but somehow things started to shift and become a bit more manageable.

But then things changed again, and her development got accelerated overnight: her company had suddenly lost a large client and within only a few weeks, a substantial downsizing was underway. Jackie 'survived' the first round, but two months later was told she also had to go. This, on the one hand, presented a very difficult predicament. On the other, though, it was also an opening, just as we have learnt earlier in the book: every crisis can be an opportunity.

When Jackie lost her job, we had worked together for nearly five months, and the truth is I felt that we had begun to stall a bit even though there was so much change on the horizon. I talked the situation through with Steve, and his idea was to ask Jackie how she saw things going. What would she need in this specific period and what should we do more or less of?

To ask for feedback was a bit daunting, but I am glad I did, because it can also be a great enabler and avoid clients 'going cold' or dropping out of therapy altogether before the time to do so is right. Jackie told me that our "journey felt nice and organic so far" and that our conversations "brought up helpful ideas and were an opportunity to talk about her fears," making her "feel less scared."

We now began to work on her job search, whilst furthering the trauma release and healing. As a next step we tried out what Steve calls the 'snow globe technique'. With their eyes closed, the client is invited to bring into their mind's eye a person with whom they have had a difficult experience. As a first step, The Bully gets a bright red clown's nose stuck on their face and is provided with an imaginary derogative name by the client.

Then, with a move of the right hand The Bully is pushed back two metres. Now the client has complete power and begins shrinking the bully down in size. Moving hands and fingers, the client gradually reduces The Bully until they are tiny. At the same time, and because of this, the voice of The Bully becomes high-pitched, almost like that of a manic chipmunk.

The client can then make The Bully bow or apologise, and in the end The Bully is being put into a snow globe, which is being shaken at the client's discretion. It may sound like a fun exercise or even silly, but although it all happens 'only' in the client's imagination, the effect can be stark and empowering.

For Jackie, it worked to a certain extent. Most importantly she enjoyed putting The Bully – the manager in her previous company – into the snow globe and shaking him ferociously. Jackie still smiled in our next session and had also joked about it with a former colleague who had suffered the same bully as well.

Continuing our sessions, Jackie brought up a situation where her previous boss had discredited her loudly and very aggressively in front of the whole team as being "stupid and not capable." This scar clearly ran deep and thinking of it could make Jackie switch in an instant from being okay and confident to finding herself in a very dark place, where she felt incapable and stupid.

We worked on what could be done when such dark thoughts came up, and over the course of two sessions, Jackie developed a remarkable mantra for herself. I believe that what she came up with could work for all of us when difficult thoughts are in danger of taking control of our inner dramas. Speaking directly to the feeling of fear and anxiety Jackie shouted:

"Dear fear: I thank you for trying to make me better.

Please allow me space to breathe & shine!

Now let's focus on what is in my control here!"

With the mantra in place, Jackie managed surprisingly well through the difficult couple of months of unemployment. And then things got better. She found a new role, as a creative specialist in a smaller advertising agency. There she learns the advertising craft, leveraging her creative talent for storytelling by developing digital video messages for clients. The start has been promising, though not easy, as the working hours are long and demanding.

Her new boss, who is female, supports Jackie in a caring and nourishing way; no more shouting or scolding in front of others. During one of our recent sessions Jackie found herself in deep thought for a while and then said: "You know what is different? I am allowed to be a person here."

This may sound simple, but it is a huge step on her journey towards releasing the difficult experiences of her past and beginning to set boundaries towards her own wants and needs.

On the personal front Jackie has strengthened her relationship with her boyfriend Damian, whom she describes as "strangely supportive throughout." Yes, a supportive boyfriend rather than a bully: Jackie is rewiring herself and with this also creates a more supportive environment around herself.

To be clear, Jackie is not skipping down the road every day. There are times of self-doubt and feelings of fear and being incapable. We continue our work, but it is worth noting that Jackie has made significant progress and continues on the path towards more self-love, greater self-respect, and setting personal boundaries. In her own words, she describes her new message to the world as: "I found myself after feeling lost for such a long time! Let's keep moving forward!"

Having worked with Jackie through regular sessions for nearly a year now and continuing our journey together, I feel that something has shifted inside myself which enables me to better support clients with difficult and complex psychotherapeutic challenges. It clearly is not an easy process but learning to be more 'like the Sun', and truly connecting and being with the client have made an extraordinary difference for me and also, I believe, my clients.

It sounds very strange that by doing less I can help my clients more. By getting out of the way rather than getting into problem-solving mode, the client feels more supported and better understood, and as a result opens up to look for ways to improve their situation and move on. Reflecting on this with Steve I felt immediately reminded of a very specific experience during my walk on the Camino.

The Journey Is the Destination – Also in Coaching

On 18th May 2012 I experienced my most difficult day on the Camino. After walking for two weeks, I felt physically and mentally exhausted. And then I broke down. Whilst it was tough, this difficult day eventually also triggered a huge liberation for me. Suddenly the need to 'perform' and 'rush to finish the Camino on time', was replaced by the notion that it was actually a huge achievement for me to be on the walk in the first place. With this weight off my shoulder, the second half of the Camino felt a lot easier and more joyful.

I would not say that I can directly compare or connect the experience on the Camino to the learning curve I am going through as a therapist and coach. But I really think that the story of the Wind and the Sun, together with the lessons of the trauma workshop, as well as the reminder to not carry other people's crosses, was in a sense a step very similar in my development as a coach and therapist to that fateful day in Sahagún where I broke down but also started to rebuild myself stronger.

This does not mean that all client sessions are now a stroll in the park, not at all, but I feel more equipped to be with the client, whatever it is and however difficult it is. Which is why I was able to work with a client like Jackie without her stopping therapy. I now have a more complete armoury of tools and techniques to support my clients, to complement the strong and effective support network through supervision and my own therapy, as well as my circle of friends, and of course Anne.

And so, I want to share one more client story. The story of a 'perfect client'. A client where – as with Hugo earlier, perhaps – working in a coaching programme together does not feel like work at all: where it feels more like co-creating a little magic in every session. Where through the various professional and personal experiences, lessons, and tools, coach and client merge into the presence of the moment and come up with new, captivating ideas and solutions together.

Bringing it all Together in 'Getting the Monkey off the Shoulder'

I met Chris, a quiet, calm, friendly, 34-year-old manager, through one of the emerging digital coaching platforms. From the start he made a very kind impression on me. In a 'fast-track' career he had grown rapidly through the ranks of a medium-sized Swedish company manufacturing lifestyle products and consumer electronics. After ten years, and based in the UK, he was now leading its global supply chain operations.

Chris absolutely loved his job. He saw it more "like a hobby," as he was completely passionate about creating improved service solutions for his clients.

But he had a massive challenge: whilst his line manager was based at the global headquarters in Sweden, out of goodwill Chris had agreed to also support the local UK service operations in the interim. This meant that for the last eight months Chris had been doing literally two jobs and it had started to take a substantial toll on him.

Chris's overall coaching goal was getting ready to lead at a higher management level and in his own words to "grow from managing 100 people to more than a thousand." But first we had to address the current situation of personal overload with some urgency.

Getting started, Chris shared that he had worked 60-hour weeks for the last 10 years. Twice he was close to burnout. Only through the intervention of a good friend and a senior mentor in the company had this been avoided. I sensed there was something we needed to understand better.

Chris is a top talent and hence participates in the company's leadership development programme. This includes a DISC insights assessment,[40] which is a psychometric tool linked to the well-known Myers Briggs assessment.[41] It measures four aspects of our personality: Dominance, Influence, Steadiness, and Conscientiousness.

The DISC profile described Chris as predominantly 'conscientious'. This means that he used an analytical, cautious approach and solved problems methodically through extensive research. He can be seen as creative and very detail-oriented, striving for perfection. Sometimes he might prefer handling tasks himself to ensure they are completed to his satisfaction.

Chris had also done a 360° assessment, where his line managers, subordinates, and peers were asked for their feedback about him. The key inputs came back as follows:

Strengths	Development Opportunities
• Attention to detail and vast supply chain expertise • Leads by example and creates trusting relationships • Engages, supports, and motivates others • Listens well and is very honest (admits mistakes) • Embraces challenges and has strong ownership • Good communicator who values diversity	• Prioritisation and time management • Stay focused, say no when needed and set boundaries

From the two assessments we could see what had made Chris so successful. He was hard-working, detail-oriented, highly knowledgeable and at the same time a 'people person'. The CEO of the company once described him as "speaking technology, business, and people in one." But his drive could also become a potential derailer as the two near-burnouts had alarmingly demonstrated.

Starting out with our sessions, we discovered another challenge. Chris was bogged down by his interim boss, the Managing Director of the UK who had "attacked" him in recent meetings. On top of working two jobs, this strained relationship created a completely new level of emotional turmoil, anger, and frustration for Chris.

He described the Managing Director as an "aggressive dictator," who was from the "older generation" and deciding everything "top-down." Chris dreaded each encounter with him, and days ahead of their next meeting, he could feel his stomach churn. The meetings usually were tense. Conversations were difficult, until at one point it all came to a head.

In front of the whole team the 'dictator' started throwing accusations at Chris and hingeing his critique on a small mistake Chris had presented in one of his slides. The 'dictator' raised his voice and, with cutting, machine-gun like remarks, he systematically dismantled Chris. Feeling embarrassed, incapable, small, and stupid, Chris shrank further and further to the point where he could not handle it and requested to stop the meeting. It was a 'car crash'. In our next session, we explored what had happened, and as we talked, Chris was still feeling deflated, helpless, and unsure how to move on.

Highly charged situations can overwhelm us. Emotions begin to run wild. At the same time, our own negative thoughts can fuel a downward spiral, leading to reactions (behaviours) that can further aggravate negative thoughts and emotions. It's a recipe for an ever-escalating disaster.

But it does not have to be that way. In the safe space of our coaching alliance, we employed the Thoughts Feelings Behaviour (TFB) worksheet. As the case was still fresh in his mind, I gently asked Chris whether he could remember the situation, and step by step we were able to put the picture together:

Listening to Chris made me think of the drama triangle. Developed by Stephen Karpman, Assistant Clinical Professor of Psychiatry at the University of California (UCSF), the drama triangle describes destructive interactions that can occur among people in conflict. It can also describe what might go on in our internal conflicts. Karpman defined the three roles in conflicts as 'persecutor', 'rescuer', and 'victim'.[42]

Talking the situation through in our session we realised an important fact. The 'dictator' had clearly acted as the persecutor in "pushing Chris far too hard and being unfair." But the actual downward spiral began as Chris inflicted punishing criticism and blame on himself for not "being able to manage the 'dictator'" and "having made that silly mistake on the slide."

Trigger	Thoughts	Feelings	Behaviours
Emotionally charged meeting with the 'dictator'	• Why is he so aggressive? • I work two jobs and only try to help him! • There is zero appreciation! • I have 32 direct reports – how is that supposed to work? • He does not do his own stuff but pushes me! • I've worked here 10 years and it has never been so bad! • How can I manage him? • My slide has one stupid mistake! • I don't know what to say! • I look so stupid! • I am a failure!	• Heart rate goes up, shallow breathing, stomach churns • I get angry and frustrated • I feel cheated and lost • I feel treated unfairly • I feel humiliated and sad	• I try to defend myself and to manage the 'dictator' • I start brainstorming what I could have done better • I lose energy and focus • I get stuck in negative thought patterns • I don't know what to do • I surf social media

Chris felt stupid for not having the right solutions at his fingertips to rescue the situation and started to load all the pressure, expectations, and responsibility onto his own shoulders. He believed he must be the 'rescuer' here. But stuck in such a negative frame of mind, he was nowhere near being able to provide a constructive way out.

With surprising speed, Chris had moved from being a 'self-persecutor' to 'rescuer' to 'victim'. He was helpless, lost, and stuck. With the current workload of his two jobs, he had no idea how to get out of this situation. He nodded when he realised that he had played all three roles when events had spun out of control.

On the positive side and with some distance now, it was liberating for him to understand what was going on and so we looked at what could be done to break this destructive cycle, which many of us may have experienced to one extent or another.

Talking through the various options, Chris's perspective started to shift. Gradually he began to replace the internal 'persecutor' with a 'challenger'. We discussed questions like 'what is it that you can learn in this situation?' and 'how will it make you grow?'

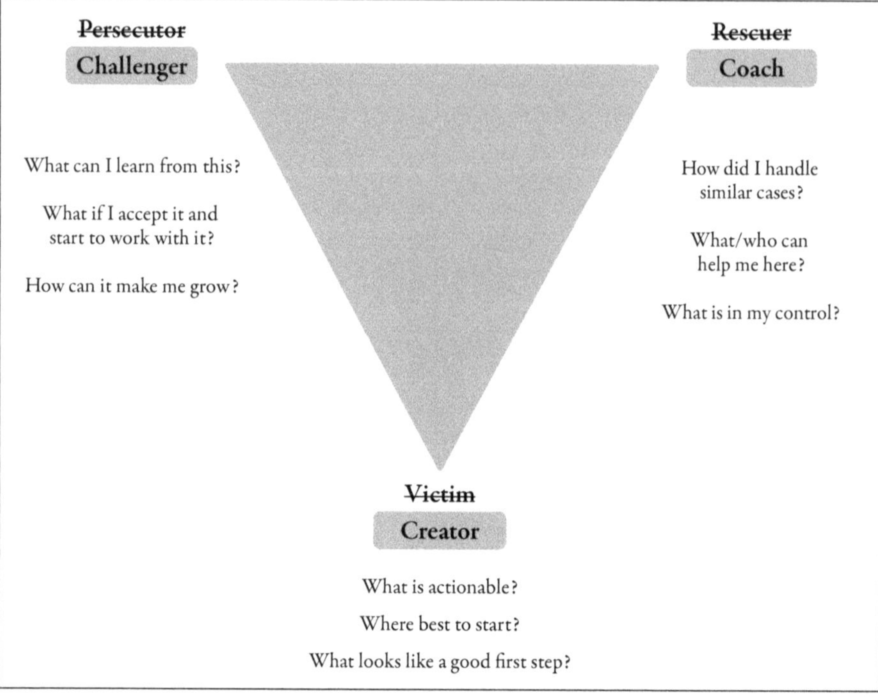

The drama triangle reversed

At the same time, he shifted the 'rescuer' to a 'coach', looking at 'what is the actual root cause of the problem?' and, 'how have you handled similar cases in the past?' With this transition, the 'victim' slowly gave way to the 'creator', beginning to explore, 'what small next steps could Chris take now to begin unlocking the situation?' The diagram above describes the process.

Working through his situation in the context of the drama triangle, Chris's perspective began to open up. He started to see what had been holding him back, and when looking at specific next steps we talked about what was in his control.

Here we turned to the CIC model, developed by Steven Covey as part of his *7 Habits of Highly Effective People*.[43] This wonderful model looks at what is in our control, what we can influence, and what is perhaps indeed our concern because it affects us, but what we can do little about, which Covey also describes as the "circle of no-control."

When looking at the three circles it became evident that Chris wanted to focus more on the things in his control in the centre circle and somewhat on those in the middle circle, more or less ignoring the outer circle.

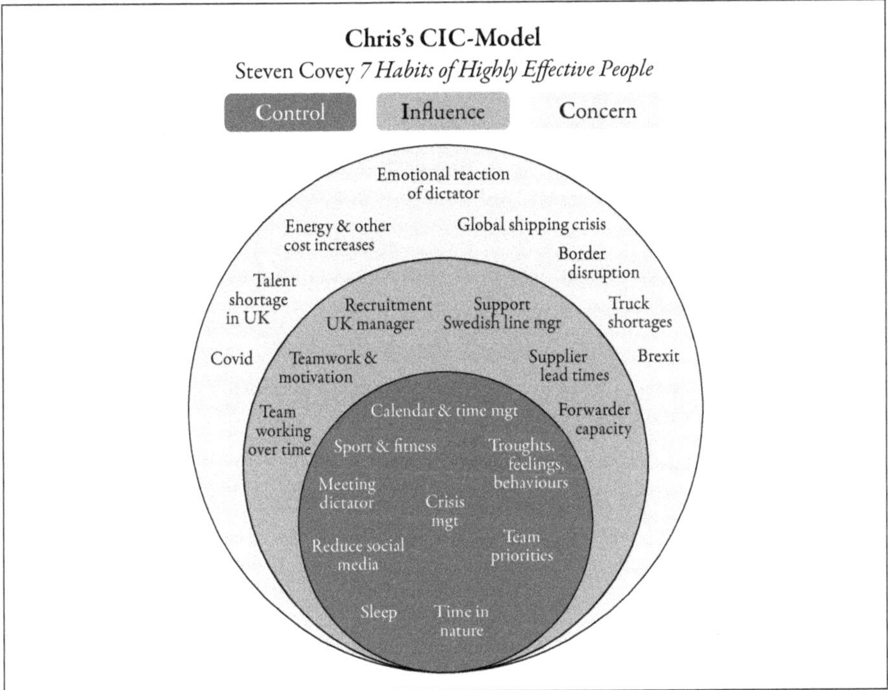

Chris's Control Influence Concern (CIC) circles

With clarity on what was within his control, Chris impressed me as he took decisive action in booking a meeting with the 'dictator' for the week after. He wanted to clear the air and clarify all the open points in a one-to-one conversation. A brave move, but we had to prepare well for the meeting, which clearly would be difficult. It was important that Chris stood up for himself in a calm and composed way to bring across all the points which were bothering him. At the same time this needed to happen in a way which would avoid another 'nuclear explosion' from the 'dictator'.

To prepare for this meeting, we applied the Non-Violent Communication (NVC) model of Marshall Rosenberg,[44] an American psychologist, author, and teacher. The model is a compelling tool to convey difficult messages. The trick is to focus on oneself rather than 'blaming' the other side. In doing so, the flow of the conversation can create a more open atmosphere of constructive dialogue.

The model consists of four steps by sharing (1) the facts, (2) how it makes the person feel, (3) what the person needs, and (4) making a request to the other side. In preparation for the 'dictator' we summarised the following:

1. Facts: We are in a crisis with our local service team due to substantial shipment delays. Some of the recent meetings were not productive and there are outstanding matters awaiting urgent decisions/inputs. This causes challenges for me to support the UK business well, especially since I am only stepping in as interim manager with 50% of my time.
2. Feelings: Honestly speaking, this situation makes me feel frustrated and left alone.
3. Need: Moving forward, I would need a closer collaboration and support from your side to effectively develop a way out of this crisis together.
4. Request: To do that, I suggest that we establish a weekly one-to-one communication, which will help to make decisions timelier, remove barriers, and get the problems under control quickly.

This sounded good, but Chris wanted to go into the conversation with the clear intention to stay calm and composed. To manifest this intention, I asked him how best he could do that? What could be a mantra, an anchor which could remind him to stay calm and composed. Chris came up with: "Stick with the facts!"

But deep down he was still very much concerned that things could blow up and get out of control, given that the recent meeting was not that long ago, and he could still feel the shock inside himself from this experience. We had to find a way to support Chris in staying the course, even if things should get heated.

Talking it through further in our coaching session, we found help in re-applying a concept from elite sports and we will see shortly why this concept spoke so well to Chris. The approach we applied has been helping professional athletes staying focused and functional in high-pressure situations. It was developed by the performance consulting company Gazing, which works with top athletes and sports teams like the All Blacks New Zealand Rugby team.[45]

The concept is called Red Head and Blue Head and the logic of the approach is effective and simple: whatever our mind pays attention to, our thoughts will follow. Our thoughts then create an emotion, which then results in a behaviour. This behaviour defines our performance.

Attention → Thoughts → Emotions → Behaviours!

If we can control our attention, and therefore our thoughts, we can better manage our emotions and enhance our performance. This is where the Red Head and Blue Head come in.

The Red Head is characterised by feelings of anxiety, doubt, overwhelmingness, and desperation. In the mindset of the Red Head, focus on the actual situation is slipping away. The possible outcome is causing us to lose confidence and our ability to perform.

The Blue Head, in contrast, enables us to clearly concentrate on the situation by staying calm, certain of the job at hand, and fully present in the actual moment, with access to the full conscious and unconscious capacity. The trick is to be able to switch from red to blue on demand.

This can be done effectively, by *anchoring* the Blue Head state to a physical trigger. James Kerr, bestselling writer, and business consultant, describes the process in his book *Legacy,* outlining the success formula of the All Blacks: "First, we put ourselves in a resourceful state: calm, positive, clear. Then we anchor that state through a specific, replicable physical action – something out of the ordinary like scrunching up your toes, stamping your foot, pinching the back of your hand, staring in the distance, or throwing water over your face. Repeat, and repeat, and repeat – until it's automatic." [46]

Anchoring ourselves to a physical trigger can bring us back to the present moment and functionality in a matter of seconds. And while throwing water in the face may not be appropriate during Chris's face-to-face meeting with the 'dictator', there are many practicable physical anchors which can help us come back from the Red Head state to the present moment, the Blue Head.

Chris tried several different anchors, but in the end, he decided to pinch the back of his left hand, together with a very long and deep inhale and an even longer exhale.

Perhaps try this out for yourself for just a moment: Pinch the back of your left hand and take a loooooong and deeeeeeeep inhale followed by an even loooooooonger exhale. Maybe you can sense how this little and quick activity brings an instant sense of calm. Pinch the back of your left hand and take a loooooong and deeeeeeeep inhale followed by an even loooooooonger exhale. Practise it regularly and you have a wonderful way to switch instantly from the Red Head to the Blue Head.

With this in place we had Chris fully prepped to meet the dictator. And it all turned out much better than we expected. The 'dictator' in the end even apologised to Chris for having been "a bit emotional," and both agreed on regular one-to-one meetings as well as a clear plan for how to get out of the service crisis.

Rupture and repair. As shared earlier in the *ho'oponopono* concept, relationships can get strengthened when we effectively work through challenging situations and conflicts together. The meeting helped tremendously to strengthen the relationship between Chris and the 'dictator' as it cleared the air, but it also brought across to the 'dictator' that Chris was not a walkover.

We still had to work out why Chris ended up doing two jobs for such a long time, risking another potential burnout. He had overcommitted himself and it would be good to find out why.

As with other clients, we started searching in the past and so the 'ghosts from the past' article came in handy. Chris had homework to do. And what he brought to our next session really blew me away, as, typical of Chris, he shared a very conscientious analysis.

Having grown up in a family of accomplished people with academic and technical backgrounds, Chris had always been very self-driven and highly motivated. But school had not come easy to him, and he experienced several setbacks early on. But then his eyes lit up. He began to talk about sports and his real passion, rugby. Having played since he was five years old, nearly every free minute he had been on the pitch with his mates. Eventually he had been spotted by one of the larger clubs and invited to join their youth academy.

Through his determined and driven approach, combined with being a people person, he quickly made it to team captain, and for many years he led his youth teams from the front. He always was a team player: he had learnt to put success and his team first, himself second.

Aged seventeen, and on the brink of earning himself a professional rugby contract, disaster struck. In a sad tone and with his eyes cast downwards, Chris described what happened. Over the course of only fifteen months, he had two successive knee injuries. "That was the end of my rugby career." He was trying to be rational, but I could still feel the devastation, pain, and disappointment in his voice, about his life-long dream of becoming a professional rugby player being shattered.

I asked him to describe himself as a rugby player. He right away mentioned that his biggest fear had always been to lose face in front of his teammates. And there were other beliefs which he had put together as part of his 'ghosts from the past' analysis. Some were very stark to me, and I felt they could explain why he was doing two jobs:

- I must be there and strong for others!
- I must do the dirty work!
- I cannot be weak!
- I want to be seen as a lion!
- I need to have all the answers!

From those statements we could see what had made Chris strong and successful. But saying them out loud in our session made him realise that his core beliefs may also have created unrealistic expectations of himself. He went as far as saying: "No wonder I worked 60 hours for 10 years and am doing two jobs now!" Shaking his head, he continued quietly: "I have to change this!" This, however, was easier said than done, as our core beliefs are deeply engrained.

I was working at the same time with another client who struggled to delegate and who had introduced me to a *Harvard Business Review (HBR)* article called 'Management Time: Who's Got the Monkey?'[47]

The article, which I now think should be a must-read for every manager who struggles to delegate, describes ways and tools how to ensure that a leader is not taking on 'monkeys': tasks which are supposed to be done by others. Chris took the article and ran with it, almost like I imagined him on the rugby fields of his past. As a result, he completely changed his time and calendar management approach, as he realised that others were "putting the monkey" on him "by regularly walking into my office for ad-hoc meetings or constantly pinging me in MS Teams with urgent requests!"

He began to block me-time and smiled when he said that he would defend this me-time "like a rugby ball." By the end of our coaching programme, Chris described his key lesson in a very simple phrase: "I don't have to!"

This did not mean that he wanted to stop working or that he did not care about work anymore. It meant that the beliefs which were instilled inside him through his professional sports career and other past experiences, that:

- He must be the one to rescue every situation
- He is the one who is solely responsible for the success of the endeavour
- He is the one who must have all the answers, and
- He must be the one who is always there for others

were simply wrong. He did not have to do any of these things if he did not want to. That was a huge liberation. The weight – the 'monkey' – had come off his shoulder. "I am only a human being and not a machine!"

This fundamental shift allowed Chris to free up his mind and leverage his many talents, including his remarkable human touch and incredible drive, in a more structured and balanced way. I am absolutely convinced Chris will go on to lead thousands of people sooner rather than later and do so in a sustainable fashion.

You may ask now, what made Chris a perfect client? For me it was the combination of his openness to reflect, learn, and adapt together with his ability to put things in motion and acting decisively, where his conscientiousness clearly helped. I also believe he was fuelled by a strong inner drive for continuous learning and growth, which made him and will continue to make him so successful.

Being a Gardener

Perhaps you recall the Chinese saying I found on my calendar more than ten years back. "If you want to be happy for one hour, get drunk; if you want to be happy for a week, get married; if you want to be happy forever, get a garden."

Every day, I am more convinced that my coaching practice is my 'garden', and I hope these individual client stories have helped to showcase how rewarding it can be to work with these human 'flowers'. How fulfilling it is to see when such a 'flower' grows a bit taller, starts to bloom, or simply holds out and bravely weathers a difficult storm. Whatever it is: I am extremely grateful, as it has been such a wonderful experience becoming a coach. It was and is not always easy. And yes, there were times when I doubted my decision, or when the going is tough. But overall, I am happy being a 'gardener' and working every day with fascinating human 'flowers' who sometimes need a little extra care, nutrition, pruning, or just some loving kindness from the Sun, to help them grow and flourish.

Maybe you remember my Sunday blues before every new week when I was still working in Procter & Gamble. I'm happy to say that the Sunday blues is gone. Perhaps that also has something to do with the fact that there is no longer a Sunday hangover, but certainly it is also because I am working on something that I am passionate about and that truly fulfils me.

In Japan there is the wonderful concept of *Ikigai*,[48] which I think quite nicely describes my current situation. Literally translated, *Ikigai* portrays 'a reason for being' and has four key components: (1) something that we love doing, (2) something we are good at, (3) something that the world needs, and (4) something we can get paid for. I personally feel that I have found my reason to get up every morning, my reason for being. And this is what I am truly happy about.

They say coaching is "two people learning and one gets paid." This means my journey continues and every day is a new opportunity 'walk the talk', to continue to learn about myself, my work, and life in general, and then putting those lessons into action. And this, in a very similar fashion, resembles what my clients do for themselves as they learn and grow, so that they are increasingly able to go their own way.

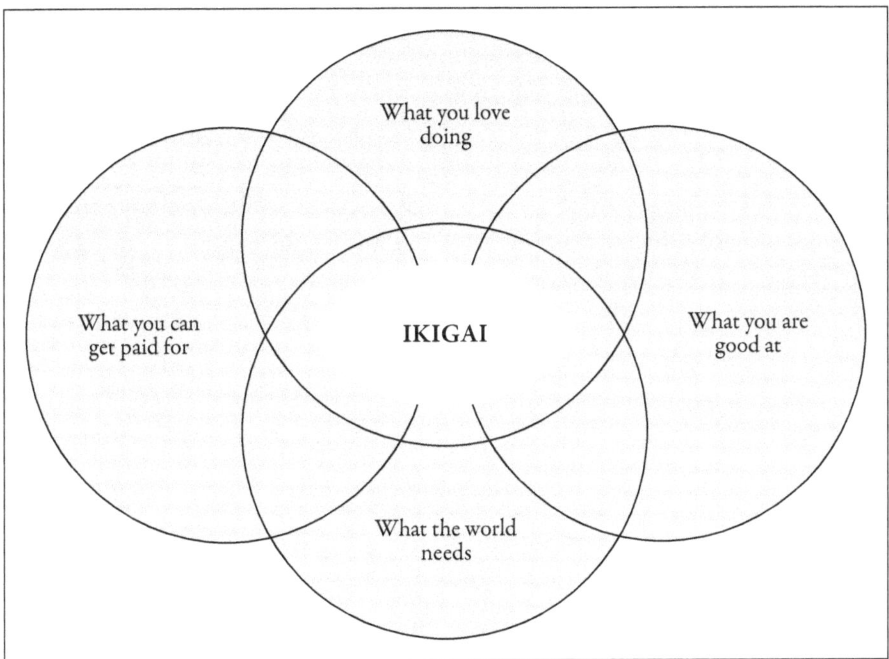

The concept of *Ikigai*

Reaching Your Goals

Back in March 2012, sitting in that 'fateful' mindfulness training, my inner voice spoke to me very clearly: "Go for the walk! Go for the walk! Go for the walk!" It was such a loud message that I simply could not ignore it.

But it was then the first step the next day – to ask my boss Jeffrey whether I could get four weeks off – that was the most difficult one. Getting over that initial barrier, to ask for something which was unprecedented at my level at that time, was something I had really dreaded.

It was taking this very first step that set a complete life change in motion. Even though my first proposal was rejected by Jeffrey, the universe jumped in and helped me with a workshop in London, after which I could set out on my journey along the Camino de Santiago in May 2012. This book has described what fundamental changes that walk triggered in my life and with this also in the life of others.

People say, "visions without actions are hallucinations," and therefore the final section of this book is about taking action and making sure that in our busy lives we march in whatever is the right direction for us. Taking action also means to listen to our inner voice, even though it may tell us something that sounds perhaps uncomfortable, because our inner voice usually knows very well what is needed for our personal development and wellbeing.

I would like to invite you now to take action for yourself. And to support you with that, you will find below a description on how to put your own Life Compass together, a tool which many of my clients have used successfully for more than ten years now. A tool, which I am convinced, can make a substantial difference along your life journey. But before we dive into the Life Compass, I need to share a little story which in a moving way describes why having a Life Compass can be so important.

What Goes Into Your 'Jar of Life'?

One day a teacher was speaking to his students, and he asked them whether they were up for an experiment. The students were eager to prove themselves and so the teacher pulled out a large glass jar and put it on his desk in front of the class. Then he carefully placed several rocks into the jar, one at a time.

After he had done this and no further rocks fit inside, he asked the class: "Is the jar full?" The class answered, "Yes, it's full!" The teacher reached under the table to grab a bucket of gravel. Carefully he began to fill gravel into the jar, and as he shook the jar, the gravel started to fill the empty spaces between the big rocks. Now he asked again: "Is the jar full?" The class answered, "Yes, it's full now!"

"Really?" asked the teacher, as he pulled out a bag of sand. Again, he very carefully added the sand, and shaking the jar it ran into the empty space among the gravel. Then he smiled and asked the group again: "Is the jar full?" The class started to understand that there was a specific teaching behind this little experiment and one student answered: "Probably not ..."

"Good!" said the teacher as he pulled out a bottle of beer, opened it and slowly poured it into the jar until it was filled to the brim. With a cheeky smile he asked the class: "Why do you think I am sharing this experiment?" The class turned silent for a bit and then launched into a fiery debate.

The teacher asked for quiet and explained: "I could have put the sand in the jar first, then the gravel. But what would have happened? The rocks would not have fitted into the jar.

Now, imagine the jar being your life. It is essential that you put into your life jar the big rocks first: those things that are absolutely crucial to you.

'Big rocks' in the jar of life

Because everything will find its place around them. But if you stuff your life full of unimportant things, the things that matter will have nowhere to go."

The students nodded in silent agreement. But one of the students held up his hand: "What's with the beer? Why pour beer into the jar?" With a big grin the teacher answered: "In life, there should always be time for a beer with a good friend!"

What are the 'big rocks' in your life? Let's work with this question and build on it, as we develop your Life Compass. We will make sure that you include all the 'big rocks' first, and then look at a simple way to stay on track.

The Life Compass

When Procter & Gamble acquired Wella in 2003, it would not only change my own life, but probably the lives of every single one of my 17,000 Wella colleagues. For me, the years and months that followed the acquisition announcement felt like doing two MBAs at the same time. It not only meant relocating to Singapore, but also operating in a totally different working culture, whilst learning new tools, systems, processes, and acronyms every day.

Among the many new things, there was one tool that stood out for me: the OGSM, which stands for Objectives, Goals, Strategies, Measures.[49] Every year, each business unit created a one-page document that defined the strategy for the next fiscal year. This powerful one-pager was deployed across all teams so that everyone was crystal clear about the road ahead and what was expected of them.

The process to arrive at the OGSM has been laid out by former P&G CEO, A.G. Laffley and Roger Martin in their 'playbook for strategy'.[50] The four strategy development questions are:

1. Where will we play?
2. How will we win and what capabilities must be in place?
3. What is our winning aspiration?
4. What management systems are required?

It is important that these questions link together, which makes the strategy development an iterative process, connecting all four choices as interdependent items. For example, we should only pick items in the 'where to play' section that are truly essential and provide us with a reasonable chance and idea of how to win (like the big rocks).

Seeing the OGSM and its development process working so well for the business every year, I had a thought: why not apply this to my personal life? And so, at the end of 2011, I sat down and developed my first personal OGSM, which I now call Life Compass. I have never stopped using it since, and that tool also has made a substantial difference in my clients' lives. Let me take you through the simple steps to create your very own Life Compass.

1. Where Will You Play?

This section is about the 'big rocks' in your life. What are the key things that you deem so important that they must go first into your 'jar of life'? What is so essential that by no means would you be able or willing to leave it out?

Take a piece of paper, reflect, and write down what comes to your mind. What are the most precious and important things in your life? For a little help, you may skip back to the stories of Alfred Nobel, or the bucket list, or the five biggest regrets of the dying. Simply think about what you definitely want to keep in focus as you go through your life.

I personally have defined four key categories of big rocks for my life. These four categories have not changed much over time and are still functioning as a powerful reminder when things get hectic and messy: My Health, My People, My Work, and Me.

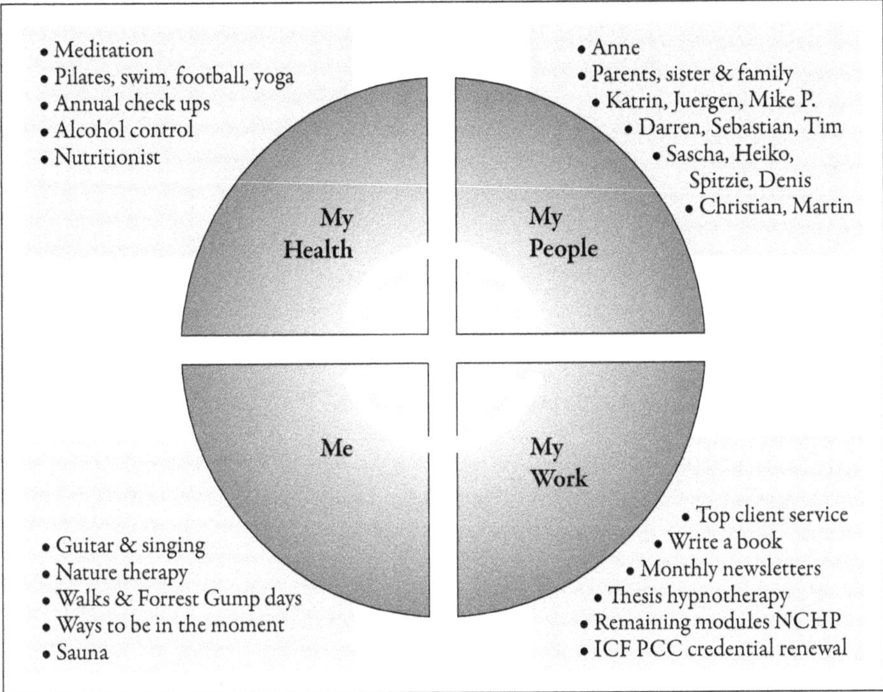

Life Compass – intention template

There is no need for you to apply these four categories. You can choose to have more than four big rocks in your life, but I suggest you don't define more than six of them. Yes, prioritising might be difficult, but this is what the 'jar of life' story taught us. We have only a limited capacity in our lives. Very much the same as the jar. Hence the big rocks need to be thought about very carefully and put in first. What are yours?

2. How Will You Win and What Capabilities Must Be in Place?

After the key categories or 'big rocks' are clear, it will now be good to develop three to four intentions for each of these areas. For me and most of my clients, these intentions include things that we want to experience, do, achieve, or reach in the coming year. As such they are the key subtasks to make each big rock successful.

When putting down intentions, please try to take a step back and look at what is truly important. Again, the 'jar of life' metaphor applies. If there are new capabilities required to be successful in any of the 'big rock' categories, you can simply include them as an intention in the respective category (for example the 'Me'-category) and make the progress measurable (such as: 'guitar – plug & slap technique in full swing'). The image above shows some examples of intensions.

In a second step, which probably looks a bit tedious, but which will be very powerful once completed, we are then trying to make each of these intentions measurable. To do that it is helpful to apply the SMART approach[51] (Specific, Measurable, Achievable, Relevant, Time-bound) so that by the end of the year you can see whether you have achieved what you wanted to achieve and/or whether a course correction may be needed as you are off-track.

Below is an example of what such an action plan can look like. Perhaps you think, is that really necessary? Yes, it may look a little overwhelming at first, but in fact it offers you the opportunity to think about all the key things you want to focus on over the course of a whole year and so having these important activities fully measurable on one page can hugely increase your chances that you do not miss out anything.

Some of my clients have decided not to go with the full-detailed action plan and rather keep the intention shared in the diagram before as a more flexible definition of what they want to focus on. There is no right or wrong and so just follow whatever feels right for your own life planning.

Where to Play?	How to Win?	Measures
My Health	Daily meditation – stillness, confidence & a positive outlook	365 days x > 30 minutes / no phone!
	Pilates, (ice) swim, football, croquet, walks, yoga	Wkly: PSFCWY, sleep > 7.5h / touch toes
	Proper BUPA health & teeth check + stay alcohol free	AF, cholesterol, blood pressure ok
	Weight loss plan, nutritionist, allergies test, less sugar	Weight goal @88kg (from 96kg)
My People	Fulfilling and nurturing relationship with Anne	MKL, pilates, swims, walks, cycling, croquet, regular quality time, meals, > 10 travels
	Regular skype w parents & sister & visits to Germany	Just do it
	Circle of friends: celebrate existing (Sascha, M&C, Juergen, Spitzie, Katrin, Heiko, Denis ...) and build new ones in London (Sebastian/Darren/Tim ...)	Regular connects existing, footie w Darren, walks w Sebastian, connects Tim ...

Where to Play?	How to Win?	Measures
My Work	Serve existing clients well	> $ X per month
	Translate & publish my book with Sebastian	Ready as Xmas present
	MKTG through monthly news-letters, LinkedIn, Website VDO	NLs & intro video on website
	Develop topic & write Hypno-psychotherapy diploma thesis	Ready by 31.07. / area expert
	Complete 4 remaining modules + CPD hours for UKCP psycho-therapist registration & CCEUs ICF PCC renewal	UKCP registered psychotherapist ICF PCC renewal until end 2026
Me	Continue guitar & singing (1 song a day keeps the doctor away)	Regular sessions with Ralf + small concert in May
	Regular walks, time for myself & in nature, sauna	Walks, Clarins-Spa, sauna
	Spiritual development – continue nature therapy w Ludwig	> 6 sessions NT / > 30% fully in moment

Life Compass – action plan template

As a picture speaks a thousand words, together with the above action plan, every year I and several of my clients, create/update a vision board. It is a fun exercise to do, and sometimes when there is not much time to run through the complete action plan, I just take a glance at my vision board. This usually brings a smile to my face and reminds me of the things I still must do, along with all the many things I can be grateful for in my life. Have a look at an example of my vision board below.

Again, there is no right and wrong here. I personally believe that visualisations can help us a lot in achieving our goals. Many elite athletes use visualisations to perfect their performance, and studies have proven that they indeed can increase their chances of success.

So, I leave it with you, whether you want to consider creating a vision board to support your action plans or prefer to just stick with some bullet point intentions for each of your 'big rocks'. Please also note, it perhaps looks like a lot of work, but once it is done for the first time, the actual effort required for updating it once a

Life Compass – vision board

year is very limited. And as mentioned earlier, it also can be a fun exercise which many of my clients even do together with their spouses or partners.

3. What Is Your Winning Aspiration?

At the top of the intention or action plan template, it will be good to define a personal motto, a challenge, a specific focus, or, in other words, a life theme for that year. As some food for thought, below you can find my aspirational life themes for the last ten years.

Year	Aspiration
2012	Nothing is good – unless I do it
2013	Enjoy & Bring Joy
2014	Every Day = A Magnificent Day
2015	Don't Over-Engineer
2016	Create 'Mumbai-Moments'

Year	Aspiration
2017	Purpose With Courage
2018	Enjoy The Journey
2019	Get Out There!
2020	Slow Down to Speed up
2021	I Am Fully Me
2022	*Fröhlich sein und Gutes tun*
2023	Perfectly in the Moment

Life Compass – aspirations

Think of a short one-line statement, which could represent an aspiration, focus, or challenge for the next period in your life. Experiment a bit and then just add it on top of the action plan template, or if you go with the intention template just add it on top of the page.

5. What Management Systems Are Required?

To ensure that we achieve what we have planned to achieve, it is essential to track the progress regularly. In our busy lives this can become a challenge, as there are usually so many things going on.

I therefore encourage my clients to always carry a small, printed copy of their Life Compass in their wallet. With this, they can take it out every few weeks, at opportune moments, for example when waiting for a bus, to reflect on how things are going:

- What is going well?
- Which areas need a little extra push?
- Where is a course correction needed?
- Where can I slow down a bit?

I personally review my progress with Anne as my accountability partner, who provides me with her kind, honest, and helpful feedback, which is a huge help. Perhaps you have a good friend, or your spouse/partner might be happy to review the progress with you regularly.

Whatever works best for you: most important is to print a copy and either place it in your wallet or in a good, visible spot at home or in your office. Some of my clients put it on the fridge or hang it near their front door, so that they are regularly reminded of the important 'big rocks'. Wherever you put it, your chances

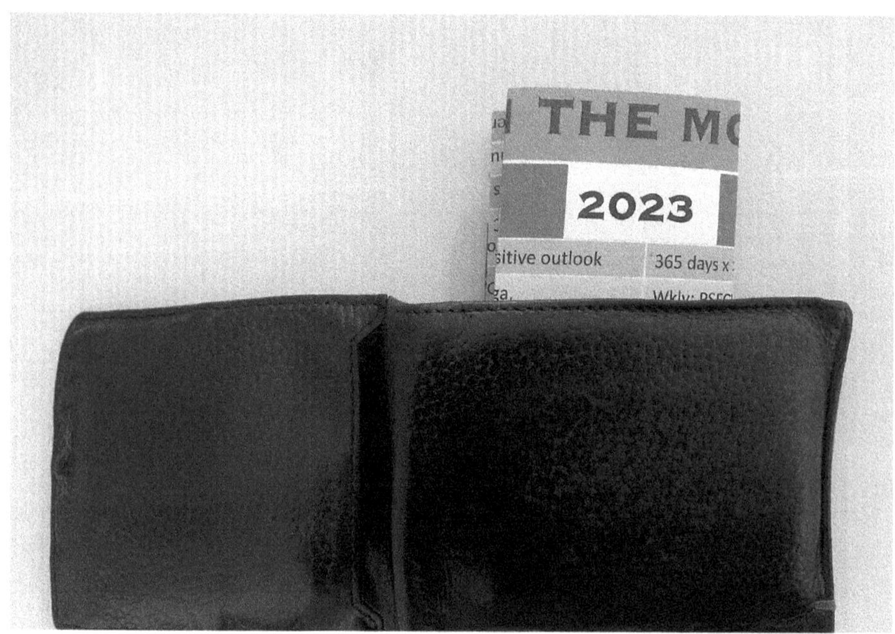

Life Compass – in the wallet for tracking

will increase substantially to live your life more closely to how you really want it to be.

I would be delighted if you gave it a shot. Perhaps you do not go all-in with a detailed action plan and a vision board, but just mapping and printing the key intentions for your big rocks will make a difference. Your Life Compass makes sure that your big rocks are covered, that you stay the course, and that you reduce the likelihood of potential regrets.

So, simply send me a quick email at info@jkcoach.com with 'Go Your Own Way' in the subject field and receive your free copy of the Life Compass template, covering all the slides shown above for easy use and adaptation. Go for it, have fun with it, and use this to go your own way!

A Message for You!

I trust and hope the Life Compass will be as helpful to you as it has been to me and many of my clients. And with the Life Compass we are also about to complete our journey together in this book. I hope you enjoyed the time we 'walked side by side', as you were reading the book.

You walked with me, not only along the 800 km on the Camino de Santiago, but also accompanying me in the decade thereafter when I completed my 'walk of change', and you were by my side and looked over my shoulder to see my clients 'walk the talk', growing as 'human flowers'.

I believe the following short story summarises nicely what happened during my walking pilgrimage on the Camino, along my own developmental journey during the ten years since, as well as in the many personal transformations of my clients.

The 'Perfect Heart' for a Life Well-Lived

The story has been attributed to Paulo Coehlo on a blog by Priya Sher.[52]

One day, a young man walked into a village square and declared he had the most perfect heart in the whole valley. A crowd gathered around him, and all admired his heart, because it was, indeed, perfect. No stains, no defects. Yes, they agreed, it was the most beautiful heart they had ever seen. The young man was proud and extraordinarily pleased with himself and his beautiful heart.

Suddenly, an old man appeared from the crowd and said, "Listen, your heart is not even half as beautiful as mine." The crowd and the young man looked at the heart of the old man. It beat powerfully, but it was also full of scars. It had spots where parts had been removed and replaced by other pieces. But some of those didn't fit well and there were jagged edges. In some places, there were deep ridges where parts were completely missing.

The people were staring at the old man. How could he claim his heart was more beautiful than the young man's? The young man looked at the battered heart of the old man and laughed. "You are joking," he said. "To compare your heart with mine! My heart is perfect and yours is a hodgepodge of scars and tears."

"Yes," said the old man, "yours looks perfect, but I would never swap mine with yours. You see, each scar in my heart stands for someone to whom I have given my love. I tore out a piece of my heart and gave it to them, and often, they gave me a piece of their heart that fit in the empty space of mine. They do not always fit perfectly. That's why I also have a few ragged edges. But I appreciate them greatly because they remind me of the love I have shared. Sometimes, I got nothing in return. These are empty slots. Giving love also means taking risks. Sometimes, those empty slots hurt, but they also remind me of the love I have felt for those people. I hope they will return one day and fill the blank spots. Do you recognise now what true beauty is?"

> The young man stood still. Tears ran down his cheeks. He reached to his perfect heart, ripped out a piece, and offered it to the old man. The old man took it and put it into his heart. He took a piece of his old, battered heart and closed the wound in the heart of the young man. It was not a perfect fit. There were a few jagged edges. The young man looked at his heart. It was no longer perfect, but he thought it more beautiful than before, because he felt the love of the old man running through it. He put his arm around the shoulder of the old man, and they walked away together, side by side.

The apparently 'perfect' heart of the young man showed a strong shortcoming in that it looked beautiful, but this neglected the fact that he had not (yet) experienced true love from others and had not yet loved someone else with his full heart. The heart of the old man, on the other hand, seemed imperfect but showed the deep love for others, the love for life, and also the love he received back from others.

In Japan there is a beautiful concept, which I believe wonderfully accentuates the story of the old man's imperfect perfect heart. It is called *Kintsugi*.[53] When a bowl, teapot, or precious vase falls and breaks into pieces, we usually throw it away. The Japanese practice of *Kintsugi* teaches us to not only glue the broken pieces back together, but to highlight and enhance the breaks by using precious metals such as gold or silver for doing so.

With every repaired piece being totally unique, *Kintsugi* is built on the idea of strength and beauty in imperfection. It is a metaphor for brokenness and healing: that embracing one's brokenness and imperfections can create something very precious, unique, beautiful, and strong.

We human beings get regular knocks during our walk of life. We all carry our cracks and our breaks deep inside. Some are already glued back together, and some are still being filled with 'exquisite metals' to heal.

On the 18th of May 2012, I had felt completely alone and forlorn on the Camino de Santiago in Spain. My shoes were falling apart, I was physically and mentally exhausted, I did not know how I would be able to walk another 400 km. In Sahagún, I had to say goodbye to two very dear fellow pilgrims who could not continue to walk. One of them, Peter, gave me a big hug and told me that it was now "time to walk my own Camino." It was tough. Not only did I feel exhausted and helpless, but I also felt completely alone and scared.

Looking back on it now, walking out of the village on that day was the tipping point of my life. Soon after that, I broke down. Walking and crying I realised that most of my life I had focused to meet other people's expectations. It was difficult to comprehend. But it also was liberating, with all those tears flowing.

Kintsugi – perfection and uniqueness in imperfection

In those moments it became clear to me that it was time to do the things in my life I felt truly passionate about. It was time to go my own way. By the end of that 'cathartic meltdown' on the 18th of May 2012, I passed by this traffic sign. Its concluding message perfectly rounded up the key teaching for me at that time. It said: 'You are very very special.'

Reading it, I sat down and in the peaceful and contemplative space of that very moment, I realised that I did not have to complete the walk. I was okay the way I am. It was a huge success for me simply being there and walking the Camino. In doing so I was taking time out from my hectic work schedule. Time to take a step back and reflect on what was really important for me on my life journey.

Sitting by the traffic sign in May 2012, I began to glue the cuts, the rough edges, and the broken parts in my heart together. 'You are very very special' helped me. It helped me tremendously, as it was that 'golden glue' which seeped into the cracks and slowly began to repair the broken edges.

Every year tens of thousands of pilgrims pass by that very traffic sign. It clearly was not a message for me only. Yes, it helped me a lot on that day, but pondering this moment many years later, I realised that the message was there so that I can bring it to you. It was there, so that I can put it in a book and share it with you! Telling you that you are unique, that you are precious, that you are beautiful, that:

You are very very special!

Perhaps sometimes it's hard for you to see it that way, and maybe there are times when you even think the opposite of yourself. But in the same way as the 'human flowers' I work with as a coach develop their true beautiful colours, you have your unique and fascinating story in this world. We are glad that you walk with us.

So, when there are times during which you are unsure about yourself or times when life becomes simply unbearable, I want to remind you, that you are very very special. And I hope you also realise that you are not walking alone. There are other 'pilgrims' who are there to support you. Look around and reach out for help if you need support. And when you can, also offer a hand to help others. Exchange pieces of your heart with others by giving and receiving love. Continue to find and celebrate the joy in your life.

We all walk on our personal Life Caminos. But we are not alone on this journey! We only have to open our eyes and look around. There are people who walk with us and who help us. There are also people whom we can help at times to make their life a little brighter. With this I wish you a continued wonderful journey: *Buen Camino!*

Make Someone's Life a Little Brighter

Amy is ten years old. She is bravely fighting her very own personal battle against cancer. She's being treated at Hasbro Children's Hospital in Providence, Rhode Island, about 50 miles from Boston. Her family, as well as the doctors and nurses, are doing their best to help her through the difficult days of chemotherapy and other treatments.

Amy is strong, but there are moments when the pain and the situation just overwhelm her. In such moments, she looks forward to 8:30 in the evening, when all the children in the hospital get a special treat. Several minutes before 8:30 pm, they usher up to their windows with flashlights in their little hands, excitingly awaiting the start of the daily routine.

Because at exactly that time, when they look outside, they see a sea of lights blinking and shining their way from all over town. And with their own lamps, the children answer by blinking flashes back into the dark night to the many people who have gathered to wish these little patients a good and restful night's sleep. It's an amazing display of people coming together and supporting each other.

A little patient and his mum looking out for the lights at 8:30pm

The daily ritual was established when Steve Brosnihan felt there had to be something else that could be done to help these children. Steve is Hasbro's resident cartoonist. He supports the little souls by drawing funny and imaginative pictures with them, so they can enjoy a few moments of playful and light-hearted distraction.

In 2016, on his way home from the hospital, Steve started to pause at a certain place. He would get off his bike and illuminate the headlight of his bicycle toward the hospital's patients. Before long, children noticed and answered using torches of their own, and soon it became an established routine.

But it did not stay with Steve. Soon former patients, their parents, police officers, and local businesses – the whole community – started to meet up at 8:30 pm at various locations to flash their lights toward the hospital.

At one point, the children even received a flashlight message that came from very far away. In March 2019, astronaut Anne McClain taped a 'goodnight' from space. She spoke directly to the kids at the hospital; suddenly, she was rotating in weightless spins while the lights were flashing. NASA gave

Steve the video to premier at an assembly of patients and staff. The little patients were stunned and in complete awe to receive their goodnight message from outer space.

Amy says: "At night, when you go to bed, you know people are saying goodnight to you. You know that they are caring for you." But this simple yet powerful gesture not only helps the children. It also helps their parents. And Amy's mother says, "After these long and difficult days in the hospital, you get yourself to the window at 8:30 pm and you have that little bit of peace and happiness."

Another young patient shared that he knows he is not fighting alone. Smiling, he says, "You can signal back to them to show them a little love too. They take time out of their day. It seems so little, but it's so meaningful!"

Acknowledgements

I want to wholeheartedly express my gratitude to the remarkable individuals who played a vital role in bringing this book to life. Their unwavering support, guidance, and encouragement throughout this challenging journey have been truly instrumental.

I would like to thank Sebastian Michael, who guided me like a big brother with his wise, kind, and supportive approach in putting this book together. My heartfelt thanks also go to Christian Henkel, who despite juggling multiple responsibilities has provided the German translation so impeccably that it truly reflects my own personal voice. Equally, I am grateful for the support of Dr. Detlef Thiel, whose critical evaluation has decisively shaped the book into what it has become.

I would also like to express my sincere appreciation to Andrea Päch and Jörg Metze, who designed and implemented the book layout beautifully and also tirelessly refined all the images and diagrams. The cover was designed by Karen Sawrey, and I am very thankful that this crucial piece of work was in her professional and kind hands.

My gratitude also extends to my proofreader, David Haviland, who played a pivotal role in enhancing the book's consistency and coherence.

The book owes its existence to its newsletters, which are the product of a remarkable global collaboration. Every month my English draft is expertly and skilfully edited by Tom Wadenfels in the US, subsequently translated into German by Christian Henkel, and given a final check for grammar and *"de Kommas"* by his brother and my good friend Martin. Celine Binder, based in Singapore, then publishes each newsletter on the website and LinkedIn, making it accessible to the world. Though this small yet powerful team has never met in person, I hope that through this book they feel a sense of pride in their consistent, wonderful monthly contributions, spanning across more than six years now. Thank you, all!

Finally, and most importantly, I want to express my heartfelt admiration for my beautiful wife, Anne, who has been by my side for nearly a decade now. Writing this book has been an adventure filled with ups and downs, some of which also touched our relationship. I am deeply grateful for Anne's unwavering support as my biggest champion and most valuable critic throughout the journey of making this book and our wonderful life together. Thank you, Baby!

References

1 Byrne, U. (2005). Wheel of Life. *Business Information Review,* 22(2), 123–130.

2 Coelho, P. (2015). The fisherman and the businessman. [online] Paulo Coelho. Available at: https://paulocoelhoblog.com/2015/09/04/the-fisherman-and-the-businessman/ [Accessed 25 Jun. 2023].

3 Marsh, N. (2007). *Fat, forty, and fired: one man's frank, funny, and inspiring account of losing his job and finding his life.* Kansas City: Andrews Mcmeel Pub.

4 Wikipedia Contributors (2019). Johari window. [online] Wikipedia. Available at: https://en.wikipedia.org/wiki/Johari_window [Accessed 25 Jun. 2023].

5 Walker, M. P. (2017). *Why we sleep: unlocking the power of sleep and dreams.* New York: Scribner.

6 Roy, S. (2016). A Conversation with Arianna Huffington, Author of The Sleep Revolution. [online] *Sleep Review.* Available at: https://sleepreviewmag.com/sleep-health/prevailing-attitudes/celebrities/conversation-arianna-huffington-the-sleep-revolution/ [Accessed 25 Jun. 2023].

7 Ware, B. (2012). *The top five regrets of the dying: a life transformed by the dearly departing.* Carlsbad, Calif.: Hay House.

8 Chalabaev, A., Major, B., Cury, F. and Sarrazin, P. (2009). Physiological markers of challenge and threat mediate the effects of performance-based goals on performance. *Journal of Experimental Social Psychology,* 45(4), pp.991–994.

9 Turner, M. J. (2016). Rational Emotive Behaviour Therapy (REBT), irrational and rational beliefs, and the mental health of athletes. *Frontiers in Psychology,* [online] 07(1423). Available at: https://www.ncbi.nlm.nih.gov/pmc/articles/PMC5028385/ [Accessed 25 Jun. 2023].

10 Wallington, M. (2014). *Five Hundred Mile Walkies.* Random House.

11 Killingsworth, M. A. and Gilbert, D. T. (2010). A Wandering Mind Is an Unhappy Mind. *Science,* [online] 330(6006), pp. 932–932. Available from: http://www.danielgilbert.com/KILLINGSWORTH%20&%20GILBERT%20(2010).pdf [Accessed 28 Jun. 2023].

12 quotespedia.org (n. d.). *I've had a lot of worries in my life, most of which never happened. – Mark Twain – Quotespedia.org.* [online] www.quotespedia.org. Available at: https://www.quotespedia.org/authors/m/mark-twain/ive-had-a-lot-of-worries-in-my-life-most-of-which-never-happened-mark-twain/ [Accessed 28 Jun. 2023].

13 Cambridge Dictionary (2022). *equanimity.* [online] @CambridgeWords. Available at: https://dictionary.cambridge.org/dictionary/english/equanimity [Accessed 28 Jun. 2023].

14 Wikipedia Contributors (2019). Kübler-Ross model. [online] Wikipedia. Available at: https://en.wikipedia.org/wiki/Five_stages_of_grief [Accessed 28 Jun. 2023].

15 Wikipedia. (2023). *Nonviolent Communication.* [online] Available at: https://en.wikipedia.org/wiki/Nonviolent_Communication#cite_note-Little-8 [Accessed 28 Jun. 2023].

16 Achor, S. (2011). *The happiness advantage: the seven principles that fuel success and performance at work.* London: Virgin.

17 Ferriss, T. (2007). *The 4-hour workweek: escape 9-5, live anywhere, and join the new rich.* New York: Crown Publishers.

18 One Year No Beer. (n. d.). *One Year No Beer.* [online] Available at: https://www.oneyearnobeer.com/ [Accessed 28 Jun. 2023].

19 Csikszentmihalyi, M. (1990). *Flow: The Psychology of Optimal Experience.* Harper & Row: New York.

20 Hougaard, R., Carter, J., Coutts, G. (2016). *One Second Ahead: Enhance Your Performance at Work with Mindfulness.* New York: Palgrave Macmillan US.

21 Harrison, D. (2023). *Talent Management technology: Acquire, Develop, Lead, Engage.* [online] Available at: https://www.harrisonassessments.com/ [Accessed 25 Jun. 2023].

22 Cameron, J. (2017). *The artist's way morning pages journal: a companion volume to the artist's way.* London: Hay House.

23 Anderson, J.G. (2013). *Plant Yourself Where You Will Bloom.* BalboaPress.

24 Bernard, K.C., Zoë (n.d.). Why Jeff Bezos doesn't believe in work-life balance: 'It actually is a circle'. [online] *Business Insider.* Available at: https://www.businessinsider.com/jeff-bezos-work-life-balance-debilitating-phrase-career-circle-2021-7?r=US&IR=T [Accessed 25 Jun. 2023].

25 Ardito, R., Rabellino, D. (2011) "Therapeutic Alliance and Outcome of Psychotherapy: Historical Excursus, Measurements, and Prospects for Research", *Frontiers in Psychology,* volume 2, pages 1–11.

26 Rogers, C. (1957) "The necessary and sufficient conditions of therapeutic change", *Journal of Consulting Psychology,* volume 21, pages 97–103.

27 Gallup, I. (2019). How the CliftonStrengths Assessment Works. [online] Gallup.com. Available at: https://www.gallup.com/cliftonstrengths/en/253676/how-cliftonstrengths-works.aspx [Accessed 29 Jun. 2023].

28 Beck Institute for Cognitive Behavior Therapy. (2015). *Thought-Record-Worksheet.* [online] Available at: https://beckinstitute.org/wp-content/uploads/2021/08/Thought-Record-Worksheet.pdf [Accessed 29 June 2023].

29 Ancona, D., Perkins, D.N.T. (2022). *Family Ghosts in the Executive Suite.* [online] Harvard Business Review. Available at: https://hbr.org/2022/01/family-ghosts-in-the executive-suite [Accessed 29 June 2023].

30 The Bowen Center for the Study of the Family. (2021). *The Bowen Center for the Study of the Family.* [online] Available at: https://www.thebowencenter.org/.

31 Eric Berne M.D. (n.d.). *Description of Transactional Analysis and Games by Dr. Eric Berne MD.* [online] Available at: https://ericberne.com/transactional-analysis/ [Accessed 29 June 2023].

32 The International Focusing Institute. (n.d.). *The International Focusing Institute.* [online] Available at: https://focusing.org/ [Accessed 29 Jun. 2023].

33 RSA (2013). *Brené Brown on Empathy.* YouTube. Available at: https://www.youtube.com/watch?v=1Evwgu369Jw [Accessed 29 Jun. 2023].

34 Gibbotson, G. (2020). *Dr. Geoff Ibbotson,* Available at: https://geoffibbotson.co.uk/ [Accessed 29 Jun. 2023].

35 www.youtube.com. (n.d.). *Caring | Ajahn Brahm | 26 May 2017.* [online] Available at: https://www.youtube.com/watch?v=HOVCsz6khAI [Accessed 29 Jun. 2023]. (mentioned at around minute 33 of the talk)

36 Chandra, N. (2022). Were you a 'parentified child'? What happens when children have to behave like adults. [online] *The Guardian.* Available at: https://www.theguardian.com/lifeandstyle/2022/sep/20/parentified-child-behave-like-adult [Accessed 29 Jun. 2023].

37 Clear, J. (2018) *Ed Latimore Quote*. Available at: https://twitter.com/JamesClear/status/1053994882346430464?lang=en [Accessed 29 Jun. 2023].

38 Cherry, K. (2023). *Which Jungian Archetype Are You?* [online] Verywell Mind. Available at: https://www.verywellmind.com/what-are-jungs-4-major-archetypes-2795439 [Accessed 29 Jun. 2023].

39 Heap, M. (2012) *Hypnotherapy – A handbook*, 2nd ed. Milton Keynes, UK: Open University Press.

40 DISCInsights (2023) Everything in the world of DISC and understanding. Available at: https://discinsights.com/ [Accessed 29 Jun. 2023].

41 The Myers Briggs Company (2023) *remote + office = hybrid*. Available at: https://eu.themyersbriggs.com/en [Accessed 29 Jun. 2023].

42 Karpman, S. (2014). *The Official Site of the Karpman Drama Triangle*. [online] Karpmandramatriangle.com. Available at: https://karpmandramatriangle.com/ [Accessed 29 Jun. 2023].

43 Covey, S. (2004) *The 7 Habits of Highly Effective People: Restoring the Character Ethic,* Free Press.

44 Rosenberg, M. B. (2003). *Nonviolent Communication*. PuddleDancer Press.

45 Gazing Performance System (2023) *How to Prepare Your Kids for Exam Pressure*. Available at: https://gazing.com/gazette-posts/how-to-prepare-your-kids-for-exam-pressure/ [Accessed 29 Jun. 2023].

46 Kerr, J. M. (2013). *Legacy: 15 lessons in leadership: what the All Blacks can teach us about the business of life*. London: Constable.

47 Harvard Business Review. (1999). *Management Time: Who's Got the Monkey?* [online] Available at: https://hbr.org/1999/11/management-time-whos-got-the-monkey. [Accessed 29 Jun. 2023].

48 Wikipedia. (2020). *Ikigai*. [online] Available at: https://en.wikipedia.org/wiki/Ikigai [Accessed 29 Jun. 2023].

49 Wikipedia. (2021). *OGSM*. [online] Available at: https://en.wikipedia.org/wiki/OGSM [Accessed 29 Jun. 2023].

50 Lafley, A.G., Martin, R.L. (2013). *Playing to win: how strategy really works*. Boston (Ma): Harvard Business Review Press.

51 Doran, G. T. (1981). "There's a S.M.A.R.T. way to write management's goals and objectives". *Management Review*. 70 (11): 35–36.

52 https://paulocoelhoblog.com/author/paulo-coelho (2010). *Reader's story: The perfect heart*. [online] Paulo Coelho. Available at: https://paulocoelhoblog.com/2010/10/04/readers-story-the-perfect-heart/ [Accessed 29 Jun. 2023].

53 Wikipedia Contributors (2019). *Kintsugi*. [online] Wikipedia. Available at: https://en.wikipedia.org/wiki/Kintsugi [Accessed 29 Jun. 2023].

Image Reference

p. 009 Personal photo

p. 016 Byrne, U. (2005). Wheel of Life. *Business Information Review,* 22(2), 123–130

p. 017 Byrne, U. (2005). Wheel of Life. *Business Information Review,* 22(2), 123–130

p. 020 Manfred Zentgraf https://en.wikipedia.org/wiki/Camino_de_Santiago#/media/File: Ways_of_St._James_in_Europe.png

p. 020 Personal photo

p. 021 Personal photo

p. 023 OpenAI (2022). Introducing ChatGPT. [online] OpenAI. Available at: https://openai. com/blog/chatgpt.

p. 023 (Table) self-developed

p. 024 Personal photo

p. 027 Personal photo

p. 027 Personal photo

p. 028 Personal photo

p. 031 Simon Shek: https://commons.wikimedia.org/wiki/File:Johari_Window.PNG

p. 035 Personal photo

p. 043 Personal photo

p. 045 Personal photo

p. 047 Personal photo

p. 049 Self-developed based on: O'Kelly, E. and Postman, A. (2008). *Chasing daylight: how my forthcoming death transformed my life: a final account.* New York: Mcgraw-Hill.

p. 051 https://www.theguardian.com/society/2014/jan/30/man-reunited-stranger-suicide-attempt-london-bridge

p. 053 Mike Hudson https://www.seriocomic.com/

p. 057 Personal photo

p. 059 Personal photo

p. 061 Self-developed based on: Chalabaev, A., Major, B., Cury, F., & Sarrazin, P. (2009). Physiological markers of challenge and threat mediate the effects of performance-based goals on performance. Journal of Experimental Social Psychology, 45(4), 991–994.

p. 063 Alamy 2JR6CCW ID

p. 068 Personal photo

p. 068 Personal photo

p. 069 Personal photo

p. 071 Drawing by Anne Kühn

p. 073 Personal photo

p. 074 Personal photo

p. 074 Personal photo

p. 076 Personal photo

p. 077 Personal photo

p. 078 Personal photo

p. 079 Adrian Tempany https://www.theguardian.com/books/2020/aug/30/the-wild-silence-by-raynor-winn-review-in-search-of-healing-and-home

p. 086   Personal photo

p. 089   Personal photo

p. 091   Personal photo

p. 092   Alamy Image ID: 2R8PF68

p. 097   Personal photo

p. 098   Personal photo

p. 129   Personal photo

p. 130   Personal photo

p. 133   Personal photo

p. 133   Personal photo

p. 133   Personal photo

p. 141   Personal photo

p. 143   Personal photo

p. 143   Personal photo

p. 145   Personal photo

p. 154   Personal photo

p. 161   Self-developed based on: Csikszentmihalyi, Mihaly, Flow: *The Psychology of Optimal Experience*. New York, Harper & Row, 1990. Hougaard, R., Carter, J., Coutts, G. (2016). *One Second Ahead: Enhance Your Performance at Work with Mindfulness*. New York: Palgrave Macmillan US.

p. 162   Personal photo

p. 163   Personal photo

p. 165   Personal photo

p. 168   Personal photo

p. 170   https://www.placesleisure.org/centres/wandle-recreation-centre/

p. 171   Personal photo

p. 178   Personal photo

p. 179   Personal photo

p. 180   Personal photo

p. 181   Personal photo

p. 190   Personal photo

p. 191   Personal photo

p. 197   Harrison, D. (2023). *Talent Management Technology: Acquire, Develop, Lead, Engage.* [online] Available at: https://www.harrisonassessments.com/ [Accessed 25 Jun. 2023].

p. 197   (Table) Harrison, D. (2023). *Talent Management Technology: Acquire, Develop, Lead, Engage.* [online] Available at: https://www.harrisonassessments.com/ [Accessed 25 Jun. 2023].

p. 201   Self-developed

p. 204   (Table) self-developed

p. 207   Rorybowman https://commons.wikimedia.org/wiki/File:TransactionalAnalysis.gif

p. 210   Self-developed

p. 223   Harrison, D. (2023). *Talent Management Technology: Acquire, Develop, Lead, Engage.* [online] Available at: https://www.harrisonassessments.com/ [Accessed 25 Jun. 2023].

p. 231   (Table) self-developed

p. 233   (Table) self-developed

p. 234   Self-developed based on: 1000Faces https://commons.wikimedia.org/wiki/File: Karp man_Triangle.png

p. 235   Self-developed based on: Covey, S. (2004) *The 7 Habits of Highly Effective People: Restoring the Character Ethic,* Free Press.

p. 241   Marc Winn https://theviewinside.me/what-is-your-ikigai/

p. 243   The Rock Jar UK https://www.facebook.com/TheRockJarUK/

p. 245   Self-developed

p. 246   (Table) self-developed

p. 248   Self-developed

p. 248   (Table) self-developed

p. 250   Personal photo

p. 253   Daderothttps://commons.wikimedia.org/wiki/File:Tea_bowl,_Korea,_Joseon_dynasty,_16th_century_AD,_Mishima-hakeme_type,_buncheong_ware,_stoneware_with_white_engobe_and_translucent,_greenish-gray_glaze,_gold_lacquer_-_Ethnological_Museum,_Berlin_-_DSC02061.JPG

p. 255   Nicquel Terry, The Detroit News https://eu.detroitnews.com/picture-gallery/news/local/oakland-county/2017/12/18/moonbeams-bring-sweet-dreams-for-hospitalized-kids/108730348/

9 798890 340825